Christian Citizens

ELIZABETH L. JEMISON

Christian Citizens

Reading the Bible in Black and White
in the Postemancipation South

The University of North Carolina Press *Chapel Hill*

This book was published with the assistance of the Fred W. Morrison Fund of the University of North Carolina Press.

© 2020 The University of North Carolina Press
All rights reserved
Set in Arno Pro by Westchester Publishing Services
Manufactured in the United States of America

The University of North Carolina Press has been a member of the
Green Press Initiative since 2003.

Library of Congress Cataloging-in-Publication Data
Names: Jemison, Elizabeth L., author.
Title: Christian citizens : reading the Bible in black and white in the postemancipation
    South / Elizabeth L. Jemison.
Description: Chapel Hill : The University of North Carolina Press, 2020. |
    Includes bibliographical references and index.
Identifiers: LCCN 2020015403 | ISBN 9781469659688 (cloth : alk. paper) |
    ISBN 9781469659695 (pbk. : alk. paper) | ISBN 9781469659701 (ebook)
Subjects: LCSH: Mississippi River Valley—Church history—19th century. |
    Evangelicalism—Mississippi River Valley. | Religion and politics—Mississippi River
    Valley—History—19th century. | Race relations—Religious aspects—Christianity. |
    Protestants—Mississippi River Valley. | Mississippi River Valley—Race relations. |
    Bible—Criticism, interpretation, etc.—History—19th century.
Classification: LCC BR540 .J46 2020 | DDC 276.2/081—dc23
LC record available at https://lccn.loc.gov/2020015403

Cover illustration: *Top*, "Scenes in Memphis, Tennessee, during the Riot—Burning a Freemen's School-House," *Harper's Weekly*, May 26, 1866 (courtesy of the Tennessee State Library and Archive); *bottom*, J. T. Trowbridge, *Teaching the Freedmen*, 1866 (courtesy of the Schomburg Center for Research in Black Culture, Jean Blackwell Hutson Research and Reference Division, New York Public Library).

To Jeanne and Frank Jemison,
and to Peggy Jemison Bodine

Contents

Map

Acknowledgments

I have incurred many debts over the course of researching and writing this book, and naming them here reminds me that academic books are hardly the solitary creation of their authors. My first thanks are to my academic mentors. Nancy Cott advised the early version of this project with her characteristic demand for excellence and the freedom to make this project my own. Her insight expanded the scope of this project, and her ability to articulate what I struggle to say clearly made me a better thinker and writer. David Hempton is an exemplary historian as well as a person of unusual grace, humor, and humility. His criticisms, always framed gently, transformed my analysis, and his deep knowledge of the devastating power of religion and violence helped me see the humanity of this book's actors. Marie Griffith is the reason I pursued doctoral study. Her undergraduate classroom transformed my understanding of religious history, gender, and critical study, and her mentoring convinced me that this was the vocation for me. She has aided this project at many stages.

Many individuals at Harvard University shaped early drafts of this book, and I thank them all. The North American Religion Colloquium at Harvard Divinity School read several early chapter drafts. For their suggestions and warm intellectual community, I thank Christopher Allison, John Bell, Casey Bohlen, Colin Bossen, Ann Braude, Catherine Brekus, Heather Curtis, Deirdre Debruyn Rubio, Marisa Egerstrom, Healan Gaston, Sara Georgini, Katharine Gerbner, Brett Grainger, Marie Griffith, David Hall, David Hempton, David Holland, Helen Kim, Dan McKanan, David Mislin, Max Mueller, Eva Payne, Kip Richardson, Jon Roberts, Leigh Schmidt, and Cori Tucker-Price. I benefited from the chance to share versions of several chapters with Harvard's Gender and Sexuality Workshop, as well as with a peer writing group, and beyond those already named, I thank Claire Dunning, Afsaneh Najmabadi, Emily Owens, Sandy Placido, Balbir Singh, and Stephen Vider for their suggestions in those settings.

At Clemson University, I have had the very good fortune to join colleagues who are serious scholars and marvelous teachers. I thank Richard Amesbury, Steven Grosby, Lee Morrissey, Mashal Saif, Kelly Smith, John Thames, and Benjamin White for their interest and support for my work. I especially appreciate Rhondda Thomas and Michael LeMahieu, who read and critiqued the full manuscript as it neared completion. Teaching Clemson students has made me a better writer and thinker, and their urgent questions about the past and present emphasize the stakes of this project.

I thank Elaine Maisner at the University of North Carolina Press. The careful criticisms and suggestion of the two anonymous peer reviewers directed major revisions and saved me from many errors. I also appreciate the many editing, marketing, and production professionals at the University of North Carolina Press who made this book's publication possible.

The scholars in the field of American religion must be among of the most generous in the entire academy, and I am indebted to many of them. Jennifer Graber gave the entire manuscript a skillful close reading in the final revision process. My Young Scholars in American Religion cohort provided generous feedback on parts of the manuscript and equally vital encouragement. I thank Brandon Bayne, Cara Burnidge, Emily Clark, Brett Grainger, Rachel Gross, Cooper Harriss, Justine Howe, Nicole Turner, and Daniel Vaca as well as our mentors Kathryn Lofton and Leigh Eric Schmidt. Years ago, Judith Weisenfeld, Anthony Petro, Ryan Harper, and Rachel Lindsey nurtured an eager undergraduate's fascination with American religion, and they continue to shape my thinking with their exceptional scholarship. I have presented pieces of this project at annual meetings of the American Society of Church History, the American Academy of Religion, and the Organization of American Historians, and I thank the audiences for their questions and comments.

I have received several grants and fellowships to support my travel to archives and my dedicated research and writing time. The Graduate Society of Harvard's Graduate School of Arts and Sciences, the Charles Warren Center for American Historical Studies at Harvard University, and the Mrs. Giles Whiting Foundation supported the bulk of my archival travel and the writing of the first version of this manuscript. Clemson University's Humanities Hub, Humanities Advancement Board, Faculty Research Development Program, and Lightsey Fellowship supported additional archival travel and final revision processes. I also thank friends and family who hosted me in their homes on archival research trips: Caroline and Joseph Antonio, Rachel and Rick Apple, Meg and Mike Bartlett, and Lee and David Bowen.

Historians would have an impossible job without the remarkable expertise of archivists and research librarians. They are the real heroes of the historical profession as they preserve, curate, and catalog the voices of the past. I extend my deep thanks to Ed Rock and Anne Grant of Clemson University's Cooper Library; Renata Kalnins of Harvard University's Andover-Harvard Theological Library; Pam Metz and Fred Burchsted of Harvard's Widener Library; Chris Brown of Centenary College of Louisiana's Magale Library; Randall Burkett of Emory University's Manuscript, Archives, and Rare Books Library; Debra Madera of Emory's Pitts Theological Library; Jessie Carney Smith, Cheryl Hamburg, Jason Harrison, and Michael Powell of Fisk University's John Hope and Aurelia E. Franklin Library; Marcia Crossman and Carole Teague of Hendrix College's Arkansas United Methodist Archives at Bailey Library; Debra McIntosh of Millsaps College's McCain Archives of Mississippi Methodism; Clinton Bagley, Grady Howell, William Thompson, and Anne Webster of the Mississippi Department of Archives and History; Taffey Hall of the Southern Baptist Historical Library and Archive; Geoffrey Stark and Megan Masanelli of the University of Arkansas–Fayetteville's David W. Mullins Library; Jennifer Ford of the University of Mississippi's Special Collections at J. D. Williams Library; Jacqueline Brown of Wilberforce University's Rembert E. Stokes Library; as well as the many excellent archivists in the University of North Carolina at Chapel Hill's Southern Historical Collection at Wilson Library, Duke University's David M. Rubenstein Rare Book and Manuscript Library, and Tulane University's Amistad Research Center. At the Christian Methodist Episcopal Church Headquarters in Memphis, Tennessee, several members of the denomination's central staff and leadership helped me access their archive while it was officially closed, and I extend my thanks to Denise Brooks, Tyrone Davis, Ruby Dyson, and Kenneth Jones.

My deepest debts are to my family. I was born into a family that cared about history, including the moral obligation to understand the intersections between religion and racial injustice. My parents have read nearly every paper I ever wrote, and their unfailing encouragement at each stage of my academic journey has been imperative. In their distinct styles, they both model an openness to new ideas and a willingness to reevaluate their own views that I seek to emulate. I was six years old when I watched my grandmother receive her PhD, and she attended my every graduation from preschool until I too earned my doctorate. Now in her mid-nineties, she requests syllabuses from my courses nearly as eagerly as she does pictures of my toddler. I dedicate this work with love to my parents and to my grandmother. My siblings, Frank and Sarah, have been careful readers and knowledgeable interlocutors about the stakes of this book. Their encouragement has buoyed me, and I love and admire them fiercely. My spouse, Andrew, has lived closest to this book and kept me anchored in the present. He talked through every aspect of this story, freed me from domestic responsibilities to write, and coparented with grace. I love our life together. Our son, Walter, slowed this book's completion but brings enormous joy to its author.

Christian Citizens

Introduction

Afterlives of Proslavery Christianity

In 1875, Rev. Charles Burch led ministers and lay members of the African Methodist Episcopal Church in Louisiana in discussing their rapidly changing political situation. African American Christians feared that their remarkable political, economic, and religious progress since emancipation was at risk amid "the counter revolution now in process." White supremacists were attacking their civil and political rights. Across Louisiana, White Leagues, new paramilitary allies of the Democratic Party, terrorized Republican voters loyal to the party of Abraham Lincoln. As Baton Rouge's senior AME Church leader, Burch denounced this "inhuman butchery" caused by "relentless . . . race prejudice" as unchristian and unlawful. As "innocent private citizens," African Americans "as a race of people . . . are fighting our foe with unequal arms." Like black citizens across the region, AME Church members merged religious and political arguments to defend their Christian citizenship and equal rights. They believed that the U.S. Constitution and the Bible together defended the equal civil and political rights of black citizens, and that it was the job of Christian citizens to protect the rights of all.[1]

Neighboring white southern Christians, such as fellow Louisianan Presbyterian minister Rev. Dr. Benjamin M. Palmer, found these arguments for racial equality incomprehensible. Palmer rejected Reconstruction's efforts "to level all distinctions and to trample on all authority" by weakening white men's authority as heads of their family. Palmer, who pastored New Orleans's First Presbyterian Church from the 1850s through 1900, had led the creation of the Presbyterian Church in the Confederate States of America in 1861, and he preserved its antebellum logic in later decades. Palmer revived an afterlife of proslavery theology when he defended the white Christian family, modeled on the slave-owning household where a white man controlled his wife, his children, and his enslaved people, as "the last hope of order, government, and law in society at large." This paternalistic family hierarchy was "the school in which men are trained for the duties of citizenship." For Palmer, the central problem of his era stemmed not from racial violence against black citizens, but from emancipation's attack on the antebellum slave-owning household's paternalistic order. Southern Presbyterian Rev. Benjamin Palmer and AME

Rev. Charles Burch both lived and preached in southern Louisiana as prominent leaders of their respective denominations, yet they held mutually exclusive ideas of their duties as Christian leaders and United States citizens.[2]

BLACK AND WHITE SOUTHERNERS both claimed that Christian citizenship
shaped their actions in the postemancipation South, yet they sought to create
entirely different societies for their region in an era of rapid transition. This
book asks how this came to be and what this meant for the South and the nation. Black and white southerners agreed that Christian identity and citizenship were closely related to one another, but disagreed on what Christian
citizenship meant. Within a framework of Christian citizenship, black Christians across the Mississippi River Valley defended their civil and political rights.
They could not separate their religious and political goals, nor conduct church
business, without addressing the unprecedented dangers facing them as newly
emancipated citizens. In their minds, American law and Christian theology together defended the equal rights of all. White southern Christians found this
model of Christian citizenship unintelligible as they defended their vision of
organic social hierarchy with its duties of submission, not rights of equality.
White southerners' understanding of Christian citizenship preserved the theology of the antebellum South as a white supremacist Christian paternalism
that justified white Democratic power and rejected Republican Reconstruction policy.

Religious arguments laid the foundation for a new South, whether in local
political debates, newly formed black churches and schools, or white supremacist organizing. Christian theology shaped self-understanding and collective
goals for communities across lines of race, class, and denomination. Bible stories offered flexible narratives that laypeople and their ministers adapted to
locate their tumultuous present in a long sacred history. Theological discourse was not limited to highly educated white men in seminaries but was
the intellectual domain of both non-elites and religious leaders. When black
and white southerners read the Bible, these women and men found models
for their nineteenth-century lives. Religious ideas shaped what it meant to
be black or white, man or woman, and determined who was worthy of civil
and political rights. During Reconstruction, African Americans asserted political and civil rights as citizens by emphasizing their shared identity as fellow Christians with southern whites. They made these arguments for their
equal Christian citizenship so successfully that white southerners attacked black
Christians as impious and undisciplined in their efforts to disenfranchise

black men. White southerners worked to discredit black Christianity in order to undermine black civil and political rights, inadvertently reaffirming the link between political and religious identity that black Christian citizens had made. In doing so, white southern Christians turned their antebellum proslavery theological ideas to a new purpose, to legitimize the creation of segregation as a modern paternalistic social order.

Although they belonged to separate churches denominated by race, black and white southerners responded to each other's arguments about Christian citizenship in newspapers, sermons, books, and political proceedings. Black Christians formed independent churches and denominations immediately after emancipation, where they advocated for autonomy and self-determination. Teaching that racial prejudice was a sin that true Christians must avoid, they argued that they deserved equal status with white southerners because they were both fellow Christians and fellow citizens. White Christians rejected Reconstruction's efforts to elevate black civil and political rights and to weaken white men's authority in families and politics. The chief problem of the day, to them, was emancipation's undermining God-given organic order. White men, especially, feared black rights as an attack on their antebellum rhetoric of mastery, and they marshaled Christian arguments to defend their racial and gendered power. White Christians legitimized racial violence as a tool to create a white supremacist social order as they destroyed Reconstruction and created segregation, while black Christians continued to argue that Christianity and U.S. citizenship together demanded equal civil and political rights regardless of race or previous condition of servitude.

This work narrates a new history of southern religion and politics from the hopes and uncertainties of emancipation to the violence of white supremacist order, by emphasizing the centrality of Christian claims in both white and black southerners' political imaginations. It uses the imperfect terms white and black, for lack of better language, to describe Christians divided by racial assumptions and by racism. Presuming a clear divide between blackness and whiteness was—and remains—a false assumption. In the postemancipation Mississippi River Valley, talking about whiteness and blackness obscured the long history of white men's sexual violence against enslaved women. Before emancipation, the distinction of enslaved versus free status mapped onto racial distinctions of black versus white to solidify the power of free white people. With that distinction erased after emancipation, southern white religious and political leaders worked to define the color line more rigidly. Their vision of white supremacy demanded that whiteness be a clearly defined category. Insofar as white Christians acknowledged the impossibility of simple white and black racial distinctions, they did so to strengthen whiteness as a sign of religious and moral superiority.[3]

This project studies the lower Mississippi River Valley region of Louisiana, Mississippi, Arkansas, and western Tennessee from emancipation to segregation. The story opens in 1863 when Union occupation brought emancipation there, two years before Confederate surrender, and it concludes in 1900, after segregation and black men's disenfranchisement had become law, setting an example for the rest of the South and the nation. The political pendulum swung more quickly and often more violently in the lower Mississippi Valley than in other parts of the former Confederacy. Much of the worst postemancipation racial violence happened there, yet several of the most hopeful moments did too. Mississippi, for instance, had a black voter majority during Reconstruction and sent the first black U.S. Senator to Washington, yet managed to disenfranchise black men statewide, first by means of extralegal violence as early as 1875, and then legally by changing the state constitution in 1890.[4] Religiously, this region was united by overlapping boundaries of denominational conferences, associations, presbyteries, and dioceses and by the circulation of religious periodicals. It was a populist religious landscape where Christian groups typically believed that a plain sense reading of the Bible sufficed to answer new religious and political questions. That assumption could produce widely different interpretations, since populist, evangelical Christian groups had fewer obligations to historic traditions or national unity than did Episcopalians or Roman Catholics. Black and white southern Christians framed their Bible reading toward their communal self-interest, resulting in diametrically opposed theological arguments.[5]

During these years, the Mississippi River Valley saw more upheaval and racial violence than much of the South, and these moments of change pivoted around the rhetoric of Christian citizenship. Mississippi's Black Code Laws, passed in late 1865, severely restricted freedpeople's civil rights, including forbidding them from preaching without a denominational license. Mob attacks on black residents in Memphis, Tennessee, in May 1866 killed dozens of people and destroyed every black church in the city. Combined with mass murders of black convention members in New Orleans's Mechanics' Institute Riot in July, this violence prompted national outrage that led to new policies of Congressional Reconstruction and the ratification of the Fourteenth Amendment to secure citizenship and equal protection for all persons born in the United States. Under Congressional Reconstruction, this region saw many black elected officials, often with close ties to black churches. Yet the

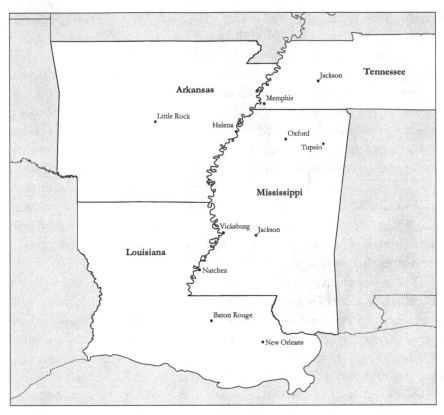

Lower Mississippi River Valley. Map created by Andrew Malwitz.

bloodiest day of Reconstruction took place in Colfax, Louisiana, on Easter Sunday in 1873, when over one hundred black citizens were killed by a white mob in what was later called the Colfax Massacre. Arkansas's nearly bloodless 1874 Brooks-Baxter War and Mississippi's violent elections in 1875 hastened Democratic political ascendancy and the end of Reconstruction before the policy officially ended in 1877. White Christians celebrated the violent seizure of Democratic power as the work of God to restore social order. Their Christian rhetoric about family order legitimized the growing lynching crisis, even as black Christians denounced white mob actions as a crime against God and humanity. Answering the prayers of white citizens in 1890, Mississippi created the first state constitution that put in place literacy tests and poll taxes in order to disenfranchise black men, providing a model for legislating segregation across the nation.[6]

The black and white Protestants whom this project examines include many denominations. Methodist and Baptist groups were the largest and fastest growing Christian groups in the region during this period. They included the Methodist Episcopal Church, South (or Southern Methodists); the Methodist Episcopal Church; the African Methodist Episcopal Church; the Colored Methodist Episcopal Church in America; the Southern Baptist Convention; the American (or Missionary) Baptist Churches; and the National Baptist Convention.[7] Additionally, Presbyterians, Congregationalists, Episcopalians, and others played significant parts in this story.[8] I refer to these Protestants collectively as "Christians," which was their preferred term and one that pointedly excluded Roman Catholics. Black and white Protestants ignored Catholic ideas in their debates over Christianity and politics. Catholic theology and social teaching, while prominent in southern Louisiana, did not engage these political issues as Protestants did. Both black and white Protestants shared anti-Catholic sentiment, and black Christians used shared anti-Catholicism to strengthen their arguments with white Christians.[9]

The modern category of "evangelical" applies unevenly to these groups because historians of evangelicalism have often assumed that white evangelicals set the norms of evangelicalism and that black Christians followed these assumptions, but this book shows that is not the case.[10] Black and white Christians often agreed on the basic framework for evangelical conversion, but they expected different behavior of the truly converted person as a church member and citizen. Even shared denominational labels such as Methodist did not indicate unity. White Methodists in the Methodist Episcopal Church and Methodist Episcopal Church, South, despised each other, while black Methodists argued that white Southern Methodists were hardly Christians because of their racial prejudice. Members of the African Methodist Episcopal Church took bolder political stances than those of the Colored Methodist Episcopal Church in America to defend black political rights and denounce white supremacy. White Christians from competing denominations could disagree sharply about predestination and free will, and yet still unite around a religiously justified white supremacist political platform. Episcopalian and Southern Baptist views differed widely on evangelical missions, alcohol consumption, sacraments, and worship styles, but they shared a commitment to Democratic political rule and hierarchical paternalism. At the same time, members of the same denominations, such as the Methodist Episcopal Church, South, sometimes disagreed with fellow members. Yet the religious and political rhetoric that these Christian groups developed in the postemancipation South would shape their region and the nation well into the twentieth century.

This book draws on a wide range of archival manuscripts and published sources, and the available materials, especially for black Christians, vary across the chapters of this book. There are fewer black-authored sources from the time of emancipation, so I sometimes read against the grain of white-authored accounts to recover black voices in these materials. As African Americans built denominations, published newspapers, and ran for office, the archival source base widens. Political records, from black men's petitions for political rights to white politicians' debates over segregation policy, often used religious arguments and explicit biblical language. Denominational meeting notes, both published and unpublished, detail clergy and lay negotiations at regional and denominational levels. Sermon notes show how ministers grounded their reaction to current events in biblical narratives. Denominational newspapers offer a much wider range of perspectives, especially those of women, and show how Christian communities understood current political events. Diaries and personal letters give more private perspectives from women and men. Organizational meeting notes, Reconstruction-era federal documents, autobiographies, devotional literature, published pamphlets, books, and legislative proceedings together allow a multifaceted approach to this history.

Sources from the few groups that attempted cross-racial religious associations are especially important. The northern Methodist Episcopal Church created a southern outpost that had both white and black ministers and mostly black congregants. Their local newspaper, published in New Orleans, avoided identifying ministers by race on principle and argued for racial unity and equality. The Colored Methodist Episcopal Church in America, created in 1870 by formerly enslaved members of the Methodist Episcopal Church, South, retained a paternalistic relationship with white Southern Methodists. Examining that relationship shows how white southern Protestants transformed their proslavery theology into a postemancipation paternalism, but it also makes the moments when the CME Church members criticized white Southern Methodists especially illuminating. Many scholars have given less attention to the history of the CME Church because it was smaller and less politically active than several other black denominations, but their history and relationship to white Southern Methodists earn closer attention here. I argue against an accepted reading of CME Church history as complacent amid white supremacy.[11]

Christian Citizenship and Racial Politics

Citizenship was an uncertain category, one that had different meanings in law and custom during the era studied. In common parlance, citizenship meant actively belonging to a place. Citizens were the free, long-term residents of a town or state who shaped its culture, governance, and laws. Legally, citizenship conferred civil and political rights and legal protection from the nation and its states. Citizenship was no guarantee of equality, however. For example, white women were citizens throughout the nineteenth century, but they, especially married women, had fewer rights to own property, vote, serve on juries, or hold public office than men did. Citizenship did not include the franchise, and the separate states, not the federal government, controlled which citizens could vote.[12] Protestant Christian identity, on the other hand, marked who belonged in society, organized influential communities, and defined what an ideal society involved. Protestant churches were the most important non-state actors in the South, especially as other voluntary societies developed more slowly there, so how Protestant groups debated belonging had a large impact on southerners' lives.[13]

Black Americans faced many barriers to legal citizenship. The U.S. Supreme Court in *Dred Scott v. Sandford* (1857) had ruled that all persons of African descent, whether free or enslaved, were not citizens. After emancipation, Congress reversed this ruling through the Fourteenth Amendment to the U.S. Constitution, ratified in 1868, which affirmed the national citizenship of all persons born in the United States, regardless of race, color, or previous condition of servitude. It also affirmed basic civil rights and forbade states from denying equal protection of the laws to any inhabitant, but it did not specify what citizenship or equal protection entailed. Citizenship did not convey the right to vote, even after the Fifteenth Amendment, ratified in 1870, prohibited states from denying the right to vote on the basis of race, color, or previous condition of servitude.[14]

Even dictionary definitions of the term were changing. Webster's *American Dictionary of the English Language* modified its definition of the word citizen in the midst of the Civil War, presumably to reflect changes in the way the word was understood. The dictionary's 1850 and 1853 editions had defined citizen with two meanings, a general concept of permanent resident and a specific meaning of a U.S. native or naturalized person who could vote or own property. In 1864, even before the Fourteenth Amendment, Webster's dropped the very general definition and instead provided a revised two-part definition, more accurately noting that some citizens—such as all white women and children—had basic civil rights, although they did not have political rights. Both the 1864 and 1866 editions defined a citizen as "A person, native or naturalized, who has the privilege of voting for public officers, and who is qualified to fill offices in the gift of the people; also, any native born or naturalized person, of either sex, who is entitled to full protection in the exercise and enjoyment of the so-called private rights." Webster's changes represented the increasing national interest in what citizenship entailed amid emancipation.[15]

Christian identity too was in flux as churches debated what they owed fellow Christians. Christian identity traditionally offered spiritual, not temporal equality. Since the Protestant Reformation, Protestants had argued that civil and political inequality could exist within churches because Christian conversion, identity, and salvation were available universally but did not affect social status. White American Christians agreed that being a Christian promised access to heaven, but not earthly freedom or political equality. All major Protestant and Catholic Christian traditions thus included enslaved people and slaveholders as fellow church members, and Christian missionaries to enslaved people argued that Christian teachings made the enslaved more obedient. Theological defenses described slavery abstractly as a peaceful, hierarchical relationship that was as legitimate as the authority of husbands over wives or parents over children. Christian antislavery voices grew to challenge these ideas, but only a few black abolitionist radicals like David Walker argued before the Civil War that Christianity and racial hierarchy were fundamentally incompatible. After emancipation, however, black Christians across the South challenged the long history of Protestant efforts to separate religious and political equality.[16]

Given the instability of citizenship and Christian identity, black and white Christians' religious and racial construction of Christian citizenship profoundly shaped the postemancipation South. Both groups relied on theological norms and biblical narratives to set the boundaries of what could be imagined. When previously inconceivable transformations happened, theological language provided tools to reframe this new reality in more familiar terms. Amid rapid, violent changes across the Mississippi River Valley, Christian citizens improvised new approaches as they faced different challenges. Yet these improvisations bore the recognizable cadences of racially and religiously specific concepts of Christian citizenship.[17]

Their very concepts of race drew on Christian precedents. Most antebellum white Christians, both antislavery and proslavery, believed that racial categories denoted heritable religious, moral, and intellectual capacities. Since the 1600s, Protestant slave societies had faced vexing questions about who had access to Christian baptism and what religious identity meant for ideas of freedom, belonging, or racial identity. Protestant missionaries reconciled Christianity with race-based slavery to assuage plantation owners' concerns about enslaving their fellow Christians and to gain access to missionize enslaved people, inadvertently creating the first Christian arguments for race-based slavery. Although racial categories were never so flexible as in the early modern period, emancipation reintroduced questions about the political implications of shared Christian identity. Black Christians seized this opportunity to argue for moral and intellectual equality across lines of race, yet even white antislavery Christians who considered themselves sympathetic to freedpeople advanced a romantic racialism that viewed African Americans as childish and in need of white benevolence.[18]

For black Christians, Christian citizenship was inextricably bound to self-determination. Freedpeople insisted that they should be equal participants in the postemancipation South because they were Christians, like their fellow residents. They created independent churches and denominations free from white oversight, and they made their churches a freedpeople's public sphere, communal spaces separate from white control. Since political citizenship was unstable and ultimately fleeting, black southerners relied on their religious identity to show that they belonged as free individuals and fellow Christians worthy of white southerners' respect. Beyond what they understood the Fourteenth Amendment to have granted, they claimed that as Christians they deserved equal civil and political rights and equal opportunity to participate in governing their community and nation. Christian behavior, black southerners argued, validated their claims to equal citizenship.[19]

White southern Christians had opposite goals for their Christian citizenship. Amid emancipation, they saw the Confederacy's defeat and slavery's end as afflictions sent by God to purify them, rather than divine judgment on their proslavery theology. To them, both before and after emancipation, being Christian citizens meant upholding biblical organic hierarchy against all religious and political efforts to make black and white southerners equal citizens. White southern Christians upheld paternalistic social order as the centerpiece of their revised theology as they adapted proslavery theology to the postemancipation South. While they claimed that true Christianity was not political, southern whites' version of Christian citizenship directly engaged politics when they saw divinely wrought "Redemption" in the white supremacist political takeovers of the 1870s. Their post-Reconstruction paternalistic rhetoric—which valued black lives even less than antebellum slaveholders had—succeeded in bringing older proslavery logic to the defense of new segregation practices.

Throughout the rapid changes following emancipation, arguments about Christian behavior placed Christian citizenship at the center of black citizens' fights for self-determination and of white southerners' countermanding efforts to establish a white supremacist society. Black Christians' success appeared not only in their limited retention of civil and political rights, but also in forcing white Christians to engage in these debates. White southerners inadvertently attested to the power of black Christian citizenship through their ongoing efforts to denigrate the authenticity of black Christianity. They attacked black churches and their ministers in local and denominational newspapers. Black communities had so successfully defended their Christian citizenship that white southerners could not ignore religious arguments when they attacked black citizens' political status. White southerners appealed to an allegedly apolitical biblicism in order to reject black Christians' claims, and their attacks on black Christian practice had strong political impact, precisely because of black Christians' concept of Christian citizenship. Because Christian identity was on the line, white southerners could not ignore black claims, even if they insisted that only their own concept of Christian citizenship was biblically faithful. Black Christian citizenship formed a vital tool in the defense of civil and political rights during the violence of "Redemption," and even after this political coup, debates about what constituted proper Christian behavior proved partial checks on white supremacist violence.

In their postemancipation communities, black Christians denounced racial discrimination as sin and prescribed a religious conversion away from racism for southern whites, but with a range of religious and political strategies. No monolithic "black religion" or unified "black church" can be found. Black ministers endorsed Republican candidates and urged political involvement, but also warned that personal piety must come before any political action. Many black churches hosted Republican political rallies, while the Colored Methodist Episcopal Church forbade member congregations from doing so. Denominational newspapers defended black political rights, yet they also preached temperance and praised marital sexual monogamy. Newspaper contributors often showed a wide range of views, beyond those of denominational bishops or other leaders.[20]

Biblical Paternalism and Organic Social Order

While many historians have assumed that theological defenses of slavery disappeared with emancipation, *Christian Citizens* demonstrates that proslavery claims had a long afterlife to justify racial hierarchy and Jim Crow segregation.[21] Southern white Christians believed the Bible presented relationships of duty and obedience, rather than rights-based freedoms, as godly means of social organization. Slavery was a legitimate element of an organic social hierarchy, similar to marriage or parent-child relationships. Northern anti-slavery Christians used rights-based language to claim slavery was inherently sinful, and southerners thought this an innovative modern heresy. Proslavery paternalism was benevolent and more biblically faithful. Southern white Christians funded missions to enslaved people as part of their paternalistic duty toward those whom they enslaved. White southerners said that their ostensibly apolitical proslavery logic marked their true piety in the face of ungodly political claims by northern churches, but after secession, their overt Confederate loyalty grew, even in the face of looming defeat. Because they rooted slavery's justification in this broader paternalistic biblical framework of family and social order, Confederate Christians preserved much of their proslavery argument after emancipation. This paternalistic theology would inspire a distinctive white Protestant political identity through the end of the century.[22]

Proslavery texts argued that slavery and marriage were parallel relationships of dependence. Like marriage, slavery allowed a white man to oversee those whom God had put under his benevolent care: his wife, his children, and his enslaved people. All four New Testament instructions for slaves to obey their masters appeared alongside statements that wives should obey their husbands, so proslavery Christians claimed that they faithfully applied the Bible to promote social order.[23] After emancipation, white southern Christians defended the benevolence of this hierarchy, preserving the logic of proslavery theology. They argued that they alone defended biblical truths in the face of black and white Republicans' politically driven innovations. Antebellum Christian paternalism defended an idealized vision of slavery, rooted in abstract biblical references, rather than the brutal reality of American race-based slavery. Though enslavement in the antebellum South was not at all like free white marriage, the claim that slavery was parallel to marriage was a powerful theological argument for slavery's legitimacy because of the near universal acceptance of women's legal subordination. Similar arguments would preserve the proslavery logic of gender and racial hierarchy for decades to come.[24]

White Christians debated the merits of slavery abstractly, not its race-based actuality, because it made for a stronger biblical case and because antislavery whites also assumed racial hierarchy. Black abolitionists like Maria Stewart and Frederick Douglass argued that racial prejudice was sinful according to the Bible, and many black Christians after emancipation would echo this point. But because few antislavery white Christians attacked the racial hierarchy embedded in slavery, most proslavery arguments did not defend racial hierarchy. Proslavery paternalism was a stronger biblical case than proslavery racial hierarchy, and this abstract defense of slavery supported white supremacist claims after emancipation under the guise of postemancipation Christian paternalism. White southerners defended Christian paternalism as a biblical mandate without having to justify white supremacy on its own terms. The seemingly race-blind defense of slavery would persist to legitimize segregation. Those later paternalistic claims undermined black religious and political self-determination in the late nineteenth century to pave the way for white supremacist segregation.[25]

In the years before the Civil War, white southern Christians defended their proslavery paternalistic arguments so vehemently that they caused schisms in all the major Protestant denominations. New southern branches produced ever stronger proslavery claims as they accused northern antislavery Christians of abandoning the Bible for modern political heresies. Methodists, Baptists, and Presbyterians would remain divided into the twentieth century because the southern denominations argued they could not reunite with their northern branches after emancipation because southern churches alone followed the Bible faithfully. Antebellum southern denominations funded Christian missions to enslaved people across the South that preached evangelical conversion and proslavery paternalism. These missionary efforts amounted to several million dollars of white Christian voluntary work, and postemancipation white southerners would look back to these antebellum missions as the best demonstration of their sincere Christian paternalism, although they never attempted large missions again. Southern white Christians refused to see black Christians as equal conversation partners, so black arguments that the Bible condemned racial prejudice rarely attracted southern whites' attention.[26]

White Christians embraced their slaveholding past as a righteous religious and historical legacy that could guide the South forward after emancipation. During their relative loss of political power in Reconstruction, white southerners limited their Christian paternalism to their families and to church organizations. But as they defended white Redemption of Democratic power in the late 1870s, they argued that hierarchical Christian paternalism should shape social and political order across the Mississippi River Valley. Paternalism justified white supremacist power. Their new paternalistic claims praised the idealized antebellum past that proslavery texts had invented, where slavery had been a loving, protective hierarchy like marriage, and then argued for continuity between that past and the 1880s and 1890s. White southerners stripped all paternalistic duties, including even concern for black lives, from their late nineteenth-century white supremacist paternalism. They used paternalism to defend their Christian duty to take over black education from government control, but they never replicated the scale of their antebellum missions to enslaved people, much less the educational goals of Reconstruction policies. As they defended Christian paternalism and biblical family order, white southern Christians made clear that they worked to protect white families, not black ones. They justified new white supremacist segregation as a paternalistic duty to care for and control those whom God had put under their righteous care, namely their black fellow citizens.[27]

Black Christians, unsurprisingly, denounced white Christian paternalism as an anti-biblical prejudice that hindered black self-determination. They challenged white paternalistic narratives by arguing that they were independent fellow Christians, not the inferior objects of paternalistic care. Black Christians understood the powerful danger that white Christian paternalism and family values arguments posed to their political rights and even their lives, while many northern white liberals underestimated their power. To counter these claims, black Christians insisted that true Christianity must necessarily be engaged in antiracist struggle because racism was sin that both contradicted the Bible and undermined constitutionally protected freedoms. Yet the final years of the nineteenth century showed that these religious arguments, without any state-sponsored backing, could not prevent white supremacist political power.[28]

Chapter Structure

This book proceeds chronologically, with five chapters that span from emancipation to the end of the nineteenth century. Amid Confederate defeat in the Mississippi River Valley, Confederate Christians, freedpeople, and northern missionaries all claimed that Christian behavior should govern their work for opposite goals, as the first chapter shows. White southern Christians believed that slavery's biblical paternalistic order justified their opposition to emancipation and black freedom, while freedpeople and Union officials celebrated God's work to end the scourge of slavery. The second chapter argues that when Reconstruction brought legal recognition of black citizenship and civil and political rights, causing stronger challenges from whites, black and white southern Christians articulated divergent concepts of Christian citizenship as the center of their responses. Black citizens argued that Christian citizenship united their religious and political identity behind their claims to equal civil and political rights, while white Christian citizenship reimagined paternalism, rooted in proslavery ideals, as an apolitical path to godly social order.

Black Christians so successfully defended their Christian citizenship that white Democrats attacked black Christianity as well as black citizenship to justify their actions in mounting violent takeovers in the 1870s. As the third chapter shows, black Christians denounced these changes and organized religious and political defenses of their rights. By the 1880s, the focus of the fourth chapter, white Christians reframed their postemancipation paternalism as a continuation of antebellum social order, albeit with little paternalistic responsibility for southern whites. Black Christians denounced white southerners' new historical narratives that claimed unchanging antebellum paternalism, and they argued that their religious and political work showed that they deserved equal rights. White southerners' paternalism gained power from lynching's terrorism, which black Christians denounced as sin that violated their most basic rights. The final chapter, "Segregation," begins with the 1890 Mississippi state constitutional convention, where white ministers blessed the work of disenfranchising black voters as the triumph of Christian family order. With the loss of civil and political rights, black Christians renewed their theological arguments that racial prejudice and violence were sins before heaven and that education and self-reliance were keys to future political success.

FROM EMANCIPATION TO SEGREGATION, black and white southerners in the Mississippi River Valley argued about the future of their region through the language of Protestant Christianity. Their claims about the rights and duties of citizens and Christians created new frameworks for understanding cultural and political belonging in the postemancipation South. Black southerners combined their religious and political power to make persuasive claims to Christian citizenship. Amid tremendous adversity, they fought for autonomy and self-determination in religious and political life. Their religious autonomy proved more successful than their political equality, but both goals would continue to shape black religious life and organizing in the next century. White southern Christians legitimized white men's authority and celebrated white family order, adapting proslavery claims to the postemancipation South without concern for black families or their civil and political rights. They repeated their antebellum skepticism toward rights-based antislavery discourse to discount all discussion of black Americans' human, civil, and political rights, to justify black disenfranchisement, and to support lynching.

By the end of the nineteenth century, black and white Christians had established new terms for religious and political debate that would shape twentieth-century contests from the creation of fundamentalism to the long civil rights movement. The newly freed people and defeated Confederates with whom this story begins did not foresee how influential their evolving concepts of Christian citizenship would be. But as these groups found religious and political power within Christianity, they were already working to create a New South from their hopes and disappointments in the final years of the Civil War.

CHAPTER ONE

Emancipation

Christian Identity amid Slavery's End, 1863–1866

On a hot Sunday in July 1863 in Natchez, Mississippi, just days after Union troops occupied the city, a church service came to an abrupt halt when "a negro man in . . . Sunday clothes came up the middle aisle to the pulpit, [and] stopped a little while there." A white man rose from the startled congregation to demand what the newcomer sought, and the man "said he came to church and wanted a seat" among the white congregants. Union soldiers present laughed as the minister and southern white congregation "looked astounded." One of those surprised white southerners, a young woman named Kate Foster, recorded the interruption in her diary. She fumed, "I was so angry" at the "impudent scamp" who interrupted her church's service, and she noted appreciatively that a white man forced him "into the gallery where the servants sit." Foster's account of this Sunday service, among stories of nearly a dozen enslaved people who fled her own and neighboring households for freedom that same week, showed that emancipation had arrived in the Mississippi River Valley. The black man who demanded a seat with white congregants was demonstrating his freedom to white Confederates who still believed him enslaved. Emancipation transformed religious, household, and political life for white and black southerners, even though the Civil War would continue for nearly two years.[1]

Kate Foster could not escape the transformations that emancipation brought to her life at home and in church, but she insisted that God supported the Confederate "war of Independence." Amid the news of neighboring Vicksburg's fall to Union troops a few days earlier, Foster appealed to "the goodness of God" because "we *all* believe He is for us and having this faith how *can* we doubt for an instant" that God would ensure Confederate victory. In fact, Vicksburg's fall was divinely ordained, as "God has let it fall to show us our cause does not rest upon the mere fall or holding of any one city." Despite this setback, Foster claimed that "not for a moment do I think we will be unsuccessful" in the war's ultimate result. In her diary entry about her interrupted church service and her anger at enslaved people's departures from her household, she insisted that "we will come out of the furnace doubly purified for the good work" of God. God's work for "the people of this Confederacy" was nothing short "of maintaining the supremacy of our Father in Heaven." Confederate Christians alone worshiped God faithfully, she argued, joining many white southern Christians' claims. For Foster, her two brothers' absence fighting for the Confederate army increased her urgent desire for Confederate victory as she feared for their safety, yet both would die near the end of the Civil War. In the decades that followed, Kate Foster led Confederate memorial efforts in Natchez and became a local officer of the United Daughters of the Confederacy.[2]

The black man who entered the white Natchez church in the middle of its Sunday service recognized the promise of freedom and equality that Confederate defeat brought to the region. He dressed for the occasion, and when he told the white congregation that he wanted a seat among them, he indicated his status as a free man. His claim to equal seating in the congregation echoed the self-determination of other previously enslaved people who emancipated themselves by fleeing to Union lines over the days before and after this Sunday. The man extended his newly won freedom to demand religious equality. While the only record of his action lies in the diary of a white slaveholding Confederate woman, her hostile prose still attested to his call for equal treatment. Foster wondered if Union soldiers goaded this man's action, just as she suspected Union misinformation would be the only reason enslaved people fled her household with their children, showing how loath she was to acknowledge black people's efforts to direct their own lives. Yet the few minutes this newly free man stood at the front of the white congregation proved to all present that massive changes were underway.

CHURCHES WERE SITES for enacting freedom and making political demands during emancipation, as were farms and towns. Christian theology and churches' physical spaces served as places to debate slavery, freedom, and Christian identity during emancipation and Confederate defeat. Finding that white southerners recognized neither their independence nor their Christian identity, freedpeople quickly formed their own churches in these years, with aid from northern white antislavery Christians. These three groups—proslavery Confederate Christians, free black people, and antislavery northern missionaries—each created their own ideas for what Christian behavior and Christian citizenship in a postemancipation United States would involve. Whether they saw the Civil War as a fight to establish a Christian slaveholding republic or as a divinely ordained end to slavery, these competing groups used Christian language and Christian institutions to shape their rapidly changing world.

In the emancipation-era Mississippi River Valley, black and white southerners and antislavery northerners used Christian theology to argue for the society they hoped to create. Each group claimed that they behaved as true Christians and rooted their actions in a sacred history reaching back to the Hebrew Bible. Throughout the antebellum period, white southerners crafted a proslavery theology that claimed that being faithful to the Bible demanded supporting slavery, and, facing emancipation, Confederate Christians doubled down on their claims. At the same time, formerly enslaved Christians used their Christian identity to advocate for educational, civic, and political inclusion as fellow Christians and equal citizens with white southerners. White antislavery missionaries positioned themselves as advocates for freedpeople's best interests, but they often exerted their own paternalism in an effort to mold black Christianity as they saw fit. These different models of Christian behavior would diverge more strongly in the years after emancipation, but they already shaped responses to the transformations of the region in 1863.

Amid emancipation, black and white southerners began to formulate the concepts of Christian citizenship that would organize their religious and political activism through the end of the nineteenth century. Confederate Christians did not consider themselves U.S. citizens as emancipation came to the region, and people of African descent, whether free or enslaved, could not be citizens based on the 1857 *Dred Scott* Supreme Court ruling. After emancipation, black residents argued in formal petitions and local interactions that they were equal Christians and should be equal citizens with white southerners. Men demanded the right to vote based on their performance of male citizens' duty in the Union army and on their Christian belief that the Bible opposed racial hierarchy. White southerners used the logic of their proslavery theology to insist that southern white men alone deserved to control the future of the South. In an abrupt shift from their Confederate loyalty, white southerners argued by late 1865 that they were model U.S. citizens and Christians. Opposing white southern Christianity, antislavery missionaries considered themselves allies of freedpeople amid emancipation, but they also wanted to direct black religious life as they saw best. Freedpeople deployed their own concept of Christian identity as they worked for freedom and equal citizenship. They welcomed aid from antislavery missionaries, but when freedpeople insisted that they deserved equal civil and political rights, even ardent white antislavery missionaries grew cautious.

Proslavery Family Order and Confederate Christianity

The Confederate cause drew support from white Christians' arguments that slavery represented a biblically based system that was morally superior to free labor. Because biblical references to slavery in the ancient Near East or Roman Empire did not involve race-based chattel slavery, southern Christians defended slavery as an abstract ideal of benevolent paternalistic social organization.[3] Protestant ministers wrote the majority of all antebellum defenses of slavery, and their zeal caused schisms in the major Protestant denominations in the years leading up to the Civil War. Methodists and Baptists were the two largest denominations in the United States before they divided in the 1840s. Southern Methodists split from the national group in 1844 to defend the ability of a bishop to own slaves, and they organized the Methodist Episcopal Church, South, in 1846. Baptists formed the Southern Baptist Convention in 1845 in a fight over whether missionaries could own slaves. Presbyterians' 1837 schism between Old School and New School factions served as a proxy fight over growing antislavery sentiment among New School adherents, and in 1861, southern Old School and New School Presbyterians together formed the Presbyterian Church of the Confederate States of America. These divisions severed the nation's largest voluntary organizations and exacerbated antebellum regional divisions. In separate southern denominations, white southern Christians redoubled their defenses of slavery as a biblically ordained paternalistic hierarchy.[4]

Slavery, southern white Christians contended, served the best interests of both slaveholders and enslaved, just as marriage allowed husbands to care for their wives. The Bible presented relationships of duty and obedience, rather than rights-based freedoms, as godly means of social organization. All four New Testament instructions for slaves to obey their masters appeared alongside instruction for wives to obey their husbands.[5] If the Bible linked marriage and slavery, white southern Christians argued, proslavery Christians were more faithful to the sacred text over newer ideas of individual rights. White women's legal subordination in marriage, where they lacked property rights, divorce rights, or protection from abuse, had widespread support as the natural order of society. Christian slaveholders' claims that they treated enslaved people like their children or wives were rhetorical flourishes, not lived reality. Neither married white women nor enslaved people saw their situations as similar. White slave-owning women welcomed the power they had over enslaved people and the labor they received from them. Enslavement was not at all like free white marriage, but the argument that it was would preserve white supremacist proslavery logic of gender and racial hierarchy for decades to come. This benevolent household paternalism formed the core of white southerners' postemancipation proslavery logic.[6]

As they connected slavery's legitimacy to that of marriage, white southerners claimed that the violence endemic to slavery did not affect its legitimacy. Southern ministers readily admitted that some enslaved people faced brutality but, by positioning this violence as comparable to domestic violence, they argued that violence against enslaved people did not undermine benevolent, paternalistic hierarchies any more than the abuse of wives or children weakened the legitimacy of marriage or parental power. Baptist pastor Richard Furman admitted in 1823 that "husbands and fathers have proved tyrants," but that did not challenge "the husband's right to govern and the parental authority." Likewise, slave owners' legitimacy did not lose validity because of its potential for brutality. As sectional tension rose to a fever pitch, white southern Christians claimed that most antislavery Christians' acceptance of gender hierarchy in marriage was selfish hypocrisy. Presbyterian minister Frederick Ross's 1857 *Slavery Ordained of God* conceded that "every fact in *Uncle Tom's Cabin* has occurred in the South," but brazenly hazarded that "he who will make the horrid examination will discover in New York City . . . more cruelty from husband to wife, parent to child, *than in all the South from master to slave* in the same time." Ross grossly underestimated the violence of slavery and ignored its many forms of physical, sexual, psychological, and cultural violence, yet his fantastic claims showed the extent to which white southern Christians tried to link slavery to marriage and parenthood to shore up slavery's legitimacy in a system of natural hierarchies. Southern ministers recognized that few critics of slavery agreed with nascent woman's rights advocates like Elizabeth Cady Stanton or Lucretia Mott, who had begun to argue for marriage reform because of women's vulnerability to abuse and deprivation of rights. Marriage, parenting, and slavery could all permit violence, white southern Christians conceded, but that abuse did not delegitimize these divinely ordained household relationships.[7]

The link between slavery and marriage existed only in the rhetoric justifying slavery as biblical paternalism, not in how white enslavers actually acted. White slave-owning women—always a small minority of white women—participated actively in the brutal coercion of slavery. White women used violence to control enslaved people in similar ways as male slave owners, although they would write of themselves after emancipation in very different ways. Slaveholding women assumed the legitimacy of slavery because they benefited from it, and they were ready to believe that God was on the side of antebellum slaveholders and the Confederacy. Kate Foster, with whose account the chapter opened, wrote angrily about emancipation when her white friend Mrs. Dunbar had "to do the house cleaning and nearly all the house work" after two enslaved women left with their children. Incapable of seeing enslaved people's desire for freedom for themselves and their children, Foster lamented that "if they had any feeling they would feel sorry for Mrs. D and remain faithful." White slave-owning women could sympathize with each other but not with enslaved women.[8]

The vast divide between the Christian rhetoric of slavery and its brutal reality emerged clearly in the aspect of slavery that most troubled slaveholding women: white men's sexual power over enslaved women. Since the seventeenth century, enslaved or free status passed through a child's mother, reversing centuries of English common law and giving male enslavers legal rights and economic incentive to rape and impregnate women whom they enslaved. Because enslaved people did not have legal control over their bodies, sexual violence against enslaved women was not legally called rape, amplifying its brutal violence. The physical and psychological horrors of enslavement defied white Christian paternalistic arguments most egregiously here. Proslavery Christian writers ignored this endemic sexual violence entirely because it would reveal the lie behind all of their proslavery Christian paternalism. After Reconstruction's violent end, these same white southerners would appeal to some black Christians as being more sympathetic figures because they had white fathers. The truth of white men's sexual violence toward enslaved women was universally known, but deliberately obscured. Frederick Douglass and Harriet Jacobs, among other formerly enslaved writers, testified that white women's inability to control their husbands' sexual lives increased these angry white women's violence toward enslaved people. This widely known reality of slavery was a telling indictment of the divide between white Christian men's rhetoric about slavery as an ideal model of family order and slavery's lived reality of gender, sexual, and racial violence.[9]

As they launched the Civil War, white southerners argued that they were fighting for biblical family order and the duty of preserving slavery. In a widely republished Thanksgiving sermon following Lincoln's election in 1860, New Orleans Presbyterian Rev. Benjamin Palmer urged white southerners "to conserve and perpetuate the institution of domestic slavery" as "the duty which . . . patriotism and religion alike requires of us all." Palmer, who pastored New Orleans's First Presbyterian Church until his death in 1902, became the first moderator of the Presbyterian Church of the Confederate States of America in 1861 and defended social hierarchy based on the slaveholding household for decades after emancipation. In 1860, he sought to "deepen the sentiment of resistance in the Southern mind" and accelerate secession because the South must defend "before all nations, the cause of all religion and all truth." Other southern clergy reminded their members that enslaved people had "the same claims for religious instruction as our children." Christian slaves with "their own personal knowledge of the Scriptures . . . in relation to the mutual duties of master and servants" would be "more faithful and cheerful in . . . their duties." Such efforts would make it possible to bring enslaved people more fully under Christian household influence.[10]

Confederate Christians claimed they fought to defend slavery and the biblical order it represented. Rather than seeing secession as disrupting social order, white southerners argued they were like the Israelites escaping Egyptian slavery, as forced members of the United States. Like the evil pharaoh in Exodus, "Abraham Lincoln . . . hardened his heart, and stiffened his neck, and would not let the people go." Lincoln here was the pharaoh who would not allow the freedom of the seceding states, rather than the Moses who led enslaved people to freedom. Southern ministers pointed to an obscure verse from the Hebrew Bible prophet Obadiah, the sole place where the King James Version used the word "confederacy," to argue that God favored the Confederate States of America, to which God gave "a solemn trust of . . . slave labor, for the benefit of the world and as a blessing to themselves." These interpretations of secession as an aid to biblical social order amounted to wartime propaganda to be sure, but as improbable as they might appear after Confederate defeat, they also represented a conceivable expansion of antebellum proslavery Christianity.[11]

Even southern clergy who were ambivalent about explicitly endorsing political events preached proslavery Christianity and Confederate loyalty to encourage social and family order. Rev. John Griffing Jones was a slaveholder who had been a respected Mississippi Methodist leader since the 1820s, when he traversed the state as an itinerant, and in the 1870s, fellow Methodists would commission his history of Mississippi Methodism, attesting to his wide respect. Where Palmer had a formal university education, Calvinist theology, and Presbyterian ordination, Jones was largely self-taught, and as a Methodist he believed in human free will rather than predestination, yet the two ministers would eventually endorse the same theological vision of family order and racial hierarchy. Because Jones believed slavery was both biblical and constitutional, he worried that secession had been misguided, yet he endorsed the Confederate cause in an appeal to the duty of following orderly governing powers. In a Confederate fast day sermon delivered in Port Gibson, Mississippi, Jones explained that the war began from two violations of the U.S. Constitution: the North's attempt to abolish slavery and the South's secession from the Union. Jones advised his congregants that their "duty as Christians is to obey the powers that be" and to "leave all events with God," because "if we are faithful as Christians" God will direct the war "all for the good of our country and posterity in the end." Without extolling Confederate superiority, Jones endorsed loyal obedience to the Confederate cause through commonplace theological claims about the duty to obey those in power. Jones connected Confederates fasting that day to fasting biblical heroes, reaching back to Moses. Although skeptical of secession, Jones preached slavery's legitimacy and his congregation's connections to God's faithful people in ancient times. After Confederate defeat, Jones would create more innovative biblical justification for white southerners' action, but early in the Civil War, he needed only to remind his congregation that Christian duty demanded loyalty to their current government.[12]

White Christians celebrated how secession allowed them to perfect slavery's model of biblical paternalism free of northern meddling, yet, as they debated potential reforms, Confederate Christians showed the limits of Christian paternalism against the realities of American slavery. In Columbus, Mississippi, Presbyterian Rev. James Lyon made a bold proposal for reform. Glossing over slavery's defense by noting that "like the existence of God, it [slavery] is taken for granted from the beginning to the end of the Bible," Lyon proposed that Confederate law recognize slave marriage and protect spouses from separation. Legal marriage for enslaved people would encourage a more truly Christian paternalism and "prohibit fornication, adultery, bigamy, incest, or even rape." Lyon published his suggestion in the leading Southern Presbyterian journal, where it immediately became clear that he had gone too far. His fellow ministers sternly rebuked him for suggesting "a revolution in the status of the slave." Slave marriage would "snap at once the tie that binds the slave to the [white slaveholding] family." The proposal was as absurd as a "marriage law for cattle . . . who are equally without civil capacity" to contract. This short-lived debate about slave marriage revealed the distance between the biblical paternalistic ideal that proslavery Christians defended and the reality of American race-based chattel slavery. Enslaved people could not marry because slavery prohibited them from forming any contracts. As Lyon's critics realized, American slavery was far from a paternalistic ideal, and reforms that would grant civil rights like marriage to enslaved people might undo the institution. Yet the same white ministers who decried the suggestion of slave marriage would, just a few years later, argue that black citizens failed to follow white marriage ideals and thus were not sufficiently moral Christians to deserve civil and political rights.[13]

Wealthy white women relied on their privileged position in a slave-owning household and worked to preserve their gender, class, and racial power. They certainly did not think of their position as similar to enslaved people's. They claimed God would vindicate the Confederate cause, yet they assumed the legitimacy of slavery rather than defending it explicitly as male ministers did. Kate Foster read the Bible to justify her desire for Confederate victory. She relished the protection her father and brothers provided for her in their wealthy household, enriched by enslaved labor. Believing that God favored the Confederacy preserved her hope that her beloved brothers would survive their Confederate army service and that her comfortable life based on enslaved people's labor would not change. Every setback—from the demands of a black worshipper to be seated among white congregants to the news of Confederate battle losses—would only make God's eventual guarantee of Confederate victory more impressive. Like many Confederate women, Foster took for granted the benevolence of proslavery paternalism, largely because she was unable to imagine enslaved people's perspectives. She repeated other white southerners' claims that wealthy white people, like her family, knew best what enslaved people and less affluent southern whites needed. Foster was angry that "the negroes are flocking to the enemy," and she described formerly enslaved people as "ungrateful" and "poor deluded creatures" whom Union soldiers must have "fooled" into emancipating themselves. In fleeing with their families for contraband camps and Union army outposts, freedpeople had "gone to what they all think a better place"; she wrote that "they will find out too late who are their best friends, Master or Massa." Kate Foster's unselfconscious claims that white southerners were superior judges of black people's best interests would reappear in the 1880s and 1890s in the white Christian paternalistic claims that justified legal segregation and extra-legal terror.[14]

Belle Edmondson, another white young woman, combined her evangelical fervor with her Confederate loyalty as she waited for God to vindicate the white South. By early 1864, she had been living under Union control for nearly two years in rural Shelby County, Tennessee, after General Grant occupied nearby Memphis in 1862. Undeterred by Union gains, she trusted God for "our struggle for Liberty," as she prayed in her diary: "Merciful Father, crown our Army's [sic] with Victory. Spare so much bloodshed of the bravest and best of our Sunny South. Enlighten the minds of the miserable Yankees, of their sinfulness; drive them from our south! Oh, just and merciful Savior, give us peace, and our independence." Despite Union control, Edmondson still energetically supported the Confederacy, for which her two brothers fought, by smuggling mail and news for southern troops away from the federally controlled area. Her evangelical faith, evidenced in her diary's prayers and records of Bible reading, supported her efforts because, as she prayed, "After you, my God, then I live for my Country. God bless our leaders in Dixie." Later, she exclaimed, "I worship Jeff Davis and every Rebel in Dixie." Like Kate Foster, Edmondson ignored black self-determination as she positioned Confederates as unjustly persecuted by Union forces. Her diary insisted that God, the "Father of justice and mercy," would "drive the wicked tyrants from our Sunny land." At any rumor of Confederate success, she was quick to celebrate: "Oh! I think the bright day for Dixie is dawning. God is just; our prayers are answered." It seemed obvious to Edmondson, as to Foster, that the Confederate cause for which her brothers fought was right. As privileged Confederate women, they could not empathize with anyone outside their social world or imagine that enslaved people deserved any of the liberties that they took for granted. Edmondson's fervent evangelical piety generated strong support for the Confederate cause, even as Confederate losses grew.[15]

As the Confederacy failed on the battlefield and home front by late 1864, Confederate Christians appealed to more obscure biblical examples to support their cause. Slaveholding Methodist minister Rev. John G. Jones, who had initially questioned secession while firmly defending slavery, preached again on a Confederate fast day in November 1864. He compared Confederates to the Old Testament story of King Jehoshaphat, who, when confronted with an enormous enemy army, prayed to God for supernatural deliverance. After Jehoshaphat's prayer, God caused the powerful enemies to fight among themselves so that they were vanquished without Jehoshaphat's army having to enter the battle. The Confederate military situation was grim, and only through supernatural intervention could Confederates hope for victory. Confederates had very few justifications for hope, but believing they belonged to God's chosen people, in whose long history God had intervened miraculously, could kindle hope in the Confederate cause. Jones left space for likely Confederate defeat in this sermon, but he did not suggest that would mean God's judgment on the Confederacy or on slavery.[16]

After Appomattox, Confederate Christians drew upon Christian resignation, but they still doubted slavery's abolition. Mississippi Presbyterian minister Rev. Samuel Agnew leaned on his Calvinist theology in April 1865 to reassure himself that "God reigns" while "Calamities . . . befall the Confederacy in every direction." He recorded news of General Lee's surrender, leaving open a slight possibility of ongoing divine intervention when he described it as "the severest blow the Confederacy has received yet," so that "humanly speaking—the Confederacy is dead." Once Agnew recognized Union victory, he chided his congregants' selective approach to the news that reached their small town because many believed news of Lincoln's assassination but not Confederate defeat. He marveled at "the multitude of lies which are circulated" to mitigate "the depression caused by the fall of Lee and his army." Yet Agnew himself doubted that Union victory meant emancipation as he noted that "the negroes themselves evidently think they are free, but they may be too hasty." Over the subsequent weeks, Agnew grudgingly acknowledged the "unpalatable truth" that "slavery is dead," yet he complained that freedpeople "got so 'high' that they would not obey my orders." Freedpeople demanded fair pay and the ability to negotiate terms for labor contracts with white employers, to which Agnew concluded, "when 'freedom' comes they will find it very different from what they suppose." Weeks after Confederate defeat, Agnew imagined that "freedom" had not come and would not mean autonomy when it did. Agnew noted that federal officials came to "draw up contracts between the master and slaves," a comment that was as close to acknowledging freedom as Agnew could imagine, though it still used the language of master and slave.[17]

In the first months after the Civil War, Confederate Christians would renew their belief in proslavery Christianity's core logic and transform it into a new white Christian citizenship based in paternalistic rhetoric. White southern Christians claimed they supported paternalism just as in the antebellum period, although actual paternalistic efforts like missions to enslaved people disappeared. Although white southerners framed their Christian citizenship in opposition to northern antislavery Christian positions, black southern Christians, not northern whites, were the first to push back on southern white Christian views by demanding that they be recognized both as free citizens and fellow Christians. Black Christians had long rejected proslavery Christianity, and they welcomed emancipation both as a miracle from God and as the result of their long prayers and striving. At the same time, northern white antislavery Christians justified their role in the emancipation-era Mississippi River Valley as a necessary corrective to white southern Christianity. Antislavery missionaries believed themselves the best aid to freedpeople, an assertion that conveyed northern white paternalism amid emancipation.

Antislavery Missionaries and Christian Identity

Antislavery northern missionaries followed Union troops to the Mississippi River Valley in the summer of 1863, excited for a tangible way to enact their Christian fight against slavery. They hailed from across northeastern and midwestern states and from many denominations, and they were funded by northern voluntary societies and churches, although some men worked at times as army chaplains for black regiments. The American Missionary Association (AMA) was the most prominent group in the Mississippi River Valley, though the northern Methodist Episcopal Church and others also played a role. As missionaries, men worked as both preachers and teachers, while women, both single and married, were teachers. They taught and preached in contraband camps while distributing humanitarian aid from the army and northern voluntary donations. Freedpeople welcomed antislavery missionaries as God's answers to their prayers, yet these missionaries brought their own racial assumptions that formerly enslaved people needed white guidance to pursue true Christianity. Missionary attitudes slowly changed during emancipation to view perceived racial difference as the result of slavery, not as inherent traits, yet this evolution was uneven. Antislavery workers did not support political rights for freedpeople, who were still classified as contraband of war. As they formulated their own antislavery Christian citizenship, northern missionaries gradually saw freedpeople less as idealized objects of missionary aid and more as individuals shaping their own lives.

Missionaries saw freedpeople as simple Christians whose guileless piety deserved northern churches' sympathy. Missionary reports on black life show idealized portraits as missionaries sought donations from a concerned northern public. Many teachers, both women and men, had graduated from antislavery Oberlin College and valued well-educated clergy, yet they praised formerly enslaved preachers with no formal education. The "talent, faith and zeal" among contraband camp preachers "would edify any . . . pulpit." Although he was illiterate, "Uncle Rufus would command respect of any audience," not just that of a contraband camp. This simplistic piety matched a hyperbolic ability to learn, especially for faithful Christians like an "old pious man" who "came one morning not knowing all his letters & by 3 o'clock in the afternoon he was reading in Noah Webster's spelling book." Missionaries reported that Christian piety could transcend race, political status, and education, yet they believed this simplistic piety needed northern Christians' direction.[18]

Antislavery missionaries saw their work among freedpeople as proof of their own true Christian identity and political loyalty. Their white Christian citizenship centered on loyalty to the Union, whose army was doing God's work to fight against the sin of slavery, but it did not allow for black autonomy. An AMA worker, Rev. George Carruthers, celebrated a Union cavalry excursion into Confederate-held territory as an effort to "break the chains of the captives and bring him into our lines a *freeman.*" Working in the contraband camp in Corinth, Mississippi, gave Carruthers the sense he was "with Moses when he was leading the children of Israel out of Egypt."[19] Missionaries' difficulties, as they endured summer heat or ate meager contraband rations, were a small price to pay "to be *identified with the Almighty God in his great work.*" God was on the side of the Union army, and so were antislavery missionaries. With God's help, the Union army and missionaries rescued people from slavery. Missionaries ignored enslaved people's own work for freedom in their accounts.[20]

Northern white missionaries employed paternalistic concepts of race and gender to distinguish between black Christian identity and black political and civil rights, yet free black Christians linked these religious and political goals as Christian citizens. When white AMA teachers wrote to their northern supervisors of the "citizens" around them, they meant long-term white southern residents of that place, and their correspondence juxtaposed "the citizens" and "the freedmen" as competing groups.[21] An important exception to this trend came from Blanche Harris, one of a small handful of black AMA teachers, who defended the influence of a powerful free black community in Natchez as she decried her white colleagues' limited racial imaginations. A graduate of Oberlin College, Harris traveled with several teachers including another black woman to Mississippi in late 1865. When they arrived, the white teacher in charge explained that while Oberlin had been an integrated space, segregation was necessary in Mississippi to protect their work. Harris objected when told she was "obliged to room with two of the domestics." She wrote the New York office lobbying for better treatment and warned national AMA leaders that "some of the old citizens (Colored)" had become dismayed by how white teachers had treated Harris and her colleague. Because of the economic power of Natchez's black community, Harris warned the New York office that the AMA had "lost the confidence of the greater, and richer portion of the colored people here." Had the AMA treated the two black teachers equally, the Natchez black community "would have given . . . means enough to have built a much larger house" for the proposed school run by the AMA. By identifying black residents as powerful "citizens" who could aid the AMA's work, Harris argued for black citizenship well before the Fourteenth Amendment. Yet her white colleagues largely resisted her calls.[22]

Antislavery missionaries connected intellectual ability and gendered leadership with racial determinism. Both men and women served as missionary teachers, but only men could be preachers or chaplains, and missionary ministers found themselves short staffed. Writing that they "cannot get *men* in these days to do the work," some missionaries in 1864 pointed to the "great substantial men" among freedpeople who could join the missionary ministers on a supervised basis. In particular, Rev. Samuel Wright proposed that Eustis Beady, a man with "gifts as a preacher" who had "been a slave all his days" but "is *nearly white*," could be the first of a new group of "the good men of color" whom northern whites could ordain and employ "until we can find better." With this proposed plan, white missionaries admitted a newly freed man as a provisional minister because they viewed his racial status as almost white, yet they suggested that they would prefer to replace him with a white man if they could. Teachers, too, puzzled over what the connection between racial identity and intellectual ability might be, as their monthly reports for the AMA asked if "the mulattos show any more capacity than the blacks." Most answered "no," but some pushed back against the question's assumption about race and intellectual ability, and one teacher wrote beside the question, "They do. *Reason*, they have always had better advantages." With ongoing pushback from teachers, the national leadership dropped the question in mid-1865. Such episodes showed that while antislavery missionary teachers supported emancipation, they brought their own paternalistic racial views and gender assumptions to bear. Black equality seemed a frightening, unwarranted change to most, although the northern white Christians who saw black Christians' identity as similar to their own religious identity would prove more capable of changing their views on black self-determination.[23]

At emancipation, antislavery missionaries refrained from fully supporting black autonomy, but over time, some would learn from freedpeople, especially when they could share the same evangelical idioms. As he proposed hiring nearly white Eustis Beady, Rev. Samuel Wright reported to a fellow minister, "My Brother, I think sometimes that I have never begun to sympathize with this people." Wright felt gratified "and humbled in the *dust* before God" when "a pious Colored brother led in prayer," thanking God for Wright's sermon and "for *just such a preacher*, for *just such truths*" as he had imparted. Wright confirmed the importance of his work and recognized shared evangelical identity, especially with "the most intelligent of the exslaves, many of whom can read." These pious freedpeople were "too intelligent & too solemn to give way to that noise & confusion so common among this people," and Wright recorded his memory of freedpeople's prayers to show this piety. One "very intelligent woman lately from bondage" prayed, "O Lord, thou hast said if we would *believe* we should see the glory of God; for long years we have prayed for this hour to come . . . we prayed and agonized that *these teachers & preachers* might come to teach us and our children glory to God, they have come. . . . Lord bless these *precious* friends." Wright reconstructed the previous evening's prayer as one that gratified him and demonstrated the freed woman's identity as a fellow Christian with the missionaries who were an answer to her prayers. Wright enjoyed the praise, which could "melt all hearts," and he shared it with distant ministerial colleagues as evidence that many freedpeople were faithful Christians.[24]

Identifying as fellow Christians with freedpeople was a start for many antislavery Christians' broader identification with black Americans. When Rev. Wright praised the Christian fervor of freedpeople, he highlighted what his fellow northern white Christians valued as true religion and worried about the less educated, more demonstrative religious worship of many black Christians. His account reiterated much of northern white Christians' own benevolent paternalism. Supporting black citizens as equally deserving of civil and political rights required far broader recognition of shared identity, yet because religious identity lay at the heart of who Rev. Wright thought belonged among white Christians, identifying as fellow Christians was an important first step toward identifying fellow citizens deserving equal rights. Not all antislavery northern Christians managed that shift, and like other Unionist whites, many opposed enfranchising black men. Yet Rev. Wright's views contrasted markedly with those of other Natchez residents, such as Confederate Kate Foster, who just months before had described emancipation as a sign that enslaved people lacked all moral character for leaving enslavers who depended on their aid. Foster and Wright lived adjacent lives with opposite views of freedpeople's moral and religious capacity, shaped by their own opposed concepts of Christian behavior. Because Confederate Christians like Foster remained powerful, Rev. Wright's identification of some freedpeople as his fellow Christians became all the more significant.

That antislavery missionaries were far removed from Confederate Christians clearly did not mean they were firm allies of freedpeople. Black Christians would work to show that they were fellow Christians who deserved autonomy to run their lives and communities as they chose. Despite their own prejudices, many missionaries were confronted by freedpeople's work for themselves and forced to see this desire for autonomy. But as they welcomed support from voluntary groups and government officials, freedpeople knew that no white ally would substitute for their own advocacy as independent people. To pursue equal religious, civil, and political identity, black communities focused increasingly on self-determination.

Emancipation and Black Christian Freedom

As they fled slavery for Union-occupied towns and contraband camps, black Christians resisted white antislavery missionaries' efforts to direct their Christian life by presenting themselves as fellow Christians, not passive objects of white benevolence. Freedpeople linked their freedom and Christian identity during the Civil War when their free status was uncertain, and they soundly rejected white southerners' proslavery Christianity in favor of a Christianity that supported their communities' autonomy. The freedman who demanded a seat in Kate Foster's white-controlled Natchez church sought to enact religious and political equality by sitting among white Christians. White southerners rebuffed his efforts, both by pushing him out of the main floor in that July 1863 service and by reiterating claims that God supported slavery and the Confederacy. But Union victories would open new religious and political opportunities. Black men joined segregated regiments of the Union army to fight for abolition and Union victory. Black Christians formed independent congregations and insisted that they deserved civil and political rights as fellow Christians and fellow citizens with their white neighbors. They organized collectively to petition for these rights, and they also pushed missionaries to recognize their desire for self-determination.

Amid the Confederacy's collapse, black Christians argued that their Christian identity and loyalty to the Union showed that they deserved equal civil and political rights. In January 1865, dozens of petitioners outlined their Christian citizenship when they urged an all-white Union Convention of Tennessee, a Unionist group shaping Tennessee's future reunited to the United States, to legislate clear protections for emancipation and black men's suffrage. They rejected white Confederate Christians' organic paternalism as they identified themselves as Christians and citizens, writing both as "men belonging to the great human family" of "God who is the common Father of all" and as "American citizens of African descent." The petitioners used their political and religious identity together, as they sought "the duties of the good citizen" including "the privilege of voting." They argued that their faithful service in the Union army and Christian devotion proved their worthy citizenship. "The color of our skin," they assured white Tennesseans, "does not lessen . . . our love either for God or for the land of our birth." These men—as soldiers and would-be voters, they were all men—insisted that they were Christian men just like the white men at the Union Convention of Tennessee. The petitioners adapted a verse from the New Testament letter to the Romans about God's love to describe their love for the Union, promising that "neither death nor life, nor angels, nor principalities, nor powers, nor things present, nor things to come, nor height, nor depth, nor any other creature, shall be able to separate us from the love of the Union." They loved the Union like God loved faithful Christians. Months before the Thirteenth Amendment would end slavery and more than three years before the Fourteenth Amendment would guarantee black citizenship, these Tennessee petitioners insisted that true Christian behavior demanded their equal civil and political rights.[25]

Black petitioners went further, arguing that racial prejudice was sinful and contrary to the Bible's teachings. If Tennessee's government claimed to be "based on the teachings of the Bible," white legislators needed to realize that the Bible "prescribes the same rules of action for all . . . whether their complexion be white, yellow, red, or black." Racial prejudice was unchristian, they argued, at a time when most white Christians, including antislavery Christians, assumed racial hierarchy. Far from being the linchpin of proslavery paternalistic order, true Christianity opposed all racial distinction. Their political petition closed with a prayer that God "may enlighten your minds . . . to act with wisdom, justice, and magnanimity," and with a warning that in the final judgment God would judge all people "by the rule of eternal justice, and not by passion and prejudice." Christian arguments for Union loyalty and against racial prejudice formed the backbone of these soldiers' appeal for equal civil and political rights for black citizens.[26]

These black defenses of Christian citizenship emerged earlier in contraband camps and Union-occupied towns, as freedpeople worked to convince white allies in the Union army and missionary groups of their Christian identity. Even when white missionaries recorded these interactions, their accounts could not fully stifle freedpeople's insistence that missionary aid was an answer to their prayers and a support to their self-determination. An older woman who fled slavery with seven family members to Vicksburg, Mississippi, received blankets, food, and clothing from a Union chaplain's wife. The freed woman responded that she knew God had sent the aid because she had prayed "many days for him to send me a friend." The missionary's timing proved apt, the woman explained, because "last night I struggled and prayed" all night for the "Lord to send me help and now it's come." Her Jacob-like struggle with God throughout the night had brought this needed aid to her. She thanked God "and you too," she told the missionary, Mrs. Eberhart, who recorded the interaction as an affirmation that "cheers me on in my arduous work." But despite Eberhart's recording the experience as proof of her good missionary work, the freed woman's own understanding of Christian identity drove the encounter, through her prayers and God's sending Eberhart as an answer.[27]

Both long free and recently emancipated black Christians demonstrated their religious identity to white missionaries through financial and educational support of white work. Natchez, Mississippi, had a significant free black population before the Civil War, and its Colored Baptist Church had erected an antebellum church building. The church invited white teachers to hold a school there, and the white missionaries praised "2 *colored teachers* whom we found here teaching" before northerners' arrival. This church with its established teachers demonstrated that black residents were partners with missionary teachers rather than merely recipients of their aid. The Natchez Methodist "colored congregation" raised twenty-three dollars when a missionary had asked for only five dollars to buy reading material for schools. Blanche Harris, the black AMA teacher who pressed her colleagues for equal treatment, rightly saw the economic power of Natchez's free black citizens when she warned AMA leaders of the cost of alienating this group because these donors supported numerous white missionary efforts around emancipation. Natchez's black community supported northern voluntary and military aid even as they defended their self-determination. A black regiment raised more than $100 to support the AMA's work, at the same time that soldiers raised money to buy an American flag for the regiment's use. As church members and soldiers, Natchez's black residents used their financial support to show they were not untutored objects of white benevolence, but fellow Christians and citizens who, as they would later advocate, deserved equal political status. Missionaries, who frequently wrote pleading letters to their northern supervisors for more funding, viewed this aid as a clear sign of black desire for self-determination, and their interactions with affluent black residents further proved black self-reliance.[28]

An affluent black Natchez resident, Brother Fitzhugh, hosted missionaries for an elaborate dinner party, and the evening showed a portrait of black achievement, even in the eyes of white missionaries who were wary of endorsing black equality. The missionary guests were amazed by his "two-story fine brick house beautifully furnished" with carpets and musical instruments. For missionaries in early 1864, who often ate government-issued contraband rations, a sumptuous dinner of turkey, oyster, beef, cakes, and more was beyond imagining. Brother Fitzhugh, whose white guests recognized him as a fellow Christian by calling him "brother," had earned his freedom when the oldest of his eight children was a baby. As the guests ate, Fitzhugh's oldest daughter played the piano and sang patriotic songs with great skill, prompting one missionary guest to exclaim: "what fools they are who continually say 'they can't take care of themselves'!!!" Brother Fitzhugh's white guests found "so much intelligence and good so that you forget you are among colored folk once slaves." The Christian identity, American patriotism, and class achievements of Brother Fitzhugh and his family set the piano-playing, brick home–dwelling family apart from most Americans, not just most formerly enslaved people. Seeing what freedom allowed one family to achieve pushed white missionary guests better to understand freedpeople's capacity for self-determination, independence, and equality, although they were cautious about advocating political equality.[29]

Black Christians across the Mississippi River Valley celebrated their freedom, but they saw clearly that southern white proslavery theology remained a dangerous obstacle. As they linked their Christian identity to nascent claims for equal citizenship, they argued that white southern Christians' proslavery theology was both wrong and powerful. After Confederate surrender, black Christians praised God for their freedom as they prayed and worked toward equal rights. Meeting in late 1865 in Little Rock, Arkansas, a state Convention of Colored Citizens condemned white southerners' belief "that slavery was divine," which had formed "the corner-stone of a bastard republic." They gathered to "thank God for the events of the past four years" and "to confer with each other as to the best means of completing the Emancipation, Enfranchisement and elevation of our race." These convention members argued that they deserved equal political rights in Arkansas and the nation. Led by several ministers and laypeople, their convention argued that God supported their right to vote in a future that "God has marked . . . with his own finger." They had "lived, suffered, found, bled and many have died" for freedom and equality, and they demanded equal civil and political rights to secure the future that God promised. Yet they warned that white southerners' belief in slavery as divinely ordained posed an ongoing threat.[30]

By late 1865, these convention delegates and their fellow black Christians considered white southern Christianity a major obstacle to their equal civil and political rights because white southerners had not abandoned proslavery Christianity. Their northern white allies remained naïve about the resilient power of proslavery theology because they misunderstood its depth and they shared many elements of the belief that proper white paternalism would best aid freed communities. Black Christians insisted on their equal Christian identity and argued that true Christianity opposed racial distinction. Northern antislavery white Christians offered theological and educational support, and federal officials gave limited support during Presidential Reconstruction. Freedpeople across the Mississippi Valley region embraced this support, but they continued to pursue political and religious independence as their crucial path forward.

Adapting Proslavery Logic after Emancipation

Southern white Christians ignored formerly enslaved people's long efforts for freedom, autonomy, and equality after emancipation in order to present postemancipation fights over Christian citizenship as between two white factions. Because they believed their antebellum proslavery Christianity was more biblically faithful than northern Protestantism, southern denominations of Methodists, Baptists, and Presbyterians refused to reunite with their apostate northern counterparts. During the Civil War, Confederate Christians had been certain that God supported the Confederacy, but by late 1865, white southern Christians claimed in an abrupt shift that they were better Christian citizens than any other group in the United States. They viewed emancipation as a divine affliction that God allowed for their purification, not a final judgment on an evil institution or evidence of racial equality. They insisted that white men alone should govern the South, and they would renew their defenses of gender and racialized social order following their proslavery logic.

In the first months after the Civil War, white southerners crafted a new model of white Christian citizenship that resurrected proslavery theology as a Christian paternalism that demanded hierarchical social order but required little of the white men at its head. Only white men had full access to this Christian citizenship, as former Confederates limited the right to vote to them. In an effort to ignore enslaved people's work toward emancipation, white southerners argued that emancipation had been the misguided work of politically avaricious northern religious and political forces. White southern Christians described freedpeople as pawns of competing white groups, not as actors in their own right, to dismiss their claims of equal citizenship. Northern whites had thrust emancipation upon contented enslaved people in these accounts. White southerners tried to dismiss black Christians' collective work to create independent churches that supported self-determination and political equality as the manipulations of northern Republican boosters, rather than organic movements. Yet, while they insisted that free black communities were pawns of competing white groups, the reality of black self-determination shaped many white actions, especially as freedpeople left white churches and negotiated with white landowners for wages.

White southerners' new Christian citizenship claimed that former Confederates were better citizens of the United States than northern whites. Writing in a widely reprinted open letter in August 1865, Southern Methodist bishops urged white members "to adjust yourselves as citizens of the United States" and linked their "duty as Christians" to that "as loyal citizens." This Christian citizenship distinguished them from their "incurably radical" northern counterparts who "preach another gospel," one "perverted" by political radicalism. White southern Christians reiterated after emancipation that their proslavery theology had been correct and that southern denominations were spiritually superior to northern denominations. Bishop Robert Paine, a coauthor of this letter, had drafted the 1844 Methodist Plan of Separation in the schism over slavery. Together with his fellow Southern Methodist bishops, Paine claimed that slavery's "abolition, for military and political considerations," did not change the "question" of slavery that drove "our separation in 1844." Only southern white churches that believed the Bible supported slavery could "spread scriptural holiness" and "oppose the tide of fanaticism" from northern churches. Expanding from the issue of slavery to a host of related social and political claims, southern Christians claimed that they alone held fast to the Bible's core teaching.[31]

Southern Methodist bishops wrote about, but not directly to, black Christians, including the many thousands who were members of their denomination, indicating that they cared primarily about white Methodists. While noting with pride that they had had over 200,000 enslaved and free black members by 1860, Southern Methodist bishops wrote vaguely about "their new condition" or "their moral training." The bishops' letter did not pastor black members but used them as evidence of white piety. White church members, by contrast, received direct address about issues affecting "your families and your neighbors." Despite this rhetoric, white southerners' accounts were full of evidence of black self-determination, especially their rapid departure from white denominations. Black Christians sought legal ownership of the Methodist churches that they had built as enslaved people to serve as missions to enslaved congregants. They argued that their labor had created these buildings for their religious education, but Southern Methodists saw that same labor as their white members' antebellum property, generously given to aid Christian paternalism. Even after emancipation, Southern Methodist bishops saw black members as their churches' property rather than their vital members.[32]

Southern white Christians claimed paternalistic oversight of freedpeople, yet the substance of that paternalism, such as teaching Christianity to black congregants, disappeared immediately. Black self-determination and southern white apathy both drove this change, but the rhetoric of white Christian citizenship assumed unchanged white paternalism from antebellum slavery, despite the evidence all around them. At the denominational level, white Christian organizations expressed surprise that freedpeople quickly left white church balconies and other spaces of southern white oversight, yet white individuals expressed relief that emancipation had freed them of their paternalistic duties toward formerly enslaved people. Mississippi Presbyterian Rev. Samuel Agnew imagined only very limited freedom for freedpeople in 1865 and complained that they would not obey him. But while he wanted them to obey his farming orders, he dropped any paternalistic religious duty to formerly enslaved people and endorsed violence against them. The same week in late May 1865 that he complained about freedpeople's being too "high" to obey him, he celebrated his first communion Sunday when neither he nor a fellow minister preached a separate sermon for black attendees. Presumably, few free or freedpeople wanted to attend a white-run Presbyterian church, and Agnew had little interest in preaching to them. But Agnew expressed far more concern over labor negotiations than changes in church life. He worried that emancipation was "fraught with sore evils to the poor negroe," yet he used the word "master" to describe his white neighbors who were "hiring their negroes." He wanted economic and political control over black lives and labor, but not religious responsibility for black souls.[33]

Over the summer of 1865, Rev. Agnew, freed from religious concern for formerly enslaved people, endorsed violence toward them. He approvingly recorded that when a freed man returned to his former enslaver to seek a labor contract, the white man "gave him a good whipping" for having run away. Union officials fined other neighbors when they "whipped a little negroe," and Agnew complained that "Yankees" believe "the negroe is a sacred animal," but "when they come to their senses they will find that the negroe must be governed in some way." Agnew had abandoned religious concern for freedpeople, yet he thought that white southerners must control them with physical violence, as an "animal," to have an orderly society. Agnew's inability to hire workers for a pittance forced him to go to work as a schoolteacher. His negotiations failed because freedpeople rejected the harsh contracts Agnew offered, preferring to rent land they could work independently. However, Agnew took comfort that Mississippi's restrictive Black Codes would not allow freedpeople to rent land. Grateful "that hiring is all they can do," Agnew predicted that "our negroes have a fall . . . ahead of them" because "freedom and independence are different things." He endorsed white male–run social order, which relied on white supremacist violence, as necessary for a proper Christian society. Agnew showed that all substance of antebellum paternalism had vanished, even though many white southern Christians would claim later in the postemancipation period that they showed unyielding concern for black southerners' religious lives and best interests. As white proslavery Christians adjusted to emancipation, they did so haltingly and with no concession that their earlier views had changed.[34]

In place of antebellum paternalism, white southerners' new postemancipation Christian paternalism tried to limit freedpeople's religious autonomy for what they claimed was black Christians' own good. Meeting in Covington, Tennessee, Southern Methodists from northern Mississippi and western Tennessee in October 1865 claimed that white ministers were "the best friends the black man ever had, or will have," even amid their "altered condition in this world." Despite emancipation, these Methodists claimed they "consider[ed] ourselves bound to preach to them the unsearchable riches of Christ." They feared that "the licentiousness of their new-born freedom" would make them "stay away from Christ and perish" because "ignorant men of their own color will . . . become teachers." The threat of independent black churches could lead to the damnation of freedpeople if severed from the guidance of southern white Christianity. Still, these Methodists considered their work among freedpeople under the rubric of "Missions," much like their hoped-for plans to send a missionary to China. Black Christians were church members, but not members as equally deserving as the white majority.

Southern states in 1865 echoed these concerns. The Mississippi Black Codes that Rev. Agnew praised restricted religious as well as economic independence by forbidding "any freedman, free Negro, or mulatto" from "exercising the function of a minister of the Gospel without a license from some regularly organized church." The law illustrated that white southerners saw black religious life as an aid to black autonomy, just as renting or owning land—other activities Black Codes prevented—could do. Black preachers threatened whites' control. Congressional Reconstruction would overturn these laws, but their creation showed that white southerners strove to limit emancipation's impact by restricting religious life. While they would later claim never to have changed their antebellum paternalistic care after emancipation, southern white Christians' actions at emancipation showed that they both lost interest in trying to guide black religious life and feared independent black Christianity.[35]

Southern white Christians argued after emancipation that slavery still had biblical support, and they used biblical concepts like affliction to argue that they suffered despite their faithfulness to the Bible, like the ancient Job. Preaching again in Port Gibson, Mississippi, on a national day of thanksgiving that President Johnson declared to celebrate the war's end, Methodist minister Rev. John G. Jones had to adopt a different tack than when he had preached the previous fall on King Jehoshaphat's miraculous victory. In November 1865, he selected Psalm 119:71, "It is good for me that I have been afflicted; that I might learn thy statutes," to call his congregation to give thanks for their afflictions as tools that God used for their spiritual growth. Afflictions, like the biblical trials of Job or Jones's own loss of his young son to death, were painful, but they arose through no fault of the afflicted. The Civil War's afflictions likewise caused pain but did not indicate white southerners' sin. These included the war's death toll and destruction of homes and farms, as well as a host of people who had become afflictions to southern whites: "Traitors: Shirkers: jay hawkers: Schalawags: Carpet Baggers and Speculators." The greatest affliction Jones described was emancipation, which "caused the ruin of the white people and the death of thousands of negroes who have been decoyed away from comfortable homes to perish from poverty and disease" in contraband camps and Union-held cities. Emancipation, Jones explained, was an affliction to both the formerly enslaved and the formerly enslaving. Slavery amounted to "comfortable homes" for enslaved people, Jones assured his congregation. While he had confessed himself cautious about secession, Jones had his white southern loyalty solidified by Confederate defeat. He would go on to declare Reconstruction an evil and white supremacists' overthrow of democratically elected Republicans in Mississippi's 1875 election to be the work of God. But in late 1865, he was content to preach that emancipation was the South's greatest affliction, which meant that slavery had been a blessing supported by the Bible.[36]

White southerners' theological dexterity ensured that the core logic of proslavery Christianity survived Confederate defeat as a new postemancipation Christian paternalism. This paternalism no longer required duties of white paternalists in return for the authority it granted them to re-create hierarchical social order. Throughout Reconstruction, white southerners across denominational lines explicitly affirmed that their antebellum theological defenses of slavery were sound theology. From that premise, they preserved the essence of those arguments: that God clearly mandated a paternalistic social hierarchy modeled after the slaveholding white family as the biblically based model for godly society. All social order and good governance rested on the model of a household directed by a white man whom his wife, children, and servants obeyed. Rights-based claims that forced equality on people who were not equal were a modern aberration from this biblical order. White southerners reiterated that the New Testament epistles still told wives to obey their husbands, children their parents, and slaves their masters. The U.S. Constitution and laws might have changed, but the Bible had not. White southern Christians would defend this vision of social order as more biblical and more just for the postemancipation South. This rearticulated paternalism meant that resisting Reconstruction's efforts to protect black citizens' equal rights meant defending God's plan for society. White southerners justified their violent opposition to Reconstruction with the same basic theological framework through which they had defended slavery. White people's self-interest remained a powerful guide for their theological interpretation.

White Christian Citizenship and Racial Violence

White Christian citizens viewed Reconstruction as tainted by northern white political Christianity in the early period of Presidential Reconstruction under President Andrew Johnson's modest plans, and even more so when Congress took charge of vigorous protections of black citizens' rights in Congressional Reconstruction. White southerners resisted the ongoing Union army presence, aided by northern voluntary groups and Republican officials, as an attack not only on their political sovereignty but on their religious structures as well. Believing, after emancipation, that slavery was biblically supported gave tacit support to violence in the summer of 1866. White southerners excused racial violence as a necessary part of maintaining social order, as it had been under slavery. Mob violence against black communities in Memphis and New Orleans would motivate Reconstruction legislation in Congress and the passage of the Fourteenth Amendment guaranteeing citizenship and equal protection under the law to all persons born in the United States, yet white southerners excused violence as a necessary response to demands for racial equality.

The Memphis Massacre brought congressional attention to white southerners' disregard for black lives, churches, schools, and communities. On May 1, 1866, a white mob in Memphis, Tennessee, attacked the neighborhood around Fort Pickering, a mustering place for black Union troops. The mob of white men burned houses, churches, and schools; killed dozens of freedpeople; and raped several black women. Every black church or school was destroyed. Lincoln Chapel, one of the largest churches, had been dedicated only five months earlier to "the immortal name of that man whose fiat has stricken the shackles from four million slaves." The church building had also housed a school for formerly enslaved people. Standing amid the building's ashes with several of his congregants in "great sorrow and depression," Rev. Ewing O. Tade of the AMA told them that "there were ashes enough . . . to build another Lincoln Chapel" and that they could meet in the shade of a large tree nearby in the meantime.[37] A massive congressional inquiry into the massacre began less than three weeks later, and congressional investigators invited black men and women to testify to their experiences of the massacre's horrors. Their accounts of violence, murder, and rape supported their need for equal protection as citizens. Enslaved women could not legally have sexual violence against them called rape, so amid this horrific violence, free black women's sworn testimonies of rape confirmed their belonging as free members of the United States.[38]

Christian language shaped all sides of the aftermath of the Memphis Massacre as federal officials, antislavery Christians, white southerners, and black residents recounted the events. The white mob had attacked every element of black self-determination, including religious life. Union General George Stoneman wrote to the city's white southern mayor, John Park, that "the people of Memphis" must "govern themselves as a law-abiding and Christian community" or face further military oversight. The U.S. army would enforce Christian behavior, by which General Stoneman meant the prevention of mob violence. Such language showed that Christian identity was an important marker of belonging and of civil participation. Black Christians' articulation of their religious identity placed them squarely among those whom Stoneman defended within this Christian social cohesion.[39]

White southerners, influenced by proslavery theology's emphasis on household order, believed that black people needed white men's paternalistic oversight in all areas of life, from religion to commerce to politics. It was unimaginable for white southerners that their black neighbors should be their political or religious equals, so they saw black churches as little more than Republican or Union political tools, not as organic institutions at the center of free communities. Once black churches were delegitimized as pawns of corrupt, coercive northern political groups, black Christians became clearer targets for their white Christian neighbors' murderous violence, as the Memphis Massacre showed. When news of the event reached Samuel Agnew a hundred miles away, two days after Union troops had restored order in Memphis, he commented with alarm that it "look[ed] like a war of the races." Calling it a war, rather than a massacre, suggested that both sides had fought equally, even though no black person had harmed a white person. In framing the incident this way, Agnew blamed black residents for inciting white mob action and suggested that white violence was merely the reassertion of order after black disturbance. White southern Christians like Agnew rejected federal oversight as an intrusion of meddlesome, misguided Christians on matters that white southerners could better handle themselves, which blunted any criticism of white supremacist mobs. White violence against black bodies formed a necessary part of social order.[40]

National outcry and congressional investigation in Memphis did not stop additional violence that July in New Orleans. In the Mechanics' Institute Riot, a white mob of police officers, Democrats, and other former Confederates attacked delegates on their way to a state constitutional convention organized to call for black men's suffrage. The white mob killed dozens of black Republicans and a few white Republicans amid carnage that prompted some black delegates to jump out of windows in desperate bids to escape. As in Memphis, the white mob also attacked uninvolved black residents around the area, injuring and killing people at work or home, before federal troops eventually restored order. Republicans lamenting the attack analogized it to the St. Bartholomew's Day Massacre, a notorious attack by French Catholics on Huguenot Protestants in 1572 to signal that the mob violence represented the worst attacks on pious Protestants by vindictive Catholics. Again, white southerners framed their actions as defending social order by opposing black suffrage and radical plots to alter the state constitution. This deadly confrontation, less than three months after the Memphis Massacre, prompted another congressional inquiry, which would fuel calls for far-reaching Reconstruction legislation. Black men, their white allies determined, must have the right to vote to protect themselves from unrepentant white supremacists.[41]

On the eve of Congressional Reconstruction, Protestant Christianity divided the turbulent postemancipation Mississippi River Valley. White Christians had revived their proslavery theology after emancipation, and black communities, more than their white Republican allies, recognized the enormous threat this theology posed to their civil and political rights and to their lives. The incommensurability of black and white southern Christianities would shape the rest of the century as Christian identity formed the contours of social and civic belonging and demarcated the boundaries of what was possible. The policies of Congressional Reconstruction and the ratification of the Fourteenth and Fifteenth Amendments, together with the exponential growth of independent black churches, would allow black Americans to assert their rights as Christians and as citizens more forcefully in the coming years. White northerners would encourage their more modest paternalism, and black citizens welcomed white aid but demanded autonomy in directing their lives and communities. White southerners would continue to reinstate a modified version of the orderly paternalism that they imagined had created a harmonious antebellum society. The logic of proslavery theology, which white Christians preserved through the first years of emancipation, would continue to guide white southerners' understanding of what Christianity offered a postemancipation South.

CHAPTER TWO

Reconstruction

Christian Citizenship and Political Equality, 1867–1874

Reconstruction policies transformed the Mississippi River Valley in the late 1860s and 1870s. Constitutional amendments declared black Americans to be citizens who could not be denied equal protection or the right to vote on the basis of race. Black Christians celebrated the fulfillment of the promise of emancipation as a communal religious and political victory. In May 1872, the African Methodist Episcopal Church brought its General Conference to the South for the first time. Meeting in Nashville, Tennessee, the AME Church bishops led the assembled delegates in rejoicing that "Liberty . . . which we gazed upon as 'through a glass darkly,' is to-day assured to us by the beneficial amendments to the Constitution of our country." Now, "all over this broad land all men are free" and "enjoy a recognition of our manhood." Freedom meant more than "physical liberty," but liberty for "the brain" to "become un-fettered and the soul emancipated so that it can bask in the pure sunlight of God's eternal countenance." Motivated by "love of the Church and the pride of the race," AME Church members anticipated ever greater religious, educational, and political gains in the years to come.[1]

As they conducted three weeks of church business, the lay and ordained delegates of the AME Church knew that many eyes watched them as the larg-est denomination of black Christians in the nation. They celebrated the growth of their Christian work with churches formed, souls saved, and schools opened across the nation, and they simultaneously praised the newly "established principle of the American government" that "every citizen of this republic shall be secure in the enjoyment of all rights in all of the states, irre-spective of race, color, or previous condition." Since their last General Con-ference four years earlier, the Fourteenth and Fifteenth Amendments had been ratified and several new southern state constitutions written, and the delegates recorded their unanimous desire to "hail with thankful hearts the growing sentiment of justice in the mind of this nation." AME Church leaders resolved that they "will never rest till, as American citizens, our race shall en-joy all rights and privileges . . . as do any other class of people." This work was their Christian responsibility, and they promised to "seek, by our labors as teachers and ministers of Christ, to elevate our race to that standard of virtue and honor which will entitle it to all the blessings flowing through the streams of civilization, moral worth and Christian truth." As Christian citizens, the AME Church considered the progress of all black Americans to be their religious duty.[2]

While they celebrated their equal citizenship in sweeping statements, the AME Church wanted elected officials to know that they were an organized group of voters who demanded attention. Delegates urged Congress "to pass the 'civil rights bill' now pending ... that equal rights may be awarded to every American citizen traveling on the highways of the nation." Traveling to Tennessee, several AME bishops and delegates faced discrimination from railroad companies that refused them the first-class seating for which they had paid, "thrusting them in second-class cars because of their color." This practice amounted to "abusing our wives and children" by denying them seats alongside white women who had purchased the same tickets. As "the largest body of Christians of the African race in this country," they voiced "solemn protest against this relic of barbarism and American slavery" that was "inconsistent with the rights of man and the principles which underlie our enlightened government." As they praised the proposed civil rights bill, they reminded all elected officials that the AME Church included 7,000 preachers, nearly 400,000 members, and more than a million in attendance, and that this large group of voters would devote their considerable "influence and energies ... to that party ... which shall guarantee to our race those sacred rights and protect us in them." As lay and ordained men, the AME Church delegates promised to vote in ways that would affirm their dignity and that of their nonvoting female members and children, as black men and women together fought for their Christian citizenship.[3]

RECONSTRUCTION USHERED IN NEW POSSIBILITIES for black Christian citizenship with constitutionally guaranteed protections for civil and political rights and independent church organizations that supported black self-determination. The national outcry over the mass murders of dozens in Memphis and New Orleans in the summer of 1866 gave radical congressional Republicans control of Reconstruction policy. Under Congressional Reconstruction, beginning in 1867, black civil and political rights, including the right to vote, gained protection through the Fourteenth and Fifteen Amendments to the Constitution and through legislation designed to enforce equal civil and political rights and to limit the power of white former Confederates. Reconstruction officials monitored new state constitutions in former Confederate states to guarantee that they protected black citizens. As a result, black voters formed a majority of Mississippi's electorate and a powerful minority in adjacent states. Black elected officials took seats in state legislatures and Congress, and the Freedmen's Bureau defended legal, economic, educational, and political interests across the South. White southerners protested vociferously against these changes, and formed the Ku Klux Klan to terrorize black citizens and their white allies. Throughout these major transformations, black and white southerners, as well as Republican federal officials in the South, argued about who deserved civil and political rights through the rhetoric of Christian citizenship.[4]

Black and white southerners clearly articulated their separate concepts of Christian citizenship for the first time during Reconstruction. Black communities defined Christian citizenship as their pursuit of equality and autonomy, and they argued that it was a religious and political goal that all Christians and citizens, including white people, should support. Federal officials, Republican politicians, and white voluntary groups served as allies to this black Christian citizenship, and while they were unequally committed to equal rights, the strongest white allies borrowed language from black Christian citizenship claims to defend black equality. Simultaneously, white southern Christians articulated a postemancipation Christian paternalism that carried the logic of proslavery theology beyond emancipation. White southerners argued that duties, not rights, should be the core of Christian citizenship. They said that Reconstruction's efforts at forced equality were unbiblical, and believed that the antebellum white household, where a benevolent paternalistic man governed his wife, children, and enslaved people, was the ideal model for true Christian citizens to follow. White Christians used this new paternalism to organize religious life during Reconstruction, amid their relative loss of political power. After they achieved Democratic "Redemption," white southerners would advance Christian paternalism in social and political order, not just family and church life. The creation of the Colored Methodist Episcopal Church in America by formerly enslaved members of the Methodist Episcopal Church, South, tested this Christian paternalism as a model for black religious life after emancipation. Although the CME Church would never attract the size or political power of the AME Church, its early history illustrated the efforts of some black Christians to work with white southerners as both navigated uncharted territory. Across Reconstruction in the Mississippi River Valley, black and white communities grappled with novel political realities, and both used the language of Christian citizenship to guide their collective goals.

As southerners developed opposite racial views of Christian citizenship in these years, they both recognized family and gender as crucial elements of identity as Christians and citizens. White southerners praised the model of a hierarchical antebellum white family, where the wife submitted to the husband, the children to the parents, and the enslaved people to their benevolent owners, as a truly Christian social organization. They had no room for free black citizens in this structure, yet they decried the structure of black families, shaped by generations of enslavement, as proof that they were fit neither as Christians nor as citizens. White southerners elevated the supposed purity of white women, the only women whom their paternalism protected, to justify racial violence after Reconstruction. Black Christians too valued families as they worked for self-determination. They sought schools for their children as they recognized an intergenerational struggle for equality. Churches preached temperance as a Christian obligation to protect women and children from the dangers of drunken men, and they saw personal discipline in religious, family, and political life as a necessary component of communal self-help. Yet black Christian citizens strongly denied that traditional gender or sexual norms, which had been prohibited to enslaved people, should be a prerequisite for their participation in Reconstruction-era religious and political life, and they argued that white Christians' family norms had less to do with Christian identity than with preserving white power. Black southerners, their northern allies, and white southerners each imagined distinct forms of Christian citizenship under Reconstruction. Black Christians achieved a remarkable transformation in these short years, while white southerners' Christian paternalism was limited to religious work, like the founding of the CME Church, as they briefly lacked broader political power.

Black Christian Citizenship

Reconstruction was a time of tremendous hope and possibility. Black Christians heralded it as God's work to bring long-delayed justice, and they worked as Christians and citizens to exercise newly protected civil and political rights and to create new churches and denominational networks. Black communities used these new church buildings for religious services, schools, and political rallies. All women and men had constitutionally protected rights as citizens entitled to equal protection, and black men now enjoyed the right to vote. Black southerners were no longer freedpeople with uncertain status, but a voting majority in Mississippi and a powerful electoral minority in other states across the Mississippi River Valley. They were optimistic about the promise that Reconstruction would usher in a racially egalitarian postemancipation era where all citizens enjoyed equal rights and privileges. Many black

Christian citizens viewed federal and state governments and northern anti-slavery groups as their allies in black self-advancement, yet they were careful to maintain control of churches and their community's goals. Despite white southerners' hostility to their civil and political rights and violence from groups like the Ku Klux Klan, this was a time of celebration and anticipation of ever greater success in the future.

Black communities quickly built independent churches in towns and rural areas, despite white supremacist violence, and these churches connected religious, educational, and political work for black Christian citizens, as the growth of black churches in Memphis showed. In 1866, the white mob in the Memphis Massacre had destroyed all of the black churches and schools in the city, but black Christians rebuilt and expanded quickly. The next year, Beale Street Baptist Church opened its new church building for a school taught by an AMA teacher. By 1868, Avery Chapel AME Church in Memphis had 600 members and property valued at $12,000. Rev. W. R. Revels was appointed the minister of Avery Chapel and the supervisor for a handful of other western Tennessee congregations. Revels was the brother of fellow AME Church minister Rev. Hiram Revels, who in 1870 would become the first black U.S. senator when he took the seat that Jefferson Davis had vacated at the start of the Civil War. By 1871, delegates of the Tennessee State Convention of Colored Men reported that Memphis and surrounding Shelby County included twenty-seven black Baptist and Methodist churches and eighteen public and church-based schools for black children. Forming new churches created connections not only among black citizens in towns like Memphis but also between Memphians and national networks of black denominations, white voluntary groups, and Republican elected officials who together aided black equality.[5]

As they built churches and expanded denominational networks, black Christians believed that individual discipline, public education, and federal intervention together would strengthen their Christian citizenship, and they valued the federal government as their ally in this work. Education, for ministers and children, was central to their religious and political goals. Black Christians relied on Congress's Reconstruction policies, and Congress supported black Christianity through direct aid including a $25,000 grant to the AME Church's Wilberforce University in Ohio. Although they lived hundreds of miles from Wilberforce, AME Church groups across the Mississippi Valley valued that grant as a sign of federal support for their religious and educational pursuits. Meeting in 1870, Tennessee's AME leaders praised Congress's gift. In the auspiciously named Citizens' Chapel in Helena, Arkansas, that state's AME ministers recorded their desire "to thank Congress for its munificent gift" to Wilberforce as they simultaneously praised "the success of the common school system in the State of Arkansas," which promised equal education to "all the children of the State." Federal and state education support came late for many black adults, including ministers who "had not early opportunities" for education, so ongoing study was key. Each minister needed to "apply himself closely" to "study not less than three hours each day" in the four-year training course set out for new preachers. Louisiana's AME Church celebrated that their members "enjoy equal educational advantages as other citizens of the Republic." Together with other civil and political rights, such as "equal participation in framing the law" and "freedom of speech" and "of the press," it was now possible for "the Hamitish race to vie laudably with their more favored Anglo Saxon brethren." As they celebrated national and state Reconstruction policy, black Christians labored to take full advantage of its promise.[6]

Black Christians found support from federal officials and northern Christian voluntary groups as they sought education. They welcomed this outside aid, but carefully controlled their church buildings as central communal spaces. Even voluntary workers who were eager to take credit for their earnest work recognized this community control, if grudgingly. One church in a small Mississippi railroad town opened its building as a school in the winter of 1867–68 when still "a half-finished church," and hosted an AMA teacher, Ms. Edmonia Highgate from upstate New York. Despite "the ground covered with snow a foot and a half deep" in an unusually bitter January, the school, "with out windows or means of warming," remained full of "scholars [who] come in five miles from the plantations." The community resisted when Highgate began "using all my energy to get a chimney built at the church" to heat the school. The black Christians who owned the building refused, explaining to her "that in a few months a stove or windows will be useless" in the hot southern Mississippi climate. Highgate did not approve of this conclusion, but she could not force the congregation to make their church more like an upstate New York church building that she considered the ideal. The black citizens of this town welcomed Highgate's lessons and the educational materials she procured from her northern sponsors, but they maintained control over the church building and the community's priorities despite her complaints. Navigating these relationships with would-be supporters, black Christians emphasized autonomy, even as they accepted teaching and other aid.[7]

Other freed communities created schools through collective effort and partnerships with federal officials and voluntary workers. In Camden, Arkansas, a small town along the Ouachita River, black Christians built a sturdy wood-frame church without any "windows, blinds, [or] benches" after emancipation. When an AMA teacher arrived, an "energetic Freedman, an expert and tasteful worker in wood," made "a fine book case and table" for the school, which the teacher hoped northern supporters would fill with donated books. At the same time, "without any missionary aid or assistance," "the Freedmen ha[d] purchased an elegant site for a school house, at an expense of $175.00," and the Freedmen's Bureau gave funds for "building a fine school house" on the lot. Camden's black community constructed the church and purchased the school lot, and they collaborated with government officials and northern missionaries to build and teach at the school. These community efforts and outside partnerships reappeared across the region.[8] Black Christians in Raymond, Mississippi, "own[ed] a large piece of land," and by 1868 were "doing every thing in their power to collect money enough to erect a building to be used as a church and school-house."[9] In Brookhaven, fifty miles away, freedpeople had constructed two church buildings, one Methodist and one Baptist, which held schools with a total of 200 students. Children and adults filled the churches for day, night, and Sabbath schools, although the "rough wooden buildings" had no stoves or fireplaces, "and the Baptist church has no windows, only shutters." On cold mornings, "the boys build fires out of doors" and students, often "not comfortably clothed and some . . . bare-footed," would take turns going outside to warm themselves by the fire while others recited their lessons.[10]

Christian citizenship led black citizens—especially men who could vote and serve as ministers—to merge their goals as citizens and as Christians in a fluid defense of their intellectual, moral, religious, educational, and political equality. Churches hosted political conventions where black men, as voters and as church leaders, demanded further protection of their rights as Christian citizens and denounced white supremacist politics. In September 1870, Tennessee's AME Church ministers gave "the heartiest and most sacred applause" to a "prayer that was full of patriotism, asking God to bless . . . African Methodism," and, from their patriotism, they called for federal intervention because of the "backward step of Tennessee" in giving each county local power over schools, thus doing "irreparable injury" to their children's education. While "almost every State in the Union" offered "Education of all the people irrespective of race or religion," Tennessee had reintroduced racial

inequality by failing to manage local Democrats or prosecute white supremacist violence, and AME Church ministers decried this.[11] Meeting in another
AME church in February 1871, the Tennessee State Convention of Colored
Men formally petitioned Congress and President Grant to overturn the state's
new education policy, created by southern whites "who claim to be of a superior race, a Christian people, and a chivalry." Aided by "outlaws and despera-
does," especially the "Kuklux," white politicians now worked to "deny colored
citizens every right of citizenship, civil and political." This dangerous "rebel
element" stripped away "every vestige of a law that looked to the education of
the colored children, and . . . the civil right of the colored citizens." These two
Tennessee meetings together condemned racial inequality in education as
"the inhuman and unchristian spirit of caste which has corrupted the church
and State." Whether as AME ministers or Colored Convention voters, black
men demanded equal Christian citizenship in similar language.[12]

Racial violence demanded greater protection of black Christian citizenship, and especially of education, by national Republicans. The Colored State
Convention in Tennessee defended equal Christian citizenship and warned
complacent Republicans that its members "will not blindly follow the lead of
any sham Republicanism which will discriminate against the colored citizens" by relying on black voters but nominating only white men to office. The
convention praised the Christian education offered by Fisk University and
Central Tennessee College as "doing more to elevate our colored citizens and
to break down the barriers to progress," to "Christianize and dispel the darkness of ignorance and prejudice than . . . the whole State of Tennessee." The
state underfunded schools for black children and turned a blind eye to "the
Kuklux outlaws" who "burn school-houses and the churches in which school
is taught" and "have broken up nearly all schools outside the large cities."
The convention cited statistics gathered by its members and concluded that
while just under half of Memphis and Shelby County's 7,000 black children
attended school, in adjacent rural Tipton County, less than 10 percent of
the county's 500 black children attended school. Parents sacrificed to send
children to school when the children's labor at home could help feed the
family because they believed education was the key to political, religious, and
economic progress. Yet the state of black education in Tennessee was dire,
especially in rural areas.[13]

As voters and ministers discussed Christian citizenship, black men praised
independent manhood and virtuous womanhood. Their Christian citizenship became synonymous with independent manhood, which meant political equality as voters, economic independence as laborers or landowners,

moral rectitude as temperate Christians, and educational achievement as lit-
erate men. As they defended this vision of manhood, Tennessee's Colored
Convention recorded the wages that men and women could earn in each
county, noting that women's work as laundresses and cooks generally brought
a quarter to half the income of a male laborer, although income for both gen-
ders varied widely from county to county. Being able to earn a living wage
and send their children to school was central to both men's and women's desires for independent Christian citizenship.[14]

Although they could not vote or serve as ministers, black women were vital to Christian citizenship as they pursued "true womanhood." The 1872 AME
Church General Conference with which this chapter opened criticized railroad
segregation as an affront to the dignity of ministers' wives, arguing that black
Christian women should receive the same respect that white women com-
manded. When Arkansas's AME Church leaders invited two white women to
speak about their work running an orphanage for black children and advocating for temperance, the male audience, who would not invite AME women
members to speak to their conference for many more years, praised the white
women's talks as deserving "prayerful consideration" and commended them
"to our wives and daughters as a type of true womanhood," hoping they would
"shape their lives after the beautiful examples set them by these cultured ladies." As black families gained more economic power, these gender norms
around independent manhood and virtuous womanhood would become increasingly important in defense of their citizenship in the face of white supremacist threats.[15]

True Christian behavior strengthened black Christian citizenship for men
and women, especially evangelical conversion and temperance. Perfecting
their Christian identity by focusing on these core Christian markers was not
a distraction from other urgent concerns but a necessary first step before engaging educational and political issues. In these areas, black Christians used
essentially the same language as white Christians, even though their political
and religious goals were distinct. Churches urged temperance pledges from all
members as vital for Christian piety and the defense of gender norms. Black
Methodists and Baptists agreed with their white religious counterparts that alcohol was the source of unnumbered evils in the family, church, and society.
Ministers' use of alcohol was grounds for expulsion from the ministry, as it was
for similar white churches. By alcohol's work, "Widows are multiplied and
Orphans increased" while "the sunshine of domestic bliss" faded before "the
dark power of husbands and fathers maddened by the influence of intoxicating
liquor." As they demanded personal abstention, black Christians praised efforts

to restrict alcohol's legal manufacture and sale, and they would urge support for ballot initiatives to prohibit alcohol sales as such measures appeared. Across denominational and political lines, black churches collectively supported temperance as a vital marker of Christian piety.[16]

Black Christians believed evangelical Christian conversion was the foundation of true piety. Individual conversion was the cornerstone of all Methodist and Baptist identity and the necessary entry point to true Christian identity and a promise of heaven after death. Black and white Christians approached conversion similarly, although they expected different behavior from new converts as Christian citizens. AME leaders insisted that there was "no stronger proof" of a church's authenticity than "that sinners are converted and saved as a result of their labors." Conversion was the essential mission of all churches and a necessary prerequisite to the work they hoped to do in black communities. Once converted, black Christians could cultivate personal piety, expand their educational horizons, and engage as politically active citizens. Yet black Christians' description of conversion was not racially or politically shaped, which supported their efforts to demonstrate shared religious identity with white people. How a converted person engaged the world varied, but what conversion was did not.[17]

Northern missionary teachers, who were often skeptical of equal civil and political rights, united with black churches around evangelical Christian conversion. Blanche Harris, an Oberlin-educated black teacher, had strongly criticized her white AMA colleagues' treatment of her in Mississippi, but she shared the same concern about the Christian conversion of her students that white teachers did. She wrote eagerly to her New York–based supervisor about the "deep seriousness" that had "settled over my whole school" and had prompted "many with streaming eyes" to ask, "What shall I do to be saved?" Harris voiced gratitude for the religious feelings expressed "among the poor" whom she and other teachers had visited. They "found those, whom sickness had brought to need nearly all the necessaries of life," but "[a]ll with very few exceptions, had great faith in God." To Harris, evangelical conversion among her black students strengthened the legitimacy of their civil and political rights. Evangelical conversion united the poor with the comfortable, the formerly enslaved with the college educated, and black with white. It laid the foundation for the educational, economic, and political advancement of all Christian citizens.[18]

Across the Mississippi River Valley, black Christian citizens argued during Reconstruction that their religious identity and political and civil rights together positioned them to participate actively in advancing their community's best interests. As laypeople and ministers, and as citizens with voting rights, black Christian men celebrated new legal protections of their civil and political rights, denounced white southerners' attempts to curtail these rights, and strengthened black educational and economic opportunities through a combination of church-based and public schools. They drew on federal and local government support while defending their community's autonomy, and they combined a focus on personal conversion, temperance, and gender norms with collective action to remind the Republican-controlled federal government that black voters must not be taken for granted. Collectively, these religious and political approaches created the foundation for black Christian citizenship advocacy throughout the rest of the nineteenth century. Black Christians sought to teach their white Republican counterparts, as well as hostile white southerners, that they were white Americans' equals as Christians and citizens. Their success in uniting their religious and political identities appeared in Reconstruction Republicans' support and even in white southerners' attacks on black Christianity as they undermined black civil and political rights.

Northern White Allies on Christian Citizenship

Black communities' claim that as Christians and citizens they deserved equal civil and political rights helped frame how white allies engaged black voters. Northern white Christians who had dedicated themselves to antislavery work and the Union cause rejoiced that they could participate further in the Christian work of expanding black religious, educational, and political opportunities. As Republican politicians campaigned in black churches, they understood their work as both a religious and a political enterprise. When they celebrated black citizenship, these white advocates centered their work on black gender and family roles, much as they had previously attacked slavery for its assault on enslaved families. These white allies, many of whom were Union veterans or voluntary workers in the Civil War, valued partnerships between the state and churches for social reform. If antislavery groups and the Union army had together ended slavery, a widespread view that minimized enslaved people's work against slavery, then white voluntary leaders could work with the federal government to reconstruct the American South. At the same time, many northern white Christians thought black citizens needed ongoing paternalistic guidance from sympathetic whites because black southerners lacked sufficient Christian discipline and because white southerners remained openly hostile to black rights. Yet across varying degrees of support for black equality, white would-be allies borrowed black Christian arguments when they defended black civil and political rights.

When Mississippi gained official readmittance to the Union in 1870, the state legislature, which now included black and white representatives, declared a Day of General Thanksgiving and invited Rev. Albert C. McDonald, a white minister from the northern Methodist Episcopal Church, to address them. McDonald, who had moved to Mississippi to organize schools for his denomination's Freedmen's Aid Society, defended black citizens' equal civil and political rights as a Christian and American necessity. Black legislators had his sermon, "Mississippi and Its Future: A Sermon for the Times," printed to circulate McDonald's ideas beyond the legislature. McDonald addressed white and black Mississippians as "a devout and Christian people" and urged them to recognize "as good citizens . . . that the contest is now ended" and slavery destroyed. Mississippi's new constitution ensured "the investiture of citizen rights" for all regardless of race, so that black citizens were "clothed . . . with the full habiliments of American citizens." White southern Christians, he urged, must abandon their Confederate sympathy and proslavery Christianity to support equal citizenship for all men and equal education for all children.[19]

Echoing black Christian citizens' claims, McDonald argued that Mississippi's new government, with civil and political rights for all and with free common schools for all children, fulfilled biblical and American promises. He addressed white Mississippians, whom he urged to support black citizens' equal rights and universal education as a Christian and American goal. McDonald claimed that the "Jewish law, representing the first government ever established, 'of the people, for the people, and by the people,' required that every child should be taught"; accordingly, "in this land, we should make the same requirement." The United States' "progress as a nation, has been peculiarly marked . . . [by] God who guided our pilgrim fathers over the wave crested billows of the wild Atlantic" and blessed the republic's formation.[20] If Mississippians would "commit anew" to America's Christian promise, they could trust that "when [their] children's children are in their graves, our country will" be "a model government for the nations of the world." He insisted that history, from ancient Judaism to contemporary America, demanded equal education for all.[21]

McDonald called for true Christian manhood from white and black Christian citizens, like that of biblical heroes. He ignored women's citizenship while he focused on Christian men as voters, legislators, and ministers. The central "duty of the leaders of Mississippi" was "to be *men for the times*." These model Christian men were those who, "brushing away the blinding mists of prejudice, have the candor to accept the inevitable" equality of all races. In his energetic defense of black civil and political rights, McDonald claimed that "the right to cast a ballot and hold official positions" had been "secur[ed] to every American citizen, irrespective of race or color." He exulted that the "whole race has been lifted to the heights of manhood" by constitutional amendments that "enfranchise[d] four millions of people," ignoring the fact that only black men, who numbered far fewer than four million, could hope to vote. Yet his focus on racial equality and its links to fabled biblical heroes echoed black Christians' claims. Mississippi needed leaders of biblical proportion to enact political change, like Moses, who "in advance of all his country men he felt the spirit of the exodus and entered on his mission" of emancipation. Likewise, "David, the warrior-king . . . made Israel the glory of the earth," and the prophet Daniel remained "true to principle" in "the lion's den" and "filled the land with Jehovah's praise."[22] In the legacy of these biblical heroes, white Mississippians should turn "from the disappointments of the irreversible past," rather than become "fossils of an age gone by."[23]

Echoing black Christian arguments, McDonald thought white Christians must disavow racial prejudice to be true Christian citizens because racial prejudice was unbiblical. McDonald challenged the "unreasoning and vindictive" racial "prejudices inwoven with their inmost life" that kept white men from supporting "all the rights of citizenship" for "a race they had regarded as below the common level of manhood." "Prejudice," he argued, "poisoned Socrates; banished Aristides; crucified the Lord of glory, and robbed Peter of the honor he might have had, and which Paul won, of being the great apostle of the Gentiles." The same unthinking resistance to change and reform with which McDonald charged white Mississippians had caused Jesus's crucifixion and Peter's skepticism of non-Jewish members of the early Christian church. McDonald promised white southerners that true Christian transformation could convert them away from racial prejudice. In these arguments for equal civil and political rights, McDonald borrowed from black abolitionists like David Walker who centered slavery and oppression on whites' unbiblical racial prejudice, as shown by the apostle Peter's resistance to admitting Gentiles to the early Christian church. In attacking racial prejudice as unbiblical, McDonald supported black Christian citizenship claims more fully than most white Republicans or antislavery Christians.[24]

State legislators welcomed Christian ministers like McDonald to address them, and black churches likewise welcomed politicians like Mississippi

Republican gubernatorial candidate Adelbert Ames. Both McDonald and Ames echoed black Christians' claims in their respective speeches. Ames, a former Union general, spoke in black churches during his 1873 gubernatorial campaign in Mississippi at the top of the state's first ticket of white and black candidates, who would be elected at the high-water mark of Reconstruction's Republican rule in the state. Ames had been Mississippi's congressionally appointed provisional governor, and in 1873 was one of its United States senators. In Tupelo, Mississippi, he "took the floor in a colored Baptist church, and spoke" for more than two hours about his vision for Mississippi's political future before "the largest audience, both of whites and blacks, ever assembled at this place." White voters attending a black church, whether out of curiosity or suspicion, showed Ames that his campaign might unite all Mississippians, at least in opposition to the incumbent conservative Republican Governor Alcorn.[25] Next, in the "village" of Booneville, Ames spoke "to a crowded house" of white voters. The "room not being large enough for all," black voters "were the ones to be crowded out," so that evening, "the colored people met in their church over the hills, a half mile away," where Ames reprised his speech for "some thirty or forty colored men and women." Ames recounted the evening as "a pleasant, yet a sad sight." Because the area had "been the scene of the Ku Klux outrages, the colored people have been deprived of almost every right." The meeting "was sad because it showed how much they had been oppressed, and how eager they were for light." In Ames's narration of his campaign stops, black voters were both oppressed and hopeful, and men and women alike came to hear what Ames and his fellow Republicans planned for Mississippi.[26]

As a New England native and West Point graduate, Ames found rural Mississippi foreign, and he borrowed the language of black Christian citizenship to articulate the significance of his encounters as he campaigned with Mississippi's ticket of white and black Republicans. His black audience "sat and cheered and laughed in turn, probably enjoying the meeting more than meetings are enjoyed even when the audience sit on velvet cushions." Ames, himself more accustomed to velvet cushions than roughly built churches, marveled at this new setting. His political delegation brought religious and political good news, and black men and women's "joy was apparent when they could meet away by themselves to hear the gospel preached by such speakers as are along with me." The Christian gospel infused the political speeches that evening. As he struggled to describe the scene, Ames analogized it to the primitive purity of the early Christian church, a model to which American Protestants had appealed since the seventeenth century as an ideal for religious and communal life. Ames reflected, "I imagine early Christians met and worshipped in the same manner—there was a sentinel to guard our building." This political meeting proved a place for political "light," even as "the stars shone through the cracks" in the "half built" church building, left unfinished because community members "were so poor they could not complete the building." The gathering appeared all the more authentic for the poverty, earnestness, joy, and hope of the men and women seated there. Ames relished the opportunity to speak to them, even as he clearly distanced himself from the deprivations of those whose votes he sought.[27]

Not all northern white residents in the Mississippi River Valley marveled at the religious and political eagerness of black Christian citizens. AMA teachers and ministers, who had first come South to aid freedpeople in contraband camps, taught schools in black churches during Reconstruction, and like Adelbert Ames, they were eager to use these churches for work that they thought would help black communities. Where Ames and Rev. McDonald heartily defended black civil and political rights, many missionary teachers proved more hesitant, especially as they shifted their focus in these years to normal schools and universities that they hoped would avoid attracting white southern violence. Instead of using black Christianity to argue for racial equality in civil and political rights, AMA teachers often argued that black Christians' simplicity and lack of personal discipline necessitated ongoing white missionary oversight of immature Christian citizens. In the many primary schools they operated in the late 1860s, black and white voices competed for authority. As white missionaries recorded the progress of their schools for their northern white supporters, they framed the schools as nonthreatening apolitical spaces where Christian piety rarely intersected with civil and political rights. White southerners viewed these northern teachers as a uniformly radical political and religious threat, but northern missionaries varied in their support for equal rights. Missionaries praised the simple piety of black Christians but cautioned that black gender and sexual norms showed that black Christian citizenship did not yet deserve equal status with that of northern white Christians.[28]

AMA teachers recorded black Christians as deeply grateful for their work, and they minimized black political activity. When 200 children and adults gathered for school in Brookhaven, Mississippi, "one of the colored ministers . . . present" opened the meeting with prayer. He prayed God's blessing on "the teachers who left their foreign homes and firesides" to "come way down South to teach his people." His prayer anticipated a time when those present "might all meet in heaven at last with Abraham, Isaac and Jacob, and Abraham

Lincoln." Adding Lincoln to the Hebrew Bible's pantheon of patriarchs showed the minister's belief that his people's struggles echoed those of God's chosen people, but also showed his endearing, simplistic piety in the eyes of the white teachers who recorded the episode. Similarly, the school's oldest pupils linked literacy to freedom and Christian identity, but never, in the records of their white teacher, to civil and political rights. One "old Aunty who [did] not know her letters yet," claimed that "if she could only read and write she would ask for nothing more in this world." Another older "Baptist minister" came to the school "very anxious to learn" so that he could "read a chapter from his testament every night." Literacy would enable economic and political self-determination in all areas of life, but Bible reading alone made it into the white teacher's report.[29]

Missionaries linked their fear of equal civil and political rights to undisciplined black churches that condoned sexually permissive behavior, a charge that southern white Christians also made. Allen Huggins, an AMA teacher, wrote that "[w]e have got to lay a foundation of correct Christlike living among them, and then keep out all the Hobgoblin, sensational . . . doctrines from . . . the church." While there were many churches near him in Jackson, Mississippi, among both white and black communities, "there is no membership with whom I could conscientiously commune" because of their improper doctrine and impious lives. The problem was so severe that he did "not think [it] can be properly understood by one living in New York." Chief among his complaints against local churches was that "polygamy and fornication are practiced with impunity in all their church organizations."[30] White southerners would make similar complaints against black churches, but Huggins and fellow missionary H. S. Beals applied them to both white and black southerners. Shortly after arriving in 1869 in Tugaloo, Mississippi, Beals lamented that among "both white and col[ored] people, here, the country seems bare of every moral sentiment." People have no "apparent ambition, except to raise cotton." Cotton "is more than King here, It is Lord." Beals thought "all the people had just awoke out of Rip Van Winkle's sleep, not of twenty five, but fifty years." Like Washington Irving's character, Tugaloo's residents were unprepared to participate in a modern nation. With an eager request for more funds and missionary efforts, Beals insisted that "Africa is scarcely more deplorably destitute, than this portion of Miss[issippi]." His work at what would be become Tugaloo College was both foreign and urgent.[31]

Because the AMA's educational work competed for funds with foreign mission groups, when Beals compared Mississippi to Africa he both sought to raise money for his work and to indicate the tremendous distance he saw between true northern Christian citizenship and the poor imitation of it by black and white Mississippians. Southerners of any race had no more grounds for political equality with northern white educators like Beals than colonized Africans did with white missionaries. From this perspective, controlling AMA institutions grew increasingly important for missionary teachers as they built southern colleges and normal schools. Fellow Tugaloo teacher Edward P. Smith described to AMA leadership his 1870 meeting with Republican Gov. Alcorn about education in Mississippi. Smith learned that "the colored people in the Legislature are going to insist on . . . a University of *their own*," and he lamented that "Gov. A's idea is . . . to put the management into their hands and appoint colored teachers and managers throughout." The AMA "should hardly care to be *connected* even with an institution under such management." While they could sell the Tugaloo College property to the state for a profit, Smith discouraged it because it was "not at all likely that the state effort to establish a Normal School . . . will be at all successful under negro management." Instead, it would cause "the aggrandizement of some Dinah & Sambo, until they have floundered through two or three years . . . of incompetency" before the school would be returned to white control with "new foundations" for "a good institution." Smith used white supremacist stereotypes about the unsuitability of black self-government to protect AMA power. While few AMA teachers resorted to such aspersions, Smith's concerns showed that AMA teachers were hardly unqualified defenders of equal civil and political rights.[32]

Black Christians welcomed a range of white partners including federal institutions, Republican politicians, and voluntary organizations as they pursued equal civil and political rights, but they defended their autonomy and self-determination in these relationships. Black legislators had Rev. McDonald's sermon printed because of his strong Christian argument that white men must accept black Mississippians' equal Christian citizenship. Black voters overwhelmingly elected Adelbert Ames and his Republican ticket, to become the state's last Republican governor for more than a century. Black Christian citizens both praised and criticized the AMA's work, depending on their particular goals in each context. The Tennessee State Convention of Colored Men in 1871 praised the AMA president of Fisk University, Prof. E. K. Spence, as doing far more "to elevate our colored citizens and to . . . dispel the darkness of ignorance and prejudice than all the powers used by the whole State of Tennessee" when they charged that Tennessee was failing to educate black children. Yet when the AMA released a particularly critical view of black Christianity in Atlanta in 1875 to justify its own work, AME

Church leaders from many parts of the South denounced it forcefully as an "unchristian assault made . . . by the American Missionary Association." Black communities clearly articulated their claims to Christian citizenship, and their strongest white allies often cited black Christians' own claims. As their educational and political power grew, black Christian citizens knew that they must continue to push the Republican officials who took for granted their electoral support and the white Christians who discounted their Christian identity. Black Christians remained clear-eyed, too, about the threat of white southerners' unrepentant proslavery paternalism.[33]

White Southern Christian Paternalism and Family Order

As white southern Christians grappled with their loss of political power and social influence, they centered their Christian citizenship on paternalism. During Reconstruction's new political order, white southerners believed Christian citizenship demanded an apolitical focus on peaceful family and religious order, to which they contrasted the political machinations of northern Christians. White southerners expressed surprise at black Christians' departure from white churches' benevolent oversight, and they reiterated that white-run Christianity was best for black southerners, though they had neither means nor commitment to attempt to re-create antebellum missions. Instead, their Christian paternalism retained the logic of their earlier proslavery theology in a form that they would expand after Reconstruction to justify white Democratic political power and the extralegal and legal suppression of black civil and political rights. Whites' grudging acceptance of black people as possible fellow Christians, but Christians who needed white oversight and guidance, became a model for viewing black citizenship as only a partial version of white citizenship. As black citizens developed stronger claims for their equal Christian citizenship, white Christians responded by emphasizing white-run paternalistic order as the best defense of Christian identity and proper social and political order.

White Christians continued to affirm that their antebellum proslavery theology had been biblically sound and remained unchanged despite emancipation and that northern and southern theological differences over slavery prohibited denomination reunion. In 1867, Presbyterian minister Rev. Robert Dabney published *A Defence of Virginia, and Through Her, of the South,* which read like an antebellum defense of slavery as Dabney scarcely acknowledged emancipation over hundreds of pages of defenses of slavery from the Old and New Testament. He argued that slavery's benevolent paternalism had been more humane than free labor. Dabney's work earned attention well beyond Virginia, and the *Daily Arkansas Gazette* called the book "invincible logic" that made "the justification of an honorable people complete," so that the "future impartial historian" would know "the course of an honest, patriotic people." These reaffirmations appeared from multiple denominations well into the 1870s. In 1874, Southern Methodists reiterated that "the existence of slavery in the Southern States" caused the Methodist schism, and that reunion of northern and southern branches was impossible because "the position of Southern Methodism on that subject was scriptural" and "our opinions have undergone no change." Southern Methodists had fulfilled their duty "to carry the gospel to the bond and to the free." Their "missions to the slaves" had "Christianized and trained" all the best ministers who now preached in black churches. White southern Christians affirmed their antebellum proslavery theology as a persistent Christian paternalism, but their Reconstruction-era Christian paternalism was nothing like the antebellum missions because neither white nor black Christians had any interest in large-scale work.[34]

To white southerners, emancipation was an unfortunate destruction of the peaceful antebellum order, and they had a duty to reestablish that Christian paternalism. Southern white Christians claimed that neither they nor enslaved people had sought this massive change, and it forced hardships on them both. In the 1880s and 1890s, they would downplay the transformation that emancipation wrought, but white southerners at the height of Reconstruction could not help seeing the magnitude of the change. Speaking in 1868, Episcopal Bishop William Mercer Green voiced concern for "those who were lately our slaves," whose "imposed freedom" caused them "poverty and suffering." With emancipation, "the tender and affecting relationship in which they once stood to us has been rudely broken," and Green hoped that all black southerners would know "to find their best advisers and protectors in their former Masters." As Bishop Green traveled across his Mississippi diocese in late 1870, he visited the Yazoo River plantation "of a beloved friend and sister," where "still stands a Chapel, once crowded with her well instructed servants, now ... fast coming under the influence of a religious teaching as blasphemous as it is unscriptural." White southerners believed that black Christians' new independent churches were religiously and politically dangerous. On this visit, Green baptized "*three* colored children," a mere "remnant of her former, faithful and affectionate household." When Green warned that emancipation had hurt the formerly enslaved, his concerns centered on the loss of paternalistic white oversight, especially on religious matters, and he ignored enslaved people's efforts in abolishing slavery.[35]

Amid their relative lack of political power, white southern Christians emphasized proper order for families and churches as core concerns for Christian citizens during Reconstruction. New Orleans Presbyterian minister Rev. Dr. Benjamin Palmer explained that church and state derived their structure from the orderly family hierarchies of husbands and wives, parents and children, and masters and servants. As he wrote essays on family order that grew into his 1876 book, *The Family, in Its Civil and Churchly Aspects,* Palmer, who had been the founding moderator of the Presbyterian Church of the Confederate States of America, articulated the essence of proslavery theology without specifically defending slavery. In a March 1874 essay on servants' obedience in the *South-Western Presbyterian,* published in New Orleans, Palmer omitted explicit mention of American slavery as he explained that "servitude, in some one of its diversified forms," must "continue a permanent relation" in "a sinful world, where man is under discipline for a holier and happier life hereafter." Palmer wrote that the New Testament "injunction to the servant is conveyed in precisely the same terms as to the child—and in both, the command is apparently absolute." Lest his readers think this a harsh statement, Palmer reasoned that "from the point of view from which God regards them," it "matters little . . . whether one is chosen to be the master, or only the slave who moves nimbly at his beck." If it mattered little to God, that distinction mattered a great deal to antebellum proslavery stalwarts like Palmer and to formerly enslaved people. Palmer's shifting between "slave" and "servant" revealed the extent to which he relied on a proslavery theological framework. His theology of family and social order taught that God expected both enslaved and enslaver to fulfill the duties of their station and maintain social order. Through religious teachings like these, white Christians argued that God designed family order—best expressed in the antebellum household where a white man directed his wife, children, and enslaved people—as the ideal model for family, social, and political organization.[36]

White women collectively embraced Christian citizenship as a duty to restore family and church order. As nonvoting citizens, they emphasized Christian piety and reverence for the antebellum past. White women formed Confederate memorial organizations that quickly gained churches' support. In 1873, the women leaders of the Southern Memorial Association of Washington County, Arkansas, invited Rev. Fontaine Richard Earle, a Confederate veteran and Cumberland Presbyterian minister, to dedicate a new cemetery for Confederate soldiers. Earle's address defended the sacred mission of the Confederacy and the religious duty to honor the Confederate dead. He praised the ladies of the Southern Memorial Association for "their undying love for those who are buried here." These "mothers and sisters and wives who gave their sons and brothers and husbands to the battle's storm and whispered 'God bless you' as they bid them 'goodbye'" exemplified noble Christian womanhood, just as the Confederate dead were "patriots" who had been "honest in their purpose" "to protect their country's honor." Earle dedicated the Confederate cemetery "in this Christian faith" and "in the name of a love for the right . . . in the name of patriotism unawed by power and uninfluenced by gold, in the name of all that is noble in the heart of man." Confederate soldiers who died to protect their households and slavery and former Confederate women who memorialized these noble dead men exemplified white Christian citizenship. As Rev. Earle praised both the Confederate dead and the white women who had created this cemetery for the remains of 300 soldiers, he strengthened the connections between the legitimacy of the Confederate cause and the duties of paternalistic Christian family order. White women proved their ongoing loyalty to this order by memorializing Confederate soldiers.[37]

White women valued this family order as they praised a theological defense of their gendered protection. Women, especially widows, felt devastated by their postwar losses, including their loss of enslaved people's labor. When Octavia Otey, a landowning widow, struggled to manage her large farm, she portrayed God as her heavenly father and male advocate for her challenging daily life. Her anxiety and grief led her to recall how much better things were when her "*husband, brother, and father, were living,*" but "now all are gone." Otey felt "so helpless, as I am." She was "so worried all the time but . . . I do wish and pray, that I could cast all my care on God." In her diary, God figured as a male protector, especially when she had to travel alone; sometimes this divine protection led her to surprise encounters with distant male relatives who offered protection and guidance. Yet, while she wished for a male protector, she did not trust the Ku Klux Klan members who visited her house. When they came in the middle of the night in December 1868 and "asked a number of questions, if the negroes were *humble* and *respectful* and obeyed me &c. I laughed and told them, that I was not certain I would tell them, if they were not." The Ku Klux Klan members assured her, "Madam you need not fear to tell us, we will see that you are protected," but the male protection Otey desired was not that of robed and masked white supremacists whose nighttime visitations she found alarming as a woman without a male protector. She longed for the kind of family that Rev. Dr. Benjamin Palmer imagined.[38]

Reconstruction brought financial difficulty to many white southerners, not only widows like Octavia Otey but many formerly wealthy, landowning men. Rev. John Griffing Jones, the respected Mississippi Methodist minister, had owned a large farm and enslaved several people before the Civil War. But during Reconstruction, he had to work as an editor of a local newspaper, the *Port Gibson Herald*, as well as a minister. With this work, Jones could still attend to "pulpit and pastoral duties," and he "enjoyed it very much," since he could "give the Herald a religious cast." Jones's newspaper work let him "study some subjects thoroughly that perhaps I never would have studied had not my editorial duties required it," such as "the ancient Ethiopian empire so often alluded to in the old Testament." He challenged the idea that "[m]any people have got to believe that Ethiopia had always been in Africa and that the present race of ignorant, savage, wooly headed negroes were the descendants of the ancient noble and warlike race of Ethiopians." His research, Jones said, "demonstrated that ancient Ethiopia was exclusively in Asia, except a little colony planted by the Asiatic Ethiopians, at a late age of their empire on the Nile above Egypt which still bears the name." Jones here excluded people of African descent from biblical sacred history. For a minister who had helped his congregants accept emancipation without abandoning their earlier proslavery theology, writing for a newspaper allowed Jones to marginalize black Christian citizens further. Here, Jones attacked the roots that black Christians might claim for themselves in the Bible, and in doing so, he attacked their Christian citizenship and reiterated racial intellectual and religious inferiority as a biblical and historical fact. When white Mississippians stole political power in 1875 through violent intimidation of Republican voters, Jones would be ready to praise that coup as God's blessed work.[39]

Because they believed black citizens were incapable of equal Christian citizenship, white southern Christians wanted ongoing southern white leadership of churches throughout Reconstruction, despite black Christians' clear desire for autonomy. Whites' paternalistic desire to control black Christianity would expand by 1890 to political and legal control with black disenfranchisement and segregation, but during Reconstruction, white Christians argued for white southern control of churches since they lacked the political power for broader goals. Southern Methodists in northern Louisiana reported to the *New Orleans Christian Advocate* in 1868 that they were trying to direct several black Methodist congregations, but these churches were "not so easily controlled." Faced with "the unanimous desire of all the negroes" to have "preachers of their own color," white Methodists warned "that to grant this desire would . . . work for their own ruin and . . . great injury to the country." These Louisiana Methodists believed it necessary that "the white man holds on to the negro and guides the helm of State and church." White control "can elevate the negro; but so soon as he turns him loose he begins to sink into greater superstition and . . . barbarism." As these local Methodists puzzled through their changing political and religious setting, they simultaneously acknowledged black Christian efforts for self-determination and the danger to religion and politics that they believed these caused. In the same issue of the regional Southern Methodist paper, stories of a "negro riot" caused by "racial incendiarism," combined with "fanaticism and partisan blindness," emphasized the danger of black independence. White Christians tried to shape black Christianity, and Southern Methodists' support of the 1870 founding of the Colored Methodist Episcopal Church in America would be the most successful attempt to create large-scale Christian paternalism in postemancipation Christianity.[40]

Recognizing that black Christians wanted only their own preachers but fearing black self-determination, some white southerners experimented with training black ministers to preach in ways that white Christians approved. Episcopal Bishop William Mercer Green reminded his fellow Episcopalians of their duty to "do what we can to make them useful citizens," lest formerly enslaved people "relaps[e] into the native barbarism and crime of the land from which their fathers came." He supported a training school for a "few, well-tried, well-chosen" "men of that color," who could be ordained deacons, a first step toward priesthood. As deacons for life who were ineligible to become priests, these men could work "as assistants to the clergy . . . or as missionaries" to black communities in a sort of second-class priesthood. The first such deacon, George Jackson, was ordained in 1874. Preaching at Jackson's ordination, white Episcopal priest Rev. William K. Douglas urged him to pursue "the pure Gospel of Christ" that would "combat superstition and grossness" and "religion which is of the emotions alone." Proper family order lay at the heart of true Christianity, and Douglas urged Jackson to teach his congregants "to look with all sanctity and reverence upon the marriage tie" and "to bring up their children in the fear and love of God." They should bring "children early to God's Altar and consecrate them in baptism to his holy service," and Jackson must teach "them what a solemn vow and profession are there made." While Douglas and his family praised Jackson's piety and intelligence, this Episcopal Church plan quickly proved unsuccessful. Jackson left Mississippi less than a year later, and white Episcopalians' hope of having black deacons keep the small number of black members within the Episcopal Church evaporated.[41]

White southerners across the Mississippi River Valley believed that their antebellum proslavery theology and their Reconstruction-era Christian citizenship defended true biblical family order against the politically moti-vated schemes of northern Republican Christians and the superstitious, emotional religion of black southerners. White Christians reaffirmed in ser-mons and newspapers that emancipation did not change the truth of their earlier proslavery theology; it only changed its context. At the height of Re-construction, white Christians deployed their Christian paternalism to struc-ture church and family life. But as white southerners destroyed Reconstruction to "redeem" white Democratic rule, they would bring this new paternalistic order to bear on the political and social framework of the postemancipation South.

Christian Paternalism and the Colored Methodist Episcopal Church in America

In December 1870, the largest experiment in postemancipation Christian pa-ternalism began with the founding of the Colored Methodist Episcopal Church in America under the direction of the white Southern Methodists. The CME Church was the only denomination formally established during Reconstruction, and its creation was simultaneously white Southern Meth-odists' strongest recognition of black self-determination after emancipation and a deeply paternalistic effort to control black Christianity. For decades to come, the ministers of the CME Church were the black leaders to whom Southern Methodists listened most closely and supported most generously. But the price of that close relationship was that the CME Church eschewed the political activity common to most black churches. The CME Church Book of Discipline specified that no church building could be used for politi-cal gatherings. In return, Southern Methodists promised to transfer deeds to the CME Church for the church buildings built, largely by enslaved labor, for Southern Methodists' antebellum missions to enslaved people. These build-ings, for which southern whites had no other use, were their primary dona-tion, showing the limits of white paternalistic aid.[42]

Despite their bishops' commitment to this apolitical Christian piety, some CME ministers and laypeople would challenge this conservatism over the years to come, especially through the pages of the denominational paper, *The Christian Index*. The CME Church's conservative, apolitical stance was too high a price for most black Methodists, and the denomination remained smaller than the AME Church; nevertheless, its efforts to secure resources and protection from white Methodists shaped Southern Methodism for de-cades to come. CME Church members may have seen their church as a safer

option amid white supremacist racial violence against outspoken congregations, or they may have believed that apolitical piety was more biblically
faithful. Because they had white Methodist observers at their early meetings,
CME Church leaders sometimes used their presence to suggest how white
southern Christians should act toward them. Amid the paternalism of its
early history, the moments when CME Church leaders signaled their independence from white oversight or criticized white southerners became all the
more significant.

As they walked in the sanctuary of the First Methodist Church in Jackson,
Tennessee, a space typically reserved for white worshippers, the thirty-five
lay and clerical CME Church delegates brought with them long ties to Southern Methodism, of which most had been members while enslaved. Richard
Vanderhorst from South Carolina had joined the Southern Methodist church
before he purchased his freedom years earlier, and he was later ordained in
the AME Church before joining the CME Church. Vanderhorst had been enslaved by two elderly Methodist sisters who apprenticed him as a carpenter in
Charleston. His carpentry skill allowed him to buy his freedom and a house
where he lived with his family. Another early CME leader, Isaac Lane, had
been born five miles away from Jackson's First Methodist Church as the enslaved child of his white slave-owning father, and he gained local prominence
as an exhorter before and during the Civil War. White mobs beat him brutally
during the Civil War for "holding [a] prayer meeting" where "Negroes were
praying to the Almighty to be set free," and later burned down a church where
he preached. He would become a bishop in 1873 after the older Vanderhorst
had died and would found a college that bore his name. Like Lane, Charles
McTyeire had been enslaved along with his mother and sister by a white
Methodist family, but unlike other delegates, he faced his former enslaver
Bishop Holland McTyeire as a presiding bishop of the first General Conference. One can only speculate about how the former relationship shaped
Charles McTyeire at the conference, but Bishop McTyeire likely saw the election of a person he had formerly enslaved as a lay delegate to the conference
as a sign of the true piety of the white McTyeire family and their faithful
Christian paternalism. Each of these men, two ministers and one lay delegate,
had been enslaved members of the Methodist Episcopal Church, South, and
they chose, among the growing religious options after emancipation, to lead
the Colored Methodist Episcopal Church in America.[43]

The symbolism of the three-day conference emphasized the orderly, mea-
sured transfer of authority from white to black Methodists, with white Methodists a constant guiding presence. The first morning opened with remarks

by white Bishop Robert Paine, who at age seventy-one was a veteran of decades of Southern Methodist debates over slavery. In the 1844 Methodist schism over slavery, Paine had directed the Plan of Separation for the warring northern and southern Methodist bodies, and in 1865 he had coauthored the Pastoral Letter instructing white Southern Methodists how to be good Christian citizens of the reunited United States.[44] Overseeing the founding of an independent black denomination in the postemancipation South would have amazed a younger Paine, yet his earlier proslavery views shaped the cautious paternalism with which he approached black Christian autonomy. He "urged upon the Conference the vital importance of a pure ministry and a spiritual membership," which his audience knew meant that they should avoid political activism. Thereafter, CME Church preachers led the opening prayer and devotional exercises each day, but the two white bishops, Robert Paine and Holland McTyeire, took turns occupying the front bishop's chair until CME Church delegates elected their first bishops, William Miles and Richard Vanderhorst, on the final day. The replacement of a white bishop by a black bishop on the final day signaled the independence of the new denomination, yet the white bishops did not leave the building even as they relinquished the chair. As they continued to look over the final proceedings, Bishops Paine and McTyeire received resolutions of thanks from the delegates, and Bishops Miles and Vanderhorst, together with Bishops Paine and McTyeire, signed the official minutes of the General Conference.[45]

Amid this paternalistic direction, CME Church delegates showed modest efforts to assert their independence, beginning with the name of the new denomination. Southern Methodists suggested the name Colored Methodist Episcopal Church, South, to show its origins within the Methodist Episcopal Church, South. The black delegates adopted a different name, the Colored Methodist Episcopal Church in America, to connect to the Methodist Episcopal Church in America, "the name first given to the Methodist Church by its Founder Mr. John Wesley." While in the past, "we regularly belonged to the South and now . . . we belong to the Colored race," the delegates chose to "simply Prefix our color to the name." Doing so distinguished them from the proslavery schismatic Southern Methodists to show that "we are in fact a part of the original Church and as old as any in America." With this name, the delegates "claim for ourselves an antiquity running as far back as any other branch of the Methodist Family on this side of the Atlantic Ocean." Claiming direct connection to the eighteenth-century founder of Methodism, John Wesley, was a common strategy for competing Methodist groups to assert their authenticity among various Methodist denominations. Their enslaved past also guided the CME Church's claims to a unique identity compared to the antebellum northern origins of the AME and AME Zion Churches, and identifying continuity between an enslaved past and free present would have reassured white Southern Methodists as well.[46]

Like other black Christians, CME Church leaders valued creating schools for black children and adults. The Tennessee Colored State Convention two months later would report on the dire state of black schools because of changing state funding and the Ku Klux Klan's intimidation of teachers. While CME Church leaders would never petition Congress and President Grant as the Colored State Convention did, they addressed the same danger of white supremacist intimidation of teachers in black schools by framing the issue as a matter of Christian education. Surrounded by white Southern Methodist leaders, the CME Church delegates called upon Southern Methodists to lend their aid, as the largest denomination in the South, to prevent violence against teachers across the region. In the final formal report delivered before the Southern Methodist bishops yielded the chair to the newly ordained CME bishops, CME delegates said that "in view of the great need of Education among our People," they "respectfully solicit the sympathy, respect, and Protection of the White People of these Southern Lands toward all persons who may be engaged in Teaching our schools let them be white or Colored." The close observation by white religious officials enabled CME delegates to defend their educational goals, albeit cautiously. If white Christians complained that black Christians and their ministers lacked the education to be truly pious, it was white Christians' religious duty to support black schools and their teachers, particularly in Tennessee, where the state was doing such a poor job of protecting black education.[47]

In the next General Conference in 1873, convened by CME Church Bishop William Miles, each debate about bureaucratic matters reflected the new denomination's position as a distinct group amid white paternalism. White Methodist leaders observed these proceedings as Miles worked to guide his church on a path distinct from that of the AME Church, whose General Conference had also met in Tennessee the previous year. In debating the location of the denomination's printing office, where *The Christian Index* and religious books would be published, Miles favored the current location, Memphis, Tennessee, because "in Memphis the Colored people would be employed by the whites and money would be more plentiful with them by which their Church would be liberally supported." In Nashville, the printing office would not hire CME members. Miles also warned against Nashville because it was home to the white Southern Methodist publishing house. He insisted that

"removal to Nashville . . . would open a door for their enimies [*sic*] to attack,"
especially those "who said they had no Church that they were under the supervision of the white people and could not stand alone." Miles persuaded
the delegates to "be separate and distinct and show that they could . . . exist
successfully as a separate body and command respect." To do so, the CME
Church must "have our own imprint on all our Publications" so they would "all
be in our name." Perhaps recognizing danger in his declaration of independence
from white Southern Methodists, several of whom were present, Miles quickly
added: "We of course desire the help of our White brethren of the Church
South and will cheerfully accept all their assistance." But, he asked, "What
would become of the literature of the Church North, the Church South and
other separate bodies without their distinct Publishing houses worked in their
own name?" Bishops Miles's concern about the printing office showed that by
1873 the CME Church had already attracted vocal critics who criticized their
ongoing relationship with white Southern Methodists.[48]

At the Southern Methodist General Conference in 1874, CME Church
leaders and Southern Methodists reaffirmed this new postemancipation relationship as what white Methodists called "the only practicable course . . . to
meet the exigences of the situation." CME Bishop Miles wrote formal greet-
ings to the bishops of the Methodist Episcopal Church, South, walking the
precarious line between paternalistic acquiescence to white leadership and
assertions of the CME Church's independence. Miles was "thankful to you as
a Church, and to God" that the CME Church was "a separate and independent ecclesiastical body." Southern Methodists' turning "over the Church
property held by them for . . . the colored members" to the CME Church
"has increased the confidence of our people in the M.E. Church, South," and
Miles hoped for further white aid for CME Church publications and education work. He assured white Southern Methodists that his church will "carry
out the design and desire of our organization in spreading Bible holiness all
over the land," and he hoped "you may never have to regret that you set us up
to manage our Church affair, and give the pure unadulterated word of God to
our people." Southern Methodists praised Miles's letter as evidence of white
Christians' ongoing paternalism. Referring to their antebellum efforts for
"the spiritual wants of the . . . descendants of Ham," Southern Methodists
proclaimed that their "interest in this cause has not ceased," although they
had "to adapt our plans to the changed condition." They called for "no slack-
ing of effort but a hearty and united cooperation of our people" with the
CME Church, but offered no specifics. At the same conference where Southern Methodists would reiterate that their proslavery theology had been

correct, they praised this new postemancipation paternalistic relationship, though they offered little aid in return.[49]

A decade earlier, Southern Methodists would not have imagined praising a letter from black Christians who affirmed their independent church organization, but emancipation forced white Christians into a new mode, one that they shaped to resemble the rhetoric of antebellum Christian paternalism. The CME Church would face much criticism into the twentieth century because its creation asked whether paternalistic Christianity and black independence could coexist. The answer was unclear, as neither black independence nor white paternalism were fully satisfied in the CME Church. Many of its early members expressed ongoing affection for Southern Methodists' antebellum missions and hesitance to join national groups with a vociferous political voice, like the AME Church. The Ku Klux Klan and other white supremacist groups targeted politically active churches and their members, so CME Church concerns about politics were likely as much about avoiding violence as about pleasing white Methodists. CME Church General Conferences eschewed political discussion as they conducted church business every four years, but in other settings, like the editorial pages of *The Christian Index*, CME Church members directly challenged white Christians' racial prejudice, especially in theological rather than political language. White Methodists' promise of aid never matched a fraction of their paternalistic rhetoric, which repeatedly pointed to antebellum missions to enslaved people as proof of their piety, while never attempting such work again. A small handful of Southern Methodist leaders supported CME ministerial education and prodded their white colleagues to recognize black people's religious and intellectual equality, if not equal civil and political rights. Southern Methodists would praise the CME Church when they turned attention to it, but they more often expressed concerns about the majority of black southerners who did not belong to the CME Church. Paternalistic control of black religion eluded white southern Christians, and they turned their postemancipation paternalism into a force for white supremacist political control by the late 1870s.

RECONSTRUCTION BROUGHT TRANSFORMATIVE new possibilities to the Mississippi River Valley. It offered previously unknown legal protections for black civil and political rights and substantive federal protection of equal educational, economic, and political opportunities for black and white southerners, but this period also saw white southerners' re-creation of a Christian paternalism rooted in proslavery family order arguments as well as white supremacist violence from the Ku Klux Klan and allied groups. Black Christian citizenship became fully articulated as a religious and political necessity, and black southerners linked their religious and political identities, which would shape their collective organizing throughout the political turmoil of the late nineteenth century. Black Christians had gained some white allies who learned to speak the language of black Christian citizenship and to argue that racial prejudice itself was sinful. All of the strongest Christian arguments for equal religious and political identity came from black Christians themselves, despite the attempts of white sympathizers to claim to speak for black communities' best interests.

White southern Christians were not among these new allies. They reinforced their biblical proslavery views explicitly as a justification for ongoing Christian paternalism in the postemancipation South. Their focus on family and social order would ground their support for violent Democratic takeovers in the mid-1870s and legal segregation in the 1880s and 1890s. White southerners' Christian citizenship valued order and duty, and they believed that legally protected equal rights undermined these goals. White Christians defended organic hierarchy as a biblical mandate, so they resisted Reconstruction policies as Christian heresy that was opposed to their political and economic self-interest. Linking their theological beliefs in biblical order to their self-interest as white citizens who did not want to share political power prepared white southern Christians to dismantle Reconstruction by any means necessary. They attempted, mostly unsuccessfully, to control black Christian communities after they lost political control of their region. With the exception of Southern Methodists' modest success in shaping the CME Church, white southerners discovered that black Christians had little interest in white-run Christianity. Nevertheless, arguments about how Christians should understand political and civil rights drove both black and white Christian citizenship, and the debates that these groups articulated during Reconstruction would continue to shape the South after the "Redemption" of white Democratic power.

CHAPTER THREE

Redemption

Black Rights and Violent Family Order, 1875–1879

Harbingers of violent political change appeared across the Mississippi River Valley in the mid-1870s. Economic pressures intensified after the 1873 depression. On Easter Sunday 1873, over one hundred black citizens were killed by armed white men in Colfax, Louisiana, and white Democrats, inspired by the event, formed paramilitary White Leagues the next year. Arkansas's contested 1874 gubernatorial race provoked armed skirmishes known as the Brooks-Baxter War that resulted in greater power for Democrats. Most dramatic was Mississippi's 1875 state election, marked by widespread racial violence and voter intimidation. President Grant declined to send the troops that Mississippi Governor Adelbert Ames requested, a signal denial of federal support for black voters more than a year before Reconstruction ended in the Hayes-Tilden Compromise. Left without federal oversight, bare-faced white mobs and Democratic militias threatened Republican voters in a strategy that became known as the Mississippi Plan of 1875. White southern Christians defended these groups as protecting family and social order. They warned of further violence and economic reprisals against any man who voted Republican. Mississippi's election resulted in overwhelming victories for Democrats across the state and the end of black men's voting power in a state that, only two years earlier, elected a multiracial Republican coalition with the support of a black voter majority.

On Sunday, November 7, 1875, five days after these violent elections, Rev. John G. Jones, a respected Mississippi Methodist minister then in his seventies, praised God for the election's result. Jones urged his congregation to "acknowledge the hand of God and praise Him publicly" for bringing about this political coup. Jones outlined God's work in directing Democratic victory by reading an entire psalm rather than his norm of preaching from a single verse. "Praise ye the LORD," Jones began, as he read Psalm 147: "The LORD ... healeth the broken in heart, and bindeth up their wounds. ... The LORD lifteth up the meek: he casteth the wicked down to the ground."[1] This psalm, Jones explained, was "very applicable to our present condition." The psalmist's Zion mapped onto Mississippi, where God had cast down "the wicked" Republicans and lifted up "the meek" white Democrats. Jones noted that white Democratic strategy had begun a year earlier and intensified in the final six weeks before the election, but he gave ultimate credit to God for intervening on the side of Democrats. He employed the language of "the broken in heart" and "the meek" to paint white supremacist actors as underdogs and servants of God. For Jones and his congregation, the week's events were "our election" and "our victory," and that morning, "our excitement" was palpable in the church.[2]

Jones preached that God had saved white Mississippians from the pain of Reconstruction and Civil War through this dramatic Democratic victory. He narrated Mississippi's glorious antebellum history, emphasizing white churches' power before "the disasters of the war," which included the dual losses of enslaved labor as "our productive property" and of Confederate war dead as "our best citizens." This juxtaposition showed that Jones saw emancipation only through the eyes of white southerners and not of formerly enslaved people, a perspective that echoed his 1865 sermon about the afflictions of Confederate defeat and emancipation. The war had left the (white) South "subdued completely," as the "negro and schalawag government" created "universal poverty" for white Mississippians. However, a new, hopeful day dawned for Mississippi in 1875, and Jones enjoined his hearers to thank God and to appreciate the hard work of Democrats over the past year, and especially the previous six weeks. In his extensive extemporaneous remarks that remain lost to the historical record, Jones may have directly addressed the violence and racial terror enacted by white supremacist mobs. Many of his fellow Christians supported this violence to protect white lives and family order. Alternatively, he could have given tacit approval by excluding mention of these tactics entirely as he celebrated the electoral results that the violence had produced. He concluded by telling his congregation that they had "obligations" of "holding on where unto we have attained," lest other forces, such as black Mississippians, white Republicans, or federal forces, push back against the Democratic victory that had been achieved that week.[3]

REV. JOHN JONES endorsed one of the most violent, unjust elections in U.S. history as God's intervention to support white Christian citizenship. Mississippi's 1875 elections marked the first major victory of the white supremacist political takeover that its advocates called "Redemption." As white southerners overtook state governments and local offices, they claimed to be "redeeming" the South from the unjust rule of black voters, white Republicans, and northern interlopers. Dignifying their work with this theological term imbued these efforts with a sense of religious mission. Redemption became the goal around which a large coalition of white southern Protestants united across class, denominational, and theological lines. The so-called Redemption of local governments across the Mississippi River Valley reinvigorated white Christian citizenship as a political strategy. As the federal government withdrew from the region, white southerners celebrated their freedom to implement godly rule, which they saw as their authority to limit black civil and political rights.[4]

Two inherent contradictions lay at the center of white Christian citizenship arguments in the mid-1870s. First, white southerners endorsed stability and order while they actively overthrew democratically elected local governments to increase Democratic power. They claimed this political transformation mirrored biblical examples of righteous government, and that it would lead to a more stable government in the future. In doing so, they invoked the rhetoric of white paternalism to discredit black communities' self-determination. Second, they insisted that Christian identity was a prerequisite for political participation as a Christian citizen, but they defined Christian identity to exclude black citizens entirely. When black Christians argued that they met whites' arbitrary gender, sexual, and class norms, white southerners discredited black Christianity through disingenuous attacks. White southerners' gendered attacks sought to undermine black Christian citizens' compelling claims that their equal rights had both biblical and constitutional support.

Black Christians believed that Christian citizenship, far from being a tool of white supremacy, demanded their full inclusion in civic and political life. They argued that U.S. laws and the Constitution guaranteed civil and political rights regardless of color or race, and that the Bible taught that racial discrimination was sinful. Backed by law and Bible, they argued that any true Christian citizen must denounce racial prejudice and defend equal civil and political rights for all. They further insisted that their chosen and cultivated personal traits as Christians demonstrated their fitness as citizens, even beyond their constitutionally guaranteed rights. They emphasized these mutable religious characteristics to fight against white supremacist claims that seemingly immutable racial differences should restrict civil and political power to white hands only. These arguments were especially important as earlier allies, like northern Christian groups and even the Republican Party, acquiesced to a new regime.[5] Black Christian citizenship arguments took many forms, but all insisted that African Americans' Christian identity, shared with white southerners, demanded their equal civil and political rights. They worked to convert white Americans away from racial prejudice and toward the legal and theological grounding for equal rights regardless of race.

Christian citizenship, for both groups of southerners, relied on gender and sexual norms as keys to who deserved civil and political rights. White southern Christians claimed they were restoring order and protecting white families amid dangerous black disorder. They grew obsessed with discrediting black men's independent manhood, and they denied black women access to the category of southern womanhood. Black Christians argued back by defending their virtuous manhood and womanhood. Black men celebrated their "spiritual manhood" as self-determination in their political and religious lives, while they fought to retain their Reconstruction-era civil and political rights. They went on to argue that white Christians, who had denied enslaved people the right to marry while ignoring rampant sexual violence from white men, had no standing to judge their marriages or families as inadequate. These claims of Christian gender and sexual norms grew more important as black civil and political rights faced increasing assaults.[6]

Southern Christians debated perennial questions of Christian identity amid Redemption, and they rooted their opposite political goals in familiar biblical stories. Black Christians denounced white supremacist politics as hypocritical and unchristian. They warned of direct divine judgment on evil behavior. They published reports of racial violence in the pages of denominational newspapers, positioning these accounts alongside devotional texts to show that the work of advancing Christianity meant both personal religious piety and broader social reform. Simultaneously, self-proclaimed Redeemers celebrated the changing political order as the will of God, brought about through human actors, just as Old Testament heroes had destroyed inhabitants of Canaan. White southerners reiterated the logic of their proslavery theology as they argued that Christians should eschew innovative modern ideas of equal rights in favor of a hierarchical paternalistic structure based on the idealized white family. By the mid-1870s, white southerners' model of paternalism had lost every pretense of concern for black lives, yet as they took political control of the region, white southerners would appeal to their antebellum authority as biblically justified, paternalistic slaveholders to legitimize Democratic control.

As they addressed their own communities, black and white Christians responded to each other's arguments about Christian citizenship at the end of Reconstruction. Dialogue across racial lines was rare, but defending a particular version of Christian citizenship necessitated arguing against its alternatives. Black citizens had linked their religious and political identity so successfully in their arguments about Christian citizenship that white supremacists denigrated black claims as both Christians and citizens as they

worked to disenfranchise black men. White supremacists dismissed black religion and politics as corrupt and insincere. Local newspapers ridiculed black
ministers as hypersexual, self-aggrandizing, and uneducated. White Christians sanctified Redemption as the work of God, and they thanked God for
the work that white supremacist organizing and the northern public's apathy
accomplished for Democratic power. In response, black citizens argued that
Christianity demanded its followers eradicate the sin of racial prejudice.
They used their denominational periodicals to catalog racial violence and
political wrongs. Some black Christians decided to cultivate a less politically
engaged religious identity, whether under direct threat from white violence
or viewing a less threatening Christianity to be a safer option, showing that
black religious perspectives covered a wider political range than white southern Christians did. Through their mutually exclusive concepts of Christian
citizenship, both black and white southerners sought to transform the South's
political landscape.

White Christians Redeem Social Order

White southern Christians expanded their postemancipation Christian citizenship to support dismantling Reconstruction through extralegal violence
and voter intimidation. After Confederate defeat, white southerners preserved the logic of proslavery theology in a new white-led paternalistic social
order for southern religious life during Reconstruction. In the mid-1870s,
white southern Christians extended this postemancipation paternalism to
justify Democratic Party power. They had no interest in protecting black
lives, as antebellum slave owners had had financial incentive to do, so their
supposed paternalism was actually white supremacist terror. Southern denominations justified this chaotic power grab as a necessary return to white
male control that would allow proper family and social order.

Southern white Democrats embraced racial violence and voter intimidation in Mississippi's 1875 election as a move toward greater white Christian
control of political affairs, and they framed egregious white supremacist violence as an effort to re-create Christian paternalistic order. Methodist Rev.
John Jones had many like-minded white Mississippians who saw this election
as a contest for Christian principles, rather than as systematic efforts to wrest
political control from the state's rightful majority of voters. Two months before the vote, on September 4, 1875, in Clinton, Mississippi, shooting broke
out at a Republican mass meeting with over a thousand people present, after
armed white Democrats had arrived. Reports differed on who fired the first

shot, but three white men and several black people died. In retaliation for what they claimed was a deliberate attack by Republicans, white militia groups traversed the area, killing dozens of black citizens over the next few days under the guise of restoring peace. White Democrats' hostility provoked the initial conflict in Clinton, and then white Democrats seized on the chaos they created to slaughter their black neighbors. Governor Adelbert Ames issued an urgent order to disband these Democratic-linked militias, to little effect. A congressional investigation the next year revealed a white Democratic plan formulated over the previous summer that "whenever a radical pow-wow is to be held, the nearest anti-radical club" of Democrats would send "discreet, intelligent, and reputable citizens" to interrupt Republican speakers and show that white Democrats were the "true friends of the negroes assembled." Armed Democrats' demands to speak to the Republican assembly caused the violence on which they would capitalize to further intimidate Republican voters over the next two months.[7]

White Christians in the region marked the Clinton violence as an attack on one of their own, and they denounced it as a radical Republican plot, exactly the opposite of what had happened. One of the three white men killed, an armed young lawyer, Frank Thompson, was the son of Mississippi Methodist minister Rev. George Thompson. The bereaved Rev. Thompson, and future Mississippi Methodist bishop Rev. Charles B. Galloway, wrote to the regional Methodist paper, the *New Orleans Christian Advocate*, relating the death of the twenty-six-year-old Thompson, in a riot of which, Galloway claimed, "the origin is scarcely known." Rev. Thompson begged "prayers and sympathy of all the good in our deep affliction." New Orleans's Methodist minister and newspaper editor Rev. Linus Parker lamented the death of this "noble Christian gentleman . . . in his manly prime." He signaled Frank Thompson's innocence in the riot where he died, although sworn testimony from black and white witnesses described Thompson as the ringleader of a group of young Democratic men in Clinton, who drank whisky amid the political speeches just before violence broke out. One white Democratic account of the event said that Thompson's pistol fired unintentionally into the ground, unleashing gunfire and pandemonium. Yet white Southern Methodists were quick to defend their fellow member as a blameless man, struck down in his youth. Doing so made it easier to justify white supremacist violence.[8]

The death of Frank Thompson amplified Southern Methodist justification of white Democratic violence as self-protection. Next to the printed letters with news of Thompson's death, Rev. Linus Parker explained in a misleading editorial to "our Conservative people" that the recent violence was organized by "the Republican leaders to stir up strife and incite the negroes to violence." Ignoring the role of armed Democrats like Thompson, Parker said that no white southerners were "blameworthy." He cautioned white readers against excessive violence, although he deemed it "necessary for communities to organize for self-defense, for the protection of families, and for the maintenance of public order while crowds of drunken, excited and misguided negroes threaten life and property." Assuring Southern Methodist readers falsely that the violence came from Republicans, Rev. Parker encouraged white Christians to arm themselves to defend family and social order for white families alone. Writing from New Orleans, Parker described Mississippi's 1875 election as a trial run for the 1876 national election over "the blight of carpet-bagger rule," and thus an urgent cause for all southern white Christians, not just Mississippians. His newspaper continued to report political unrest, attributed to either Republicans or unnamed instigators, until a final notice in November 1875 that in Mississippi, the "Democrats have swept the State, electing their entire ticket in nearly every county," and, the paper assured white Methodists, "All is peace, and no disturbance is reported anywhere." In one of their leading religious newspapers, white Christians claimed they were preserving social order and protecting their families by advancing white supremacist Democratic power.[9]

The Mississippi violence that white Christians like Rev. Linus Parker justified was not among strangers but neighbors, and the intimacy of white supremacist terror made it more powerful. The days after the violence in Clinton, white men "hunted the whole county," shooting at black men "just the same as birds," as black farmer and Republican state representative Eugene B. Welborne explained. Armed white men "would go right to their houses . . . and kill them if they could," without consequence. Ann Hodge, a young black woman, testified that this happened to her husband Square. Ten armed white men rode on horseback to the home of Square Hodge, a black man who had been shot in the arm the day before in Clinton. His wife Ann met them at the door, and she later recounted to congressional investigators the names of seven of the men who came there. Her older brother John explained where many of the men lived, most a mile or two from the Hodge family. These white neighbors were well known to the Hodge family. One of them, Henry Quick, appeared throughout her narrative as Mr. Quick, suggesting that the Hodge family either worked for him or rented land from him. The white men encircled the house waving pistols, and then began to fire under the house where Ann's two young children hid. Ann pled with them not to kill the children, and they pointed pistols at her, threatening to "shoot your God damned brains out" if she did not reveal her husband's hiding spot. When the men found Square, Ann struggled to put shoes and a coat on her injured husband as he was dragged away. Mr. Quick shouted at Square that if he had listened to his advice, it would not have come to this, indicating that as his employer, he had warned Square against attending political rallies. After the white mob forced Square Hodge from his home, Ann did not find her husband's body for a week. He lay in a swamp, miles from home. Buzzards had disfigured him, but she recognized that Square's shoes were tied just as she had done when the white vigilantes took him from home. Mr. Quick, his white supremacist rage quenched, loaned Ann a wagon and a pine box so that she could retrieve and bury her husband's mutilated body.[10]

This intimate terror, which Rev. Linus Parker justified as a defense of family and social order, destroyed black families' efforts to live as free citizens. As a free man and a voter, Square Hodge had traveled several miles to hear Republican candidates speak in Clinton, and after being shot, he made his way home after dark with his arm in a sling. He avoided telling his wife details of the event for fear that they might endanger her life. Ann Hodge testified under oath to congressional investigators the next summer that, yes, she and Square were married. She named her brothers, who had been present, under a different last name, Jones. Ann and Square Hodge, with their two young children, tried to live as independent citizens, yet white Democratic neighbors destroyed the life they were building for their family in the name of peace and order. As she hid her husband under loose boards in the bedroom, Ann urged her brothers who were in the house to hide because as men with voting rights, they were all in danger from white supremacist vigilantes. Ann's mother concealed her five grandchildren—Ann's two children and three others—under the house, perhaps as she might have hidden her own children from danger when she was enslaved. As her adult children attempted to save Square from the white mob, Ann's mother tried to protect her family's first generation to be born as free citizens. The Hodge family's tragedy showed that in Mississippi in 1875, black voters, households, and families were not safe from the murderous rampages of white Democratic men pursuing white supremacist family order.[11]

Across Mississippi in the fall of 1875, white Christians from many denominations endorsed Democrats' white supremacist power grab as a return to social order from chaos. Such claims showed that white Mississippians had no respect for black self-determination and independence as citizens, Christians, or families. Mississippi Presbyterian Rev. Samuel Agnew endorsed Democrats in the same way his Methodist neighbors did, even though Agnew devoted many evenings to reading theological treatises on why Presbyterian theology was better than that of Methodists or Baptists. The denominational differences paled amid a growing political urgency as Agnew praised Democratic candidates and endorsed the intimidation of Republican voters. After hearing Democratic Congressman L. Q. C. Lamar's stump speech, he praised the Confederate veteran as "an admirable orator, eloquent and gifted with the power of expressing his ideas beautifully." A few days later, Agnew joined a mass meeting in Guntown, Mississippi, for Democratic supporters who were preparing strategies for election day. He praised the town's merchants for collectively deciding "not to credit any black or white man who votes the Radical [Republican] ticket." The mass meeting was less than twenty miles from the church where, two years earlier, Adelbert Ames and his multiracial Republican coalition held a political rally among black citizens that Ames praised as like the early Christian church. Now, white merchants collectively threatened Republican voters with economic ruin, and the visible support of ministers like Rev. Agnew signaled local white Christians' support for these threats. When Democrats swept state offices the next week, Agnew welcomed the outcome as a promise that "Mississippi will once more have a decent Legislature." As a minister, farmer, and teacher, Agnew's white Christian citizenship led him to endorse the political coercion that would bring in Democratic rule.[12]

Processes similar to Mississippi's 1875 election were underway in neighboring states, where white ministers and their congregations constructed theological support for white political power and black men's disenfranchisement. In Arkansas, conflict in the spring of 1874 between rival Republicans, both claiming to be the rightful governor, became known as the Brooks-Baxter War, although it was nearly bloodless. With the victory of Elisha Baxter, a Republican who had earned the support of most of the state's Democratic voters, the path toward Democratic control of the state had been set, and a Democratic governor would be elected in the next election. In this setting, Confederate veteran and Cumberland Presbyterian minister Rev. Fontaine Richard Earle preached a thanksgiving sermon for the political changes underway. He selected a verse from Proverbs: "When the righteous are in authority, the people rejoice: but when the wicked beareth rule, the people mourn." From this text, Earle explained to his congregation that God's power extended over all political factions and nations in ancient times and present. Emphasizing God's sovereignty more than Methodist Rev. John Jones had done, Presbyterian Rev. Earle maintained the necessity to give thanks to God for the political changes, even though it was "impossible for us to say how much is due to the direct agency of the Lord and how much to man." Whether God's work or human labor, Earle pronounced the changes good.[13]

As Earle enumerated the challenges of Reconstruction, he encouraged his listeners to "give thanks to-day" because Republican "manipulators" had been vanquished "like Haman." Linking federal officials and Republican politicians to the biblical figure of Haman, a villain who had conspired to kill the exiled Jewish people, according to the Old Testament book of Esther, was a powerful reference that would hardly have needed explanation to his congregation. Yet Earle surely dwelled at length on the story of Haman, an adviser to King Ahasuerus, who plotted to kill all the Jews in Ahasuerus's Persian kingdom. King Ahasuerus had selected the Jewish girl Esther as his wife without knowing she was Jewish. When Haman plotted to kill all Jews, Esther's bold appeal to her husband the king ended with Haman's execution on the gallows he had prepared for Jews' execution. This well-known story offered Earle the opportunity to link federal officials, Republican politicians, and black voters to the deposed and executed biblical villain Haman. Comparing black voters to Haman could imply that, like Haman, they had had murderous intentions against God's chosen people. Although Haman had been second to the king, a divinely inspired political transformation led to his execution—an outcome that could have chilling implications for black and white Republicans in mid-1870s Arkansas. Through this comparison, Earle insisted that white Democrats followed the legacy of the exiled Jewish people. Linking widely known stories to contemporary events allowed ministers like Earle or Jones, across denominational and state lines, to connect the events of the mid-1870s to biblical narratives. Seeing themselves as the modern-day Hebrew people escaping the murderous intentions of their oppressors, white southerners felt emboldened that not only was their political Redemption justified, it continued the legacy of biblical heroes like the courageous Queen Esther.

White southern Christians defended their destruction of Reconstruction governments as ultimately protecting social and family order despite the violence and intimidation that white vigilantes used to overthrow democratically elected state governments. New Orleans Presbyterian minister Rev. Dr. Benjamin Palmer published his *The Family, in Its Civil and Churchly Aspects* in 1876, and in nearly 300 pages, the book outlined how the whole of church and civil order derived from family authority in marriage, parenting, and servitude. The work read like an antebellum defense of slavery because it legitimized power for white men as husbands, parents, and masters more than a decade after emancipation. Palmer explained that "the Family is . . . an empire under law" in which "the husband rules, the wife submits; the father commands, the child obeys; the master reigns, the servant ministers." In these relationships, individuals were bound into organic unions and were saved from "the monotony of equality" by being taught obedience, deference, and submission. Writing the book over the years 1874–76, Palmer warned that there was "no folly" worse than that "which seeks to level the distinctions in society, and to reduce all classes to a uniform grade." Instead, "the gradation of rank in the Family" was what creates its "value as a school for training" individuals to understand God's orderly plan for hierarchy in church and civil government. Without invoking contemporary events, Palmer implied that Republicans failed to see that forcing equality was dangerous and against God's plan. Biblical order derived from duties, not rights.[14]

Family order was God's design, and godly Christians in the nineteenth-century South should restore this order after more than a decade of disorder. Like antebellum proslavery authors, Palmer was unafraid to emphasize the deep inequality of wives, children, and servants as the necessary subordination that God's plan for family, church, and society required. He drew on the New Testament epistles where he claimed that, in marriage, the wife "never exists afterward as an independent person," but is "merged, civilly and legally, into the man," until death. A woman begins "as the peer of her future lord, until the [marriage] bond is sealed," but a child "from the dawn of its reason" must learn to "express the whole moral nature" in obedience to parents. Palmer next turned to servitude, a category that included slavery as "involuntary servitude." Servitude was the means "by which the poor find relief from the pressure of their necessities; whilst the rich, by their exemption from the drudgery of life, have leisure to push the world forward in refinement and civilization." The relationship between servants and masters advanced society, Palmer claimed. Although he chose not "to perplex this discussion by . . . the vexed question of slavery," Palmer explained how the logic of servitude was most perfectly demonstrated by American slavery, where "the slave is the owner's money" as "capital." Accordingly, self "interest binds the master to promote his well being," including "food, shelter, clothing, care in sickness, [and] the protection of his children," so "that the owner may have a return from the investment he has made." In 1876, Rev. Dr. Palmer explained in a lengthy, erudite text that slavery should be seen as the model of the Bible's plan for family, church, and social order.[15]

FAMILY ORDER ARGUMENTS extended beyond ministers' voices to local newspapers. Alongside arguments that white Democrats' strivings restored Christian order to southern society, white southerners claimed that black Christianity was impious, undisciplined, and uneducated. Recognizing the power of black Christian citizenship, white southerners attacked black

Christianity to discredit black citizenship. Such claims were not merely the province of ministers or church publications, but appeared from many white southern voices, especially Democratic-supporting newspapers. White supremacists' attacks on black Christianity revealed the centrality of gender and sexual norms, especially premarital chastity and sexual fidelity within marriage, to white Redeemers' concepts of Christian citizenship. Such sexual morality, which they argued black churches ignored, became a prerequisite for voting rights. Democratic newspapers attacked black Christianity and its allegedly deficient sexual morality in order to undermine black men's franchise and equal citizenship. Throughout scores of articles attacking black Christians' sexual practices, white Democrats never acknowledged centuries of white men's sexual assault on enslaved women or the ongoing sexual violence that white men could perpetrate with impunity. Black families, not those of white southerners, faced these attacks alone.[16]

Criticizing black Christians' sexual morality and family structures was a central part of Democratic strategy in the 1875 Mississippi elections. "That the negro has a ballot in his hand is a small achievement," a Mississippi Democratic paper pronounced in July 1875, "unless he can have integrity in his character." The "religion of the black race" proved merely "a religion, after a sort," whose adherents were frequently "swept headlong into sensuous sin by their emotions." Black churches were "little better than caricatures," with their "sad lack of virtue," as they preached political ideas rather than sexual morality. Instead of the ballot, black people needed "the Gospel of chastity, honesty, and industry," with an emphasis on "the seventh commandment," which forbade adultery. Eschewing "mere emotional piety," black churches should teach personal moral discipline rather than political ambition, because "the Gospel must be made more . . . than Republicanism." The next summer, after Democratic victories, the same paper ridiculed a recent Republican meeting in a black church with a sarcastic merging of political and religious meaning. Several dozen black voters came to the church to hear Republican speakers. The "expectant darkeys" came "to receive the bread of Republican life from these holy men," but, because the speakers never arrived, the crowd "went home hungry and disappointed." Instead, a local judge and deputy sheriff spoke briefly, and the attendees received only the judge's "sacerdotal benediction." By claiming that black churches were little more than Republican recruiting grounds, white newspapers dismissed black Christian citizens' ability to be either true Christians or equal citizens.[17]

A rare exception to the onslaught of negative stories about black Christianity was one piece that further proved the reach of white supremacist arguments that black voters should vote Democratic or not at all. A Jackson, Mississippi, Democratic newspaper published an "Appeal of an Able Colored Minister to His Race," which typified the Christian paternalism that white Mississippians thought black ministers should teach. The letter so closely mimicked Democratic claims that it seemed the author might have written it under duress, or perhaps that the paper's white editors fabricated it. However, amid the growing violence, the author may have decided to appease white southerners by supporting Democrats. The letter, attributed to Rev. J. G. Johnson, urged black voters to listen to their "white neighbors" because "from childhood you have grown up as the members of one great household, in the bonds of common sympathy and good will." Since emancipation, "you have found your white friends true to you." White Mississippians "have planted with you for your prosperity, they have aided you when in trouble or distress, and when death has entered your households . . . their tears have been mingled with your own." Yet misguided black voters ignored white counsel, so that "white friends at home are made your political enemies." Even sympathetic northerners wondered if "enfranchisement has not proved a curse instead of a blessing." The attacks that black men faced on their voting rights resulted from their own poor decisions, not from any external hostility. Black communities bore responsibility for "the blood of the white man and of the colored man so needlessly spilled." They needed to "join hands with the white people in redeeming from the spoiler your common country," and so to "be worthy the name of freedmen." Black voters should see that their "interests and the interests of the white people are identical." This letter urged the same action white vigilantes did and echoed white arguments that the antebellum past proved white Democrats should govern white and black southerners.[18]

Far more often, Democratic newspapers presented black ministers as moral and political failures, even murderers of their family members. News stories across 1875 alleged that black preachers destroyed families, even their own, and therefore could not be equal citizens. Several Louisiana papers reprinted a story from Delaware in which a black preacher murdered his wife, then hid in the church attic during her funeral, before being found and arrested. These papers rarely printed news from as far away as Delaware, but the story of a preacher murdering his wife aided the papers' overall mission. In a gruesome tale from rural Shelby County, Tennessee, a black preacher nearly killed his wife by attempting to hang her. Worried that his two children might report him, the man enlisted an older black preacher and his wife to help him cover up this domestic abuse. The older couple murdered both children, whose bodies were found on the banks of the Mississippi River.

The *Memphis Daily Appeal* reported the story on the same front page as a laudatory report of a Mississippi Democratic gathering where speakers "with manly fortitude" urged their white neighbors to "shake off the shackles of Radical" Christianity. The "vile and diabolical party" of Republicans, in league with these murderous ministers who had no respect for marriage and family, had to be defeated.[19]

Through the late 1870s, local papers across the Mississippi River Valley alleged corruption and sexual impropriety on the part of black ministers in unverified, lascivious stories. In Memphis, Tennessee, a preacher attempted to rape a twelve-year-old black girl until the girl's cries roused neighbors' attention. On a New Orleans streetcar, "a negro preacher" who "does not exactly follow the precepts of Christ" stabbed a white man in the back. Several papers reported the hanging of an Arkansas preacher who had confessed to murdering his wife. A Texas minister, the Shreveport *Times* testified, had been arrested while preaching, for having stolen two horses. In Mabelville, Arkansas, "a colored preacher" grew "jealous of a young man in his congregation" because of a rivalry over a young woman whom the minister "conceived to be his own property." The minister allegedly lured his rival after dark and fatally stabbed him in the chest, and then escaped by drawing a shotgun on a local policeman. A Monroe, Louisiana, paper told a story from Alabama in which a black minister raped and murdered a white woman and her seventeen-year-old daughter and then killed her fourteen-year-old son in order to steal eighteen dollars. The minister preached the next Sunday on the importance of personal piety, before being arrested and then killed by a white mob. Another "big burly black negro preacher" confessed his desire to marry a white woman, coming to her door when her husband was away to explain that he had been dreaming about her. The respectable white woman fired a revolver at the preacher and missed, but she "waved her bonnet at some gentlemen who were near," who arrested him. That night "a body of masked men" murdered "the scoundrel" before he could stand trial. In story after story, southern papers insisted that "the most consummate rascals are, as a general rule, the negro preachers," who "have about as much idea of piety as a hog has of Sanscrit." Waves of these stories helped Democratic papers justify extralegal attacks on black equal citizenship by arguing that black Christianity was insincere and sexually dangerous.[20]

Newspaper stories that rendered black speech in dialect illustrated black citizens' supposed lack of religious, sexual, and political fitness. Most southerners' vernacular speech could have been rendered a dialect of standard English, but these accounts contrasted the standard English of white narrators to a black dialect. In Arkansas, Lizzie Huggins, "a pudgy, fat-faced, fiery-eyed little colored woman," publicly accused her minister of having an affair with a woman in the congregation. Huggins interrupted the minister's sermon by shouting: "What bizness you got 'zortin' [exhorting] . . . sinners to come to the mourners' bench. Better clean your own self before you get up there 'zortin' sinners—you had. You an' 'Manda Tuggett goin' 'roun' and doin' your dev-ilishness an' then you comin' here an' 'zortin'!" The minister did not deny the affair, but according to the article, he successfully pressed charges against Huggins for disturbing his congregation. The story made the church a farce of un-disciplined religious and sexual lives. Lizzie Huggins appeared brash and disorderly, rather than as a Christian woman upholding accepted sexual norms. Portraying black speech in dialect marked it as a racialized "other," especially when it had no pronunciation change, as in "bizness" and business.[21]

In similar dialect stories, white newspapers maligned black ministers' treatment of black women to link religious authority with sexual license and disregard for the law. A minister seduced the wife of a man in his congrega-tion after Sunday dinner in the couple's home. This story turned a standard trope of hosting a minister for a meal into a scene of black male sexual aggres-sion and female lasciviousness. Another told of a minister who stole a mule and was defended by an inept black lawyer before an ignorant black judge, or of a minister who encouraged his fourteen-year-old daughter to fight and throw rocks at another girl, cheering her on from the sidelines as she hit and bit the younger girl. Another minister, accused of stealing a mule, had alleg-edly turned to work in the church after his earlier efforts in politics had failed. These recurrent themes of thieving and sexually unrestrained ministers who destroyed women's feminine and sexual virtue argued that black Christians and citizens could neither understand nor participate in equal citizenship.[22]

In newspapers across the region, white southerners argued that black sex-ual and gender practices disqualified black residents as equal citizens or Christians. Outside explicitly religious periodicals, these stories underlined the links between black Christianity and citizenship, and between sexual discipline and political fitness. That white supremacists chose to focus their arguments on black religious character in denying their equal citizenship further demonstrated the power of black Christian citizenship. These articles warned that black minis-ters abused their power for personal gratification and self-aggrandizement, par-ticularly through sexual misconduct. White southerners, who only a decade earlier had decried a Confederate Christian proposal to legalize slave mar-riage, argued that failed marriages and lack of premarital and marital sexual discipline proved that black religion failed to adhere to the basic sexual norms that undergirded Christian practice. Together with white Christians' explicit endorsement of Democratic victories as the restoration of Christian social order, white southerners discredited black Christian citizenship by claiming that black people were fundamentally incapable of Christian family order.

Black Christian Citizenship under Attack

Black Christians responded directly to these white supremacist attacks by insisting that the U.S. Constitution and federal laws defended their equal civil and political rights and that true Christianity forbade racial discrimination. To be fully Christian meant to disavow all racial prejudice. With both the law and true Christianity on their side, black Christian citizens demanded protection of their civil and political rights from white supremacist extralegal attacks. Black Christians also defended themselves against charges that they failed to meet gender and sexual norms, but as they rebuked white claims, they denied that these questions of proper manhood or womanhood affected their equal citizenship. Black Christians argued they were the intellectual and moral equals of white Christians, but insisted that neither educational achievement nor conformity to gender and sexual norms should be a prerequisite for equal civil and political rights. White southerners, who had denied enslaved people access to marriage and who had perpetrated sexual and familial violence upon generations of enslaved people with impunity, bore the blame for any failure of black families to live up to Christian norms. As they argued that true Christian citizenship demanded equal religious and political standing for all, black Christians believed that recording white supremacist violence was a Christian duty, and they used their religious periodicals to do this.

After the hopeful moments of Reconstruction, the mid-1870s brought what AME Church ministers identified as an "inhuman and unchristian assault made upon our race."[23] Black Christians taught that white supremacist violence and the racial prejudice that drove it were deeply unchristian, and that Christian practice demanded active attention to the political and social crises facing their communities. The AME Church believed that fighting for political equality belonged within the Christian mission of their denomination. AME Bishop John M. Brown, speaking in January 1876 in Louisiana to black and white ministers from the AME and Methodist Episcopal Church, placed the fight against racism squarely in the center of the ministers' collective responsibilities. Brown used martial language to describe the ministers' duty as "battling in the same arena" to "move . . . in one unbroken phalanx." This battle was against racism since "Negro hate is not an anglo-saxon instinct.

It is the result of early teaching." Racism had been taught to white people, and like any false idea, Christian ministers needed to correct it. Brown insisted that the systemic powers of racism proved the greatest challenge for Christian evangelism, and to solve it, he prescribed religious-based heart change. He enjoined his listeners that Christian salvation and ending racial prejudice worked together because "the spirit of Christ, the grace of God, the blood of Jesus, is able to cleanse the heart, sanctify the soul, and give us proper ideas concerning our fellow man." Where his southern white ministerial counterparts claimed that protecting social and racial order was a Christian duty, Brown taught that Christian conversion was key to ending racial prejudice. "The world," he preached, "must be evangelized by the preaching of the glorious gospel of God." Ministers, "as brethren beloved and as soldiers of the cross," needed to "set our faces as flint and steel against the sins of caste, prejudice and wickedness in high places." Brown explained that the chief sins of the day—racial prejudice and abuse of power—could be overcome through collective action and God's help. Promoting this Christian citizenship and working to convert white Americans away from racism was a central mission of the AME Church in these years.[24]

While excoriating racial prejudice as sin, black Christians also directly challenged white southerners' claims that black churches were disorderly, their ministers uneducated, and their members impious. Racial prejudice was sinful, but it was also unfounded because black Americans were the equal of white Americans, although they faced the assault of white supremacy. To disprove the "preconceived idea of negro inferiority and religious laxity," the AME Church ministers in Louisiana voted in January 1876 to have the sermons preached in their Annual Conference printed in full. These sermons exemplified the "hundreds of eloquent, soul-stirring, logical and theological sermons" preached by "honorable, intelligent and pious colored ministers weekly." They covered ubiquitous Christian topics like the doctrine of the trinity or the church's mission, and made no mention of black experience or current political events. They were filled instead with historical references to Josephus's and Eusebius's histories of the early church, to Luther's role in the Augsburg Confession, and to John Wesley's founding of American Methodism. These sermons could have come from any leading white Methodist minister, which was precisely the point of their publication: showing that AME Church ministers were as educated and eloquent as any white minister.[25]

Black Christians also showed their equal Christian piety by writing themselves into broader currents in American Protestant culture. Antebellum Protestants had worked to distribute Bibles, particularly through the American Bible Society, founded in 1816. AME Church ministers noted that while enslaved, black Christians "as a race did not directly contribute to this great work, yet, indirectly we did; because by our labor we furnished means to those who did." Their enslaved labor gave wealth to northern and southern white Protestants, who had in turn funded Bible distribution. From this past, current AME Church leaders pressed for further work "circulating the Bible to our poor, despised and suffering people" because Bibles were in great demand in black communities. Because "our people are commonly charged double prices for all they purchase," ministers wanted to ensure that Bibles were affordable. Even issues that seemed purely devotional or religious in content, such as the ubiquitous Protestant focus on Bible distribution and reading, allowed black Christians to claim equal Christian piety with white Christians who prided themselves on a long history of Bible distribution and to fight unjust practices like price gouging.[26]

Black Christians recognized education—from primary to higher education— as a part of their Christian work as they fought for full inclusion as equal Christians and citizens. Education would help build their case for shared Christian identity with white southerners, although black Christians denied that formal education should be a prerequisite for equal identity as a Christian or citizen. Local church conferences worked to educate ministers and laypeople through Sunday school programs. They built on black churches' earlier work hosting and supporting schools after emancipation and recognized, especially as Reconstruction ended, that public schools for black children were essential but inadequately funded. Earlier allies like the American Missionary Association turned over primary schools to local public control and focused instead on educating teachers and ministers in normal school and university settings. AME Church ministers set standards for educating their new preachers in preparation for ordination on topics ranging from English grammar, modern geography, and arithmetic, to the Bible, moral philosophy, and pastoral theology. Black Baptists were more loosely organized than other groups, but they organized regionally to create schools for members and ministers so that "brightness of mind" would come equally to "the man who has the darkest face" because "God made all men . . . of different hue or color of the same blood and faculties." Members of the CME Church pushed white Southern Methodists to support their efforts to educate ministers. Black Christians from many denominations worked for better educational opportunities for primary schools, Sunday schools, and ministerial education. While they worked resolutely to improve the educational status of their members, they resisted white southerners' claims that educational status—including literacy—demarcated who could be a true Christian citizen.[27]

Recording instances of racial violence was an important way that black Christians fought growing threats to their civil and political rights. Denominational newspapers, especially the Methodist Episcopal Church's *Southwestern Advocate*, later retitled the *Southwestern Christian Advocate*, published in New Orleans, reported on racial discrimination and violence as part of its religious mission. As a mission of the Northern Methodists in the Mississippi River Valley, the denomination included both white and black ministers and almost entirely black congregations, and its ministers purposely wrote for the paper without identifying themselves by race. All considered it their duty to fight against white supremacy. Drawing upon local reports as well as articles from sympathetic northern and midwestern newspapers such as the *Chicago Inter-Ocean*, the *Southwestern Advocate* explained that Louisiana's White Leagues held "the avowed object of depriving negroes of all political rights, th[r]ough the establishment of a white man's government," much like the Confederate government that had "been voted down and fought down at the cannon's mouth and at the point of the bayonet." These arguments emphasized the continuities between the Confederate vision of a slaveholding republic premised upon the logic of proslavery theology and the white supremacist vision of black men's disenfranchisement and white male rule that white Christian citizenship advanced. Doing so enabled the paper to stress that black identity as both Christians and as citizens deserved solidarity and protection.[28]

Reporting "the outrages perpetrated upon innocent, inoffensive citizens . . . by members of the so called White League" became an increasingly important goal of religious reporting as "these outrages . . . increased to an alarming extent" in the late 1870s. In White League attacks, "Men have been shot, hung and burned on account of their political opinions, and because their skins were not of the same hue as that of the devilish and cowardly assassins." Even closer to the minds of the editors were reports that "[n]ewspapers have been threatened" for opposing the White League's actions.[29] Nevertheless, the *Southwestern Advocate* reported lists of White League activities including names of murder victims across the state, reports of sixteen murders in one rural parish, and notes of civil servants and ministers who had been driven from their offices and sometimes their homes. By positioning these articles alongside the standard fare of devotional meditations, religious poems, and exhortations to holy living, the paper showed that bringing attention to these violent acts was central to the paper's larger mission for Louisiana- and Mississippi-area Northern Methodists.[30]

While other papers in New Orleans, like white Southern Methodists' *New Orleans Christian Advocate*, reported that Mississippi's 1875 election peacefully yielded massive Democratic victories, the *Southwestern Advocate* declared that "[t]he election in Mississippi went Democratic not because there are a majority [of] Democratic voters in that State," but because of "intimidation and violence." Lest any reader misunderstand the election's results, the paper explained that "colored republican voters . . . were given to understand they must vote with the Democrats or not at all." In some counties that had had large Republican majorities, "not a single Republican vote was cast." This political coup had not emerged spontaneously, but "the plan was laid months ago, and has been fully carried out to carry the State *peaceably if possible, by force if necessary!*" The paper looked to other electoral races across the country for more hopeful results, and from these races, insisted that Republican success elsewhere "prove[d] that the people of this nation prefer to trust the Republic in the hands of the party which saved it, rather than in the hands of those who sought to destroy" it. These results, particularly in northern cities' local elections, forecasted that there was "no doubt" that a Republican would win the 1876 presidential race. Although that prediction would prove naïve, the statement demonstrated the Methodist Episcopal Church paper's commitment to Republican politics and to black men's enfranchisement.[31]

As they denounced attacks on their voting rights, black Christian ministers asserted that they were true men who deserved the same self-governing rights as white male citizens. Across Louisiana, AME Church ministers insisted that "our independent manhood, and our reliance on God, has brought forth from our enemies the highest encomiums." This independent manhood meant both economic independence with the goal of landownership, and marriage with its opportunities for overseeing dependents like a wife and children. When Simeon Taylor, an AME Church minister, died in 1875, his fellow ministers eulogized him by praising his work "to plant the seeds of spiritual manhood in the soil of the Mississippi Valley." This manhood collaborated with "the strong arm of God," which "strikes down the barriers of caste, prejudice, and enmity, and rears upon the ruins of vassalage and ignorance an African church where God . . . gives life and vivacity." Black manhood was a powerful force to establish Christian citizenship and combat white supremacist power.[32]

Likewise, women's gendered virtue and black Christians' sexual norms proved that they were virtuous Christian people, despite white Democrats' spurious allegations. To such critics, AME Church leaders responded: "We would have them understand that amid our females, virtue produces her most beautiful blossoms: and where ever our standard has been hoisted these infamous charges have melted and passed away into oblivion." The AME Church repelled charges of sexual impropriety as abhorrent, but to broader charges of having "not reached that high standard of practical religion taught in the Bible," they blamed the legacy of slavery. "[W]e would have ... the world to know that if degradation [or] dishonesty" is found among "our people, it emanates from that class and race of people who *branded* us with it. If there be dishonesty among us, it came from having been *robbed of our daily bread* by vampires and leeches of the so-called *dominant race.*" Any faults that white observers found in the propriety of black churches had been forced upon them by slavery and racial inequality, and because of that, the ministers insisted, "We hurl back into their faces their infamous charges and will teach them by our onward Christian march that such slanders ... must not stop or impede our progress." That progress toward independent manhood and virtuous womanhood stood at the center of the religious mission of the AME Church, and in pursuing these goals, they relied on the promises claimed by their belonging to a nation where the "Fatherhood of God, the brotherhood of man, is shouted along our lines from Maine to the Rio Grande." The United States' laws and Constitution stood on their side, as did true Christianity's denunciation of racial prejudice. Black Christian citizens claimed the independent political and economic identity of all citizens.[33]

Black Christians held fast to their belief that the U.S. Constitution and laws and true Christianity supported their equal civil and political rights as Christian citizens, but with the federal government's failure to defend black civil and political rights, white Democrats continued to gain power. Meeting in western Tennessee in 1879, AME Church ministers addressed the crisis of white supremacy and the benefits of emigrating away from the South. White southerners, "since they ... resumed political power," relegated "the Southern black man" to "a servile substratum." Black Christians were "law-abiding citizens" who asked only for "the observance of the Constitution and the laws," but they recognized that these basic rights were diminishing. They appealed to "the God of Battles, ... the King of Kings," and "to the loyal people of the nation" to aid them, but they also taught self-reliance. "Let us not wait for something to turn up," they encouraged each other, "but go forth and make chances" for their equal rights. They appealed "to the independent manhood of the black man" to "stand man to man in their political organization ... until the rights of all men are secured, enforced and respected in every state ... in the starry Union." Black Christian men deserved the rights of all men, and while they hoped that, "as sure as God rules in the heavens," their rights would be protected, they also recommended that their members might find emigration to other regions their best chance for "happy release and safer abode." To preserve their Christian citizenship, black Christians needed to take matters into their own hands rather than waiting on divine or human intervention, even if that required leaving the South entirely. As they preached self-reliance, black Christians recognized that white allies had fled and that southern white Christians posed a dire threat with their white supremacist paternalism.[34]

Reinventing Paternalism amid Redemption

When white southerners seized Democratic power across the Mississippi River Valley by the late 1870s, they claimed they were creating a new paternalistic family order out of the chaos of Reconstruction. Their Reconstruction-era Christian paternalism had appealed to antebellum examples to govern black and white religious life in the postemancipation South, but now white Christian Democrats expanded this vision to social and political order following what they claimed was an antebellum model. The relationship between white southern Christians in the Methodist Episcopal Church, South, and black Christians in the CME Church illustrated the limited extent to which black Christians could marshal support for their religious, educational, or political goals by appealing to white Christians' paternalistic goals. The path of the CME Church, a smaller group than the AME Church or Baptists, showed deliberate appeals to white paternalism, but it was not the complete capitulation to white paternalism that its critics alleged. CME Church leaders appealed to long-standing Christian piety as they articulated their apolitical stance, and they specifically invoked white Christians' paternalistic arguments to claim spiritual equality as fellow Christians with white Southern Methodists. The relationship between the CME Church and white Southern Methodists demonstrates how powerful white southern Christians' white supremacist paternalism grew in these years, and also illumines the range of political strategies that black Christians adopted in the face of this power.

Every four years, the CME Church's General Conference conducted church business and set goals for their denomination amid white onlookers. CME Church leaders focused on educational and publishing work as a core religious endeavor and never mentioned political changes in the South. As they advocated education, piety, and personal morality, rather than black civil and political rights, CME Church leaders argued that Christianity's proper sphere was "to mold and shape and sanctify the moral nature of man." In an approach that paralleled the AME Church's publishing sermons to refute white claims that black ministers' sermons were unsophisticated and overly emotional, the

CME Church leaders gave lengthy speeches and read letters from absent ministers to show their elevated religious and educational work. All of these elements mirrored similar AME Church efforts to demonstrate the educational achievement and literacy skills of their clergy despite the different political approaches of these two denominations. Amid its paternalistic relationship with Southern Methodists, the CME Church joined fellow black denominations in illustrating black competence to prove racial equality.[35]

CME Church leaders, like many fellow Protestants, both black and white, warned against new religious trends and celebrated Bible reading as distinguishing Protestant characteristics. They called forth "renewed energies to meet the aims and ends of our advancing civilization" because "our people are becoming a reading people and are beginning to understand the new position in society." Simultaneously, they expressed concern over the "rupturing of society and civil life" by "new forms of unbelief, and laxed morals," against which the CME Church labored to maintain "good spiritual Christianity." These concerns over morality and education demanded "an educated and intelligent leadership in the church." They further bolstered their educational work by contrasting it with Roman Catholicism, vilifying Catholics for wanting to keep black people uneducated, while Protestants, "since the day of Martin Luther," had presented the Bible and literacy to "the common people." This anti-Catholic view echoed white Southern Methodists' anti-Catholicism, a shared prejudice that linked the two groups. CME leaders argued to white Methodists that opposing black education made them like Catholics and failed a basic Protestant goal of universal Bible reading.[36]

The CME Church's acquiescence to paternalism emerged strongly when they adopted resolutions that described white Southern Methodists as "our foster mother in the past" and "our true friend of the present and for time to come." With Southern Methodist officials present, CME Church leaders averred that their "prayers will ever be that that church may continue to manifest their love for us."[37] The deaths of white Southern Methodist leaders offered an opportunity for CME Church officials to express ongoing gratitude for Southern Methodist leadership. They praised the late Rev. Thomas Taylor, whose "heroic labors" as the superintendent of Southern Methodists' "colored work" after the Civil War had prepared for the 1870 founding of the CME Church. In a glowing memorial, CME Church leaders praised the "untiring fortitude" and "extraordinary character" of "that sainted servant of Christ," who had been "a true friend, an able counselor and Christian worker."[38] When noted Southern Methodist proslavery activist Rev. Thomas O. Summers died during their General Conference, CME leaders paused the business of their conference to pass a resolution of "sympathy . . . in the loss of this great and good man" in whose "death we have lost a father and a friend." Ignoring his support of slavery and his ongoing leadership in a denomination that had defended proslavery Christian claims after emancipation, CME Church leaders mourned his death and helped to appease white Southern Methodists concerned about the CME Church's goals.[39]

White Southern Methodists valued these gestures, and they wrote approving accounts of the CME Church in their newspaper, praising the CME Church's apolitical piety in contrast to other black denominations. The CME Church worked "to keep their religious assemblies from that complication with political parties and demagogues that has been so damaging to the spiritual interest of the colored people of the South" by making a "rule . . . that their church houses shall not be used for political speeches or assemblies."[40] Other articles singled out Bishop Isaac Lane for his exemplary focus on religious piety rather than politics. Lane's "plain and direct" sermons dwelled on "morality and virtue," and he emphasized to his hearers that "till their standard of morality was raised higher they might not expect to rise higher as a people."[41] Lane's sermons on personal discipline rather than politics earned Southern Methodists' approval. Isaac Lane seemed a sympathetic figure to white Southern Methodists for an additional reason: Lane was the son of the white man who had enslaved him. His virtues appeared to be written into his body, which was "tall, erect, and showing in his general appearance a preponderance of the Anglo-Saxon blood," according to a white Southern Methodist minister's report. Here Lane's being the son of his former enslaver, a fact to which Lane's autobiography testified, rather than exposing the sexual violence that slavery encouraged and the vulnerability of enslaved women, rendered Lane a less threatening black leader. Bishop Lane emerged then as a liminal figure who physically looked like white southerners and resembled white Southern Methodist piety in his preaching, yet because he never attempted to identify with white Christians, he could be viewed as an ideal black minister. His fellow ministers, Southern Methodists urged, should "imitate him, and avoid the corrupting influences of politics" as they navigated the post-Reconstruction South.[42]

CME Church leaders used shared evangelical idioms to identify with white Southern Methodists. In a story reprinted in several white Southern Methodist papers, CME Church Bishop Lucius Holsey praised Southern Methodist Rev. W. A. Parks, recalling that two decades before, Rev. Parks's sermon and his praying with Holsey, then an enslaved young man, led to Holsey's conversion. Retelling this story when Parks visited his CME congregation in 1879, Holsey turned to Parks and "said, with much emotion, and his finger pointing up to heaven: 'Mr. Parks, when you get to heaven, and the Lord Jesus places a crown upon your head, I will be one star in that crown.'" Parks was overwhelmed by "emotions of joy" at the story. The account positioned Holsey's conversion as equally valuable as that of any white Methodist, while also drawing connections between the Southern Methodist past under slavery and the ongoing relationship between the CME Church and the white Southern Methodists. The next day, Bishop Holsey was invited as an honored guest to a meeting of white Southern Methodist ministers and their bishop, and the group assured Holsey of their "abiding interest in [the] present and future welfare" of "the church and race he represents." Holsey reported these statements, although promised support rarely emerged from these white offers.[43]

When Southern Methodists held their next General Conference, Bishop Holsey addressed the several hundred ministers and laymen with "a message of love and Christian fraternity." He earned applause with his assurances that the CME Church remained "proud of our ancestry and noble parentage" from Southern Methodists, as he asked for financial support. Holsey cautiously sidestepped Southern Methodist claims about the justification of slavery by pointing out that "[w]hether God designed the institution of slavery or not . . . it does not now exist," a maneuver that showed how widespread proslavery logic remained for Southern Methodists long after emancipation. CME Church members, if often "servants," were now "citizens" with white Methodists, and they had a unique claim on Southern Methodist aid for help "in redeeming your friends and former slaves from . . . darkness and degradation." If white Christians wanted a paternalistic society, then they needed to provide the support that paternalistic duty demanded. Borrowing language from a Pauline epistle, Holsey insisted that his congregants were "fellow citizens with the Saints, who are of the household of Methodism, and built upon the same foundations of grace and truth in common with yourselves." Black Methodists were uniquely capable of practicing "an active, living and spiritual Christianity" because they had avoided the "foul blotch of infidel" ideas spreading among late nineteenth-century white Protestants in the form of biblical higher criticism and theological liberalism. He and his fellow ministers remained "aloof from the corrupting and entangling alliances of party politics," because "the evangelical work of the gospel" could not coexist with "the intrigues of the politician." For that work, Holsey sought "your helping hand, your prayers, your cooperation, and your money." Evangelical piety and Christian paternalism demanded white aid, although the CME Church would receive only a small measure of what they requested.⁴⁴

The CME Church's example demonstrated that eschewing political activism earned whites' approval as a better form of religious practice, yet far less institutional or financial support flowed from this recognition than white Christians' own logic suggested. These conservative responses to white supremacist Redemption had a long history in Protestant Christian identity across massive social inequality. The tactics of the CME Church represented a deliberate approach to Redemption politics, one that would remain crucial as black franchise and equal citizenship rights diminished over the rest of the nineteenth century. Becoming white Southern Methodists' favored group of black Christians conveyed some benefits to the CME Church, although white Christians failed to live up to their paternalistic promises. As the next chapter will discuss, after the threat of black political equality had disappeared, Southern Methodists led other white southern Christians in fledgling efforts to build schools and colleges for black people. Many of these had special ties to the CME Church, and CME Church bishops and other leaders occupied senior positions within the schools' leadership, yet these efforts never approached Reconstruction-era universal public education goals.

THROUGHOUT THE WHITE SUPREMACIST political coup in the mid-1870s, white southerners defended themselves as creating a new political order in which they would finally be free to reenact true Christian paternalism. They upended democratically elected Republican governments through violence and voter intimidation in the name of social and family order. White Christians endorsed white supremacist violence as necessary to protect white families, particularly white women. They used the white Democratic press to attack black Christians and their ministers as sexually permissive threats to white order, never as fellow Christians whose concerns deserved attention. Black Christians resisted white southerners at every turn, arguing that U.S. law and Christianity together opposed white Democratic action. Yet with scant federal support, black citizens had shrinking legal and political recourse. Black Christian citizens argued that as fellow Christians, they deserved unprejudiced treatment from white Christians. As their civil and political rights were stripped from them, black Christians' religious arguments for racial equality, however inadequate to protect civil and political rights, grew more central to their legal and political arguments.

In the 1880s, white southern Protestants fashioned a paternalistic order that transformed idealized antebellum paternalism and the logic of proslavery theology into a new political system. As they had justified Redemption's white supremacist violence as a means to achieve greater family order, white Christians relied on extralegal violence and intimidation to create a new political structure that empowered white men to control the Mississippi River Valley. White Christians argued that antebellum proslavery paternalism served as their model for a new Christian paternalism in the post-Reconstruction South, yet they stripped their antebellum paternalism of its modest duty to aid black Christianity or protect black lives. Sanctifying white power without demanding any paternalistic duties of whites, white southerners moved to justify the forced racial separation and inequality of Jim Crow segregation with the same logic as their earlier justification of proslavery's household intimacies.

CHAPTER FOUR

Paternalism Reborn
New Southern Histories and Racial Violence, 1880–1889

Under the pen name Iola, twenty-six-year-old Ida B. Wells urged her fellow black Christians in 1889 "to meet the crisis that is coming" in the dangerous "public sentiment which some of these Negro-hating papers are arousing against the Negro as a laborer and a citizen." She argued that black Americans must buy land because property ownership offered the best means to "defend ourselves" and "to protect our man and womanhood and . . . our rights." Those rights were under renewed assault as white supremacist "charges are receiving new life instead of slumbering and there is room for grave fears" because "the southern white man is looking a long way ahead." Wells quoted a recent speech in which a white Memphis attorney had said that "the white man must take steps to prevent Negro supremacy by restricting his (the Negro's) suffrage." Writing in the CME Church's *Christian Index*, Wells urged ministers to mount vigorous opposition to this political threat and to center their religious mission on the civic and political education of their congregations. The "minister who teaches his people best how to live on earth" served his community better than one focused only on heaven. "Let every teacher and preacher awake to the necessity of teaching our people to think [and] act for themselves," Wells called, so that each individual may be "a true citizen." Christian and citizen identity joined together in Wells's prescription for protecting the independent manhood and womanhood of black citizens living in the Mississippi River Valley as white supremacist political power grew.[1]

Ida B. Wells exemplified black southerners' defense of their Christian citizenship as southern Democrats moved to create legalized segregation a decade after Reconstruction's collapse. Wells's own life evinced the challenges facing black southerners in these years. When she was sixteen, she lost her parents and baby brother in 1878 to the nation's worst yellow fever epidemic, forcing her to move from Holly Springs, Mississippi, to Memphis, Tennessee, to provide for herself and several younger siblings by teaching and writing. She faced myriad challenges as a single black woman making her own way in 1880s Memphis. Her column in the *Christian Index* started as a women's religious column, but Wells quickly shifted her focus to politics, arguing that

Christian womanhood required protecting black civil and political rights. After her good friend Thomas Moss was murdered by a white lynch mob for operating a grocery store, Wells would rise to national prominence with her investigative reporting on lynching in 1892, yet she was already raising the alarm about the multifaceted white supremacist attack on black Christian citizenship in the 1880s.[2]

BY THE EARLY 1880S, federal involvement in the former Confederate states had ended, leaving black southerners with few resources to defend their civil and political rights against white supremacist southerners. In 1883, the U.S. Supreme Court declared much of the 1875 Civil Rights Act unconstitutional. The court ruled 8-to-1 that Congress lacked the authority to prohibit racial discrimination by private businesses. White southern Christians turned with new fervor to address what they called the "Negro problem," by which they meant their challenge to expand white supremacist control of the region given the strength of black religious, political, and economic self-determination. White southerners had used extralegal violence and intimidation to regain Democratic political power, but they still wanted to create legal restrictions on black civil and political rights without arousing federal intervention for violation of the Fourteenth and Fifteenth Amendments. This challenge of converting white supremacist political power into white legal authority was their "Negro problem."

As they sought legitimized legal authority, white southern Christians invented historical narratives of continuity with the antebellum period. These new accounts were white supremacist fantasies that ignored the previous two decades and disregarded black citizens' exercise of political and civil rights. They rooted white Christians' vision of the future of the South in an imagined past that connected the persistent logic of proslavery theology to emerging segregation. White Christians' history grudgingly acknowledged emancipation, but insisted that white leaders' antebellum experience as slaveholders or as children in slaveholding households gave them unique insight to control black communities. These newly invented histories constructed fictions in which enslaved people had been happy recipients of their white owners' generous benevolence. Enslaved and free children had played together on plantations before gracefully assuming their adult roles as property and property owner. Ironically, these fantastic visions of the antebellum past drew upon the intimacies of slaveholding households and the close contact between white and black household members under slavery in order to argue for an increasingly segregated society. The expertise that white southerners claimed to have in knowing black people's best interests drew upon a form of intimacy that they sought to erase.

These new historical accounts studiously avoided acknowledging black self-determination. During Reconstruction, white southerners had lamented black citizens' independent churches and political rights, but in the 1880s they pretended as though black Christians, whom they had kept from voting by violent intimidation, had never sought self-determination in religious or political life. Instead, southern white Christians claimed that northern white Republicans had been their opposition and had used black voters as pawns during Reconstruction. Discounting black self-determination made white Christians' paternalistic claims fit better to their segregationist goals. Omitting their massive extralegal fight for political power in the 1870s, white southerners imagined an unchanging past where antebellum paternalism remained the best model for southern society. White southerners framed their attacks on public schools for black children as a Christian duty to return education to its rightful place under white Christian, paternalistic control. Their most developed paternalism in the 1880s—Southern Methodists' partial funding of Paine Institute—did not begin to approach the size of their antebellum paternalistic outlay in enslaved missions. Neither of these examples of southern white benevolence, as southern white Christians classified both antebellum enslaved missions and 1880s education support, attempted the scale of Reconstruction-era educational programs operated by government and voluntary groups, which southern whites' violence and northern apathy had ended.

Black citizens judged white Christians' narratives of antebellum continuity in the 1880s to be nonsensical. They defended their civil and political rights through their model of Christian citizenship and decried racial prejudice as sinful and unchristian as well as a violation of their rights for equal protection as U.S citizens. As Ida B. Wells's columns showed, black writers and leaders argued that their gendered conduct as Christian men and women proved that they richly deserved the civil and political rights due them as citizens. Faced with these white fantasies and a growing threat of extralegal terroristic violence, black Christians insisted on their belonging as citizens and Christians through alternative religious and historical narratives. These narratives centered on their active, loyal contributions to the South and the nation. They argued that they were better Christians than whites, whose religious faith was marred by unchristian racial prejudice. God, they insisted, wanted justice and thus supported black Christians in the myriad dangers that they faced. If white southerners saw a "Negro problem" in the 1880s, its solution was simply "to give to the negro his civil and political rights. . . . If the negro can but receive his just rights there will be no need of agitating this great problem any longer."[3] Black Christians recognized that "the great Southern problem" occupying white people's attention was "how to disfranchise the Negro within the forms of Constitutional requirements," namely the Fifteenth Amendment's prohibition of denying franchise on the basis of color, race, or previous condition of servitude. Black citizens argued, "it can't be done" without violating their constitutional rights, but they recognized that white Christians were determined to try.[4]

By the 1880s, black and white Christians increasingly operated in separate silos with vastly different understandings of the history and present situation of the Mississippi River Valley, based on their mutually exclusive ideas of Christian citizenship. Southern white Christians rebirthed their antebellum paternalism with historical claims of continuity from slavery to the 1880s. They argued against all rights-based claims as unbiblical and in favor of an organic paternalistic social order that required very little of white paternalists. Even more than antebellum proslavery paternalism, this new white supremacist paternalism did not value black lives. By contrast, black Christians argued that no true Christian could embrace racial prejudice. They claimed with greater urgency that their Christian identity, American loyalty, temperance practice, and educational efforts demonstrated that they fully deserved the equal civil and political rights that Reconstruction legislation and constitutional amendments had promised. The rise of lynching highlighted the dangers of this new paternalism, where claims of protecting white women justified the extralegal terroristic murders of black men. Black Christians denounced lynching as a sinful tool of white supremacy, but nearly all white Christians remained silent, grateful for how lynching strengthened white supremacist power in the name of protecting white family and social order.

White Christians' Reimagined Antebellum Paternalism

As they sought to legitimize the religion and politics of a region now firmly under white Democratic control, white southern Christians created a new model of paternalism that defended white supremacist practices while limiting the paternalistic obligations that white southerners held. In their reimagined antebellum paternalism, white southern Christians carried the persistent logic of proslavery theology into the 1880s, ignoring two decades of intervening history. They used the idealized vision of slavery that proslavery theology had defended, rather than slavery's actual history, as their historical baseline in these new accounts. Doing so obscured the gendered and sexual-ized violence endemic to slavery, especially white men's assault on enslaved women, at the same time that white southerners advanced new fears of sex across the color line. These new concerns centered on black men's alleged threats to white women, which became a white supremacist call for mob vio-lence. White southerners also reintroduced their antebellum claims that white southern denominations alone held biblically faithful views on politics and social change, and they argued that rights-based claims had no place in a biblical social order. Amid this new paternalism, some white southern Chris-tians voiced a limited paternalistic duty to fund schools and colleges for black education that white southerners could direct. White Christians hoped such schools would provide greater white control of black religious life.[5]

White southern Christians, who had rejoiced in the "Redemption" of southern state governments from Republican control in the 1870s, insisted in the 1880s that they held deeper commitments to black well-being than any other group of white Americans. Northern Republicans had only cared about black potential voters, and northern Christian groups had been tainted by Republican politics and weakened by their naïveté about black inferiority. By contrast, white southerners, because they had been raised in a slave society, could implement better educational and religious programs for black south-erners. Their antebellum efforts to convert enslaved people to Christianity, they argued, showed their commitment to black people's best interests. White Christians invoked their antebellum past with scarcely a nod to the tremendous changes of emancipation and Confederate defeat. Instead, they maintained that their "work done among the colored people . . . before the war" gave "sufficient proof" of their commitment, and that "the best material, in preachers and members . . . among the blacks in the South to-day" were those whom white Christians had converted before emancipation. Repeatedly, southern whites invoked "the *antebellum* past and its history of faith and zeal in behalf of the colored people," and white ministers claimed authority to know what was best for black southerners because, as one minister explained, "in the days of slavery I preached to them."[6]

White southerners' claims about the antebellum past disregarded black self-determination, even as their ongoing efforts to create legal structures of white supremacy showed that they urgently targeted black autonomy in prac-tice. In their new narratives of the antebellum past, enslaved people had not sought freedom. A white Mississippi Methodist, asserting that he was an ad-vocate for black education, wrote in 1883 that black southerners' "present condition" of freedom was "not in any degree a matter of their own procuring." Enslaved people had been "faithful to the Lost Cause.... The whites were not more true." Upon emancipation, freedpeople's condition showed "the excellent care, discipline, preservation of health, abundant food, suitable clothing, and general protection" that slaveholders (enslaved people's "benefactors" in the white minister's parlance) had given them. This account ignored the history of Reconstruction, and skipped to the late 1870s, since which time black southerners' "conduct ... demonstrate[d] the solid improvement they have made in ... true civilization." This narrative erased black citizens' exercise of political and civil rights, their election to public office across the region, and the white supremacist violence that drove the transformation to the state of affairs that white Christians praised.[7]

Emancipation and Reconstruction became unfortunate, temporary interruptions to southern whites' benevolent care for black southerners at a time when northern Republicans manipulated black communities for their own interests. Reversing what they had said during Reconstruction, white Christians dismissed black self-determination entirely as they celebrated their own religious superiority to northern denominations. After the Civil War, a "wide chasm yawned between the whites and blacks of the South," not because of slavery, but because of federal interference. Northern whites imparted "crude ideas of citizenship, and the rights it involved" to black people and "alienated" them from white southerners, "who were their best friends, and knew best how to develop them into thrifty, industrious and useful citizens." Northern Republicans disrupted the harmonious relationship between antebellum southern whites and enslaved people with dangerous political ideas that undermined white southerners' control. No group "had stronger reasons for treating the Negro fairly" than white southerners because "they had grown up together on the same plantation; they have played, hunted, fished, and often worked together." These antebellum intimacies made white southerners understand what black southerners truly needed, and "the white churches that ... labored for the blacks so earnestly and successfully previous to the war" had produced "the best elements in all the negro churches" in the 1880s. Northern Christians had "prejudice[d]" black people "against their Southern benefactors, ... the people who had brought them to Christ." By relying on "military aid, [and] by operating upon the prejudices of the negro," northern Christians "took our colored work out of our hands." Black communities had been unwitting tools of northern white groups, rather than centers of organized opposition to the religious and political goals of former Confederates.[8]

These new historical claims were false, and white southerners in the late 1860s or early 1870s could not have imagined making them. In the 1880s, white Christians had to look hard for evidence of unchanging Christian paternalism after emancipation. Since white denominations no longer operated the substantial black missions that they did in the antebellum period, they wanted to show paternalistic oversight without actually putting funds behind large-scale religious or educational work, so they pointed to their self-interested political work in destroying Reconstruction in the 1870s as their paternalistic duty. Mississippi Methodist Rev. W. T. J. Sullivan disputed charges that white Christians had "failed in our duty to the colored people" since emancipation because "Southern people have done a great deal for the colored people" by "resisting false political creeds" and "saving the country from negro rule." The idea that white southerners aided their black neighbors after emancipation by undermining black political power illustrated how severely white paternalistic claims twisted black collective action. As they "secur[ed] civil and social, as well as industrial, salvation" for the South, white Christians' attacks on black civil and political rights and economic independence showed their paternalistic duty and served black southerners' best interests.[9]

The history of the CME Church gave white Southern Methodists their best opportunity to claim ongoing paternalistic care for black Christians. The Methodist Episcopal Church, South, had supported the creation of the CME Church in 1870, hoping to counter the growth of independent black churches like the AME Church or independent Baptists. White Southern Methodists pressured the CME Church not to engage in Republican organizing, as most independent black churches did, but offered almost no financial support, apart from providing some of the church buildings built for Methodist missions to enslaved people. These buildings, used exclusively by black congregations, were of little use to white southerners, but as late as 1878, Southern Methodists noted that several properties had yet to be transferred from white ownership. In the 1880s, white Southern Methodists shifted their description of the CME Church to fit more fully within their new paternalism. With the "close of the fearful and fateful war between the States" and emancipation, which white southerners euphemistically termed "changed relations," Southern Methodism's "wise men" had struggled over how best to maintain their paternalistic duty toward freedpeople. The creation of the CME Church had been southern whites' best attempt to "advocate their [black] religious interests" and was never meant "for the purpose of securing honorable relief from responsibility" for the religious oversight of black southerners.[10]

These new accounts of the founding of the CME Church ignored black Methodists' advocacy for an independent denomination and made the CME Church a clear ally to white paternalistic goals. Southern Methodists touted the CME Church's commitment to "teach their people to be quiet and law-abiding citizens, and to cultivate the closest friendships with our church and the Southern people as their natural and providential allies." Yet southern whites ignored the ways that they had initially promised to give aid comparable to the hundreds of thousands of dollars they spent on antebellum missions, and then did almost nothing. Even cautious Bishop Holsey noted that the CME Church had been promised far more than this pittance in exchange for their political caution. While their ongoing ties to Southern Methodists and their dearth of political activism earned criticism from other black churches, the members of the CME Church labored to distinguish themselves as an independent denomination. In the 1880s, they criticized southern whites, including Southern Methodists, more strongly in their denominational newspaper, as Ida B. Wells's columns conveyed. Nevertheless, Southern Methodists positioned the CME Church under the new claims of their ongoing paternalism from the antebellum period into the 1880s.[11]

Through this re-created paternalism, white southerners in the 1880s adapted their antebellum proslavery theological commitments to shape the postemancipation South into a racial and gendered hierarchy in which white men governed dependent members of society. As white southern Christians voiced fears of rapacious black sexuality, they demonstrated the centrality of sexual discipline and marriage to their understanding of Christian identity. Citing highly selective concepts and ignoring other evidence, white southerners argued that black religious and sexual lives showed the need for Democratic political rule and white southern religious influence. Proper Christian manhood demanded performing paternalistic duties, though southern white Christians acknowledged far fewer duties to black communities than their antebellum predecessors had done. This paternalistic rhetoric meant that only white men could be full Christian citizens who directed southern political and religious life correctly. Increasingly, white southern Christians viewed Christian citizenship as the ideological justification for white Democratic power.

White southern Christians rejected all rights-based claims, especially those of northern denominations, as they solidified their new white supremacist paternalism. When Presbyterians and Methodists discussed closer ties between northern and southern denominations, white southern Christians opposed such moves and argued that their northern counterparts were impossibly corrupted by rights-based political views. Southerners' renewed paternalism was more biblical than this individualistic, innovative politics, and southern Christians restated their irreconcilable differences with northern denominations more than fifteen years after Confederate surrender and slavery's end. Southern Methodists warned that Northern Methodists might appear similar to their southern counterparts, but "they are not the same people." Southern churches alone bore the responsibility "to keep clear of the partisan and secular spirit, [and] to preach the gospel in its purity" since northern Christians had abandoned this work.[12] Similarly, in 1883, New Orleans Presbyterian minister Rev. Benjamin M. Palmer published a lengthy summary of the "open hostility and acts of aggression" that Northern Presbyterians had committed since 1865. Palmer, who had led the creation of the Presbyterian Church of the Confederate States of America in 1861, argued the difference between the two denominations was Northern Presbyterians' "mingling of politics with religion." These different views on "the relations . . . between the Church and State . . . compels" each denomination "to be separate from the other." Fellow Southern Presbyterian James A. Waddell echoed Palmer's concerns when he argued that Northern Presbyterians had "converted their Church into a political machine, to propagate political dogmas." While Waddell and Palmer had defended slavery and secession and opposed Reconstruction, they argued their northern counterparts' politics corrupted true religion by introducing rights-based claims instead of organic biblical paternalism. Southern white Christians showed superior religious devotion through their re-created paternalism.[13]

Southern white Christians used education to argue that Christian paternalism, not politically motivated church-state partnerships, should guide southern policy. Northern Protestant groups had become too politically active by advocating for black citizens' equal civil and political rights. Instead, Christians should work for black education in church-sponsored contexts. In practice, this meant that southern white Christians opposed black voting rights and undermined black public education while teaching a politically conservative message of personal moral discipline in a much reduced educational project targeted at creating cautious clergy and disciplined laborers. This Christian education would correct the problems unleashed by emancipation and aid white southerners' "*material* interests" by training black students to "*learn to work,* as well as to study books." These white-run Christian schools would train black ministers to be more like antebellum "white pastors" than current black preachers, who were mostly "field hands, without education or . . . discipline." It might have been "the United States, who set them free," but "the Christian church," meaning white southern Christians, should guide that freedom and "furnish Christian teachers for their schools and educated ministers for their pulpits." White southerners believed that proper black education defended white paternalism, rectified the chaos unleashed by emancipation's promises of equality, and promised to support white economic interests.[14]

White southern Christians supported this paternalistic education work in rhetoric but not substance, and white churches never appropriated significant funding for this work. Southern churches announced a duty to support black education, as they had missions to enslaved people, but even by comparison to antebellum missions, much less to Reconstruction-era goals of universal public schools for all black children, this 1880s educational work amounted to a pittance. Still, white southern Christians viewed all progress that black communities had made by the 1880s as the result of southern white missionary endeavor, rather than black self-determination or federal defense of civil and political rights. Mississippi Methodist Rev. C. K. Marshall claimed that white southerners "as citizens and as Christians" deserved credit for raising black southerners from the status of "benighted heathens" in Africa. Slavery had helped people of African descent. "All they are to day above their savage ancestors" came thanks to "the white people of the South." White Christians' work throughout the antebellum past was the greatest of "missionary enterprises conducted by the united powers of Christendom." Rather than being their fellow citizens, black Christians were the objects of white southerners' missionary endeavors, more like the colonized people missionized in European empires than neighbors with equal civil and political rights. From this imagined past, white southerners could mount new Christian education that would counter misguided public schools. If white southerners would consent to work as teachers, Rev. Marshall suggested that they could be paid by northern voluntary groups' donations but have southern white control of this education's content.[15]

White southern Christians across denominations endorsed the idea that they should manage funds given by northern Christians for paternalistic oversight of black southerners. Episcopal priest Rev. J. L. Tucker took advantage of belonging to the one denomination that had reunited nationally after the Civil War to press his northern coreligionists to fund southern efforts for black education. Because southern Episcopalians best understood "the vast mental and moral differences between the races," they must address the problems created when "the North made citizens of a race utterly unfitted for citizenship, and then failed utterly . . . to educate the race into fitness for citizenship." Tucker, even more vociferously than other white southerners, argued that all people of African descent were morally, intellectually, and religiously inferior to white people, and therefore required firm guidance from southern white Christians. After the Civil War, Tucker explained that "negro churches sprang up everywhere, built largely by Northern money," but filled with "a form of Christianity without its substance." Tucker ignored black communities' work to build their own churches as he complained that these churches were full of "shouting, praying, singing, all manner of excitement, hysterics, trances, loud calls upon God; but . . . no religion, at least none of that kind which has its issue in a holy, humble and obedient walking before God." To solve this problem, Tucker called for inviting black Christians back to segregated balconies in white churches where they could learn true religion. He thought this idea plausible if white churches offered free schools, employment centers, hospitals, and orphanages, all of which Tucker thought northern Episcopalians should fund and southern Episcopalians should operate. Tucker proposed these church-run services as an alternative to state-sponsored agencies. Christian paternalism, enacted by southern white Christians, should carry the day.[16]

Tucker's speech earned much attention, including widespread criticism. He delivered the speech initially to a national conference of the Episcopal Church, but expanded it for publication along with printed endorsements from several dozen prominent white citizens, including many Episcopal priests, other Protestant clergy, judges, attorneys, doctors, and more. The published speech had many more pages of endorsements than of Tucker's words. Yet Tucker earned criticism from both white and black readers for his gross racial stereotypes of black inferiority. Southern Methodists joined these criticism, and Rev. C. K. Marshall wrote a lengthy rebuttal as "The Colored Race Weighted in the Balance." Presenting himself as an expert on black Methodists, Marshall defended black people as not altogether morally and intellectually inferior to white people. He pointed out that many of the charges against black superstition or exuberant religiosity could be matched by white people's reliance on good luck charms or fortune tellers, or by Catholic excess at Mardi Gras. Marshall also attacked Episcopalians' religious formalities and skepticism of evangelical revivals as he argued for the superiority of the more humble and evangelical Methodists over wealthier Episcopalians. Even though Marshall soundly criticized Tucker, both southern white Christians shared the belief that white southerners should manage educational and voluntary work to instruct black southerners on their duties to follow white leaders in religion and in politics.[17]

Southern Methodists held up Paine Institute, a Methodist training school for ministers and teachers in the CME Church, as a model for this new paternalistic education. Southern Methodists believed that Paine was a Christian paternalistic ideal that proved their ongoing care for black southerners' Christian education. But one partially funded institute for higher education could hardly replace the public school systems that southern white Democrats undermined in state after state. Reconstruction had prescribed universal public schooling equally for black and white children, and Southern Methodists proposed nothing of this kind. Their fundraising framed donations as part of whites' paternalistic duty to black religious and moral needs. An 1885 pamphlet explained that the school was "reaching out after the masses who sit in the darkness of ignorance and sin in our immediate midst" with "the refining process of Christian education."[18] The CME Church deserved support because of its political conservatism and respect for white paternalism, and it, alone among black denominations, had not received financial support from northern churches or Republicans, and thus "had no one to look to for help, except the Southern Methodist Church." Paine Institute was "the supreme opportunity that God has opened to our church to do a great missionary work for the negroes of the South by the establishment of these training-schools." Whites should fund this school to help black spiritual, not political, needs and as a voluntary missionary enterprise, not as an educational right due to fellow Christian citizens. Praising this school, which provided secondary and higher education to some CME Church members as the best way to discharge their paternalistic duty to black southerners, showed the gap between their rhetorical promises of taking over the work of public and Freedmen's Bureau schools with new Christian paternalistic education, and the meager financial support actually backing these ideas.[19]

Even the most expansive proposals for black education drew on antebellum paternalism and undermined black civil and political rights. Southern Methodist Rev. Atticus Haygood, a founder of Paine Institute, was an outlier among white Southern Methodists because he argued for black intellectual, moral, and religious equality with white Americans. Haygood explained that seeming inferiority resulted from slavery, not racial inferiority, and pointed to traits shared by many rural southerners and by poor laborers around the world. His 1881 *Our Brother in Black: His Freedom and His Future* called for white southerners to recognize their black neighbors as equal Christians and to support their education as white Christians would support education for white southerners. The book was deeply controversial, in particular for its attempt at a somewhat balanced history of the Civil War and Reconstruction, including cautious praise for elements of Reconstruction alongside criticism of black men's suffrage. Yet the antebellum past still shaped Haygood's claims. His boyhood affection for the people whom his father had enslaved helped him to appreciate the needs of black citizens after emancipation. While insisting that his father treated enslaved people with love and care, Haygood said that his views had changed, and he saw slavery as wrong. Unlike many fellow white southerners, Haygood recognized emancipation as a dramatic rupture and wanted his readers to better appreciate emancipation's transformation of the South. *Our Brother in Black* called white southerners to work for "the right education and elevation of our black brother, the free negro, in our midst." In doing so, it criticized a range of prejudicial attitudes toward black Christians, while avoiding condemning antebellum whites or the Confederate cause.[20]

Unsurprisingly, many white southern Christians resisted Haygood's claims, especially his argument against innate racial difference in intellectual or religious ability. Southern Methodist Bishop Christian Keener's scathing review insisted that "the term [brother in black] is chosen with much skill, and it is full of error and sentimental nonsense, calculated to deceive." Haygood's "sentimental use of language, which ignores the real difference between the races" represented a willful manipulation of white readers.[21] Few white Christian advocates for black education could conceive of brotherhood between southern white and black citizens. Even southern Christians who embraced Haygood's claim that black Christians were their "brothers in black" maintained that "the difference between the negro and the white man is more than skin deep."[22] It was, most white Christians insisted, because of the self-evident inferiority of black people and their religious deficiencies that Christian paternalistic education proved so important.

Even those rare white southern claims that defended equal intellectual and religious ability regardless of race did not imagine equal political rights. Mississippi Methodist minister Robert G. Porter, writing under the pen name Gilderoy, said that "No sane man will deny the fact that the negro can learn anything and everything that white men learn." That equal ability showed that "God has not been as partial as many of us suppose in the bestowment of mental capacity." Porter argued that "negro teachers are more competent than many of us are willing to allow." He cited a white school supervisor who had "no negro mania" but came to recognize that black teachers and students had equal ability as their white counterparts even though his "prejudices were stung by this fact." This equal intellectual capacity was matched by equal religious capacity. White southerners' Christian duty, Porter explained, required that they acknowledge that "God has poured the Holy Spirit upon some Negroes just as copiously as upon some white men." Porter claimed that believing in racial religious and intellectual inferiority represented sinful prejudice. He borrowed a favorite antiprejudice Bible story from black Christian arguments, the story of Peter's rejection of prejudice against Gentile would-be converts to Christianity. The story from Acts 10 had been used by black activists since David Walker to criticize antiblack racism, and Reconstruction-era northern white Christians had supported black civil and political rights with this same biblical passage. Porter quoted Peter's speech to tell Southern Methodists, "God is no respecter of persons, but that in every nation he that feareth God and worketh righteousness is accepted of him." As Peter learned that no food was unclean despite kosher law, white southerners should recognize that "no work," including teaching black students, was "unclean work" if it had "the approval of God upon it." Porter criticized belief in racial intellectual and religious inferiority as sinful prejudice, but he never suggested that black citizens should have equal civil and political rights.[23]

To encourage white southerners to consider teaching in schools for black students, Porter and his allies argued that it was like the work of Christian missionaries in Africa. This comparison supported arguments for Christian duty while reinforcing links between black American citizens and seemingly uncivilized foreign groups. White southerners had no more obligation to recognize the political rights of black fellow citizens than missionaries to colonial African countries had to their colonized pupils; they only needed to help them gain a Christian education. Atticus Haygood's *Our Brother in Black* pointed out the hypocrisy of white southern Christians' praise for missionaries in Africa, such as David Livingstone, when contrasted with hostility toward teachers in southern black schools. He devoted a chapter to explaining why teaching formerly enslaved people should be valued as important Christian service. Similarly, Southern Methodist Bishop Charles B. Galloway criticized the "travesty" of the "disposition to canonize missionaries who go to the dark continent, while we have nothing but social ostracism for the white teacher who is doing a work no less noble at home." Others proposed that southern white unemployment could be reduced by teaching in black schools. Teaching Christian piety was the goal, not promoting dangerous forms of political or social equality.[24]

The specter of social equality, with its connotations of sex across the color line, loomed large in white southerners' discussions of black Christian education in the 1880s. Many white Christians voiced fears that if black southerners had access to equal education, black men would demand both political equality and equal access to marrying white women. When Southern Methodists raised funds for Paine Institute, they presented Paine as a force for maintaining racial distinctions and preventing sex across the color line. The irony that many of the CME Church leaders, such as Bishops Isaac Lane and Lucius Holsey, had identified themselves repeatedly as the sons of their former enslavers disappeared entirely in these accounts. While reiterating that the CME Church was "singularly free from all political alliances" and focused on "giving the gospel in Methodist simplicity to their people," white southerners praised the church further because its leaders "have maintained their Church in harmony with us in keeping the two races apart, socially, and in the marital relations." Southern Methodists praised CME bishops for defending "the purity of their African [blood] as we do for our Anglo-Saxon blood." The idea of the "purity" of African or Anglo-Saxon blood was a myth, but its invocation by white Southern Methodist supporters of Paine Institute showed how important a rigid color line was for white Christians. Here, they praised CME Bishops Lane and Holsey for identifying themselves firmly on the black side of a color line and upholding a clear racial divide that their own parentage proved a lie. The pains to which white southern Christians went to insist that black education would not encourage "social equality" demonstrated the centrality of sex to concerns about racial separation in these years of nascent segregation practices.[25]

As southern Democrats consolidated their political power in these years, they relied on white Christians' new narratives of historical continuity between the antebellum past and the 1880s. Christians from a variety of denominations constructed white supremacist fantasies that linked the present dominance of white political power to visions of peaceful plantations and happy, dutiful slaves. These historical narratives represented a new version of proslavery theology's logic in the guise of a Christian citizenship that justified segregation and racial discrimination. From these appeals to antebellum benevolence, white southern Christians supported black educational efforts with the goal of producing morally disciplined Christians who did not seek political equality or its dangerous corollary, social equality.

Black Christian Activism in the 1880s

Black Christians thought the idea that the antebellum past should be a model for the late nineteenth century was absurd and dangerous. They countered white southerners' new narratives of historical continuity and paternalistic

Christian citizenship by arguing that true Christian practice could not coexist with white supremacist goals. Although white Democrats had seized power across the region, black southerners pointed to legal and constitutional support for their civil and political rights and decried early segregation efforts, especially after 1883 when the Supreme Court struck down the Civil Rights Act of 1875. To defend these increasingly precarious rights, they recounted the dramatic changes that emancipation and Reconstruction had wrought. They emphasized vital black contributions to U.S. history, beginning with the valor of Crispus Attucks, an enslaved man whose death in the 1770 Boston Massacre made him the first American casualty in the Revolutionary War. These contrasting narratives claimed that black Christian citizens deserved civil and political rights based on their upright moral conduct and their loyalty to the United States and to the South. Black Christians defended their Christian manhood and womanhood as fully within gendered religious norms. For those black men still able to vote, voting with white Christians for prohibition ballot initiatives demonstrated their Christian piety as well as their citizenship, class, and educational identity. Pressing for economic self-help and racial solidarity, black Christians worked to help their own communities as white southerners' promises of educational aid rarely materialized.

Recognizing their loss of northern allies, black Christians in the Mississippi River Valley condemned attacks on their civil and political rights from both northern and southern white people. In 1884 in Vicksburg, Mississippi, AME Bishop Henry McNeal Turner said that "the status of the Negro" made him "indignant," especially "those Justices of the Supreme Court, who dared to strike down black man's rights." Turner invoked divine judgment on the United States as a whole: "May the God of Heaven lash, rebuke, chastise and humble this nation till it shall learn to recognize the negro's manhood." Other Mississippi AME Church ministers showed "a keen sense of the injustice done to an unoffending people" in "the wrongs and outrages perpetrated" by white people, North and South. The evils facing black Christian citizens in Mississippi stemmed not only from "violent and unlawful" white Mississippians "who in 1875–76 overthrew the state government by force of arms," but also from the Supreme Court's decision that, "as a climax of our debasement," stripped "from our shoulders our defensive armor in the form of the Fourteenth Amendment and the Bill of Civil Rights." White Americans across the nation refused "to settle . . . the status of her citizens, and to ensure all her sons and daughters the equal protection of their persons and rights." The problem lay with the whole "race that has fattened itself on the unrequited labor of an unfortunate people," not just southern Democrats. Black Christian citizens condemned all racism among white people across "the boasted land of the free and home of the brave" as they sought to chart their path forward."[26]

Black Christian citizenship was even more important in this hostile national climate, and it demanded condemning racial injustice, cultivating pride in black identity, and engaging local issues. Ministers had a particular responsibility because "the preacher is no less a citizen than others," and he "must agitate the public mind" and be his congregation's "temporal and spiritual adviser." The AME Church's central mission was "to foster in the race a due self-respect, to make the colored man ambitious, [and] to give him stamina." Race pride was essential for this, and all black Christians must know that "to be black is no disgrace." While they could not hope to sway the Supreme Court, the North Mississippi AME Conference tried to shape local issues, such as Alcorn College, the state's institution for black teacher training, which was underfunded and poorly run. In a petition to the governor that fifteen AME Church ministers delivered in person, they explained that "the colored people of Mississippi can not afford to allow Alcorn college to . . . die." While churches might fund private colleges like the AME Church's Wilberforce University, it was the job of "*the State* to make liberal provisions for her citizens" in this public institution, which needed to be controlled by "colored men" as white Mississippians had little reason to operate the school effectively.[27]

In their increasingly fragile political position, AME Church leaders in Mississippi proved more willing to seek allies wherever possible. They invited Vicksburg Southern Methodist minister Rev. C. K. Marshall, along with several other white ministers, to join their meeting, out of gratitude for his criticism of Episcopal Rev. Tucker's arguments about black inferiority. Introducing Rev. Marshall, the AME assembly called him a "hero" for having "dared to weigh the negro in the balances, and found him not altogether wanting." Such high praise for a relatively modest statement showed how AME ministers shifted their rhetoric when several prominent white ministers were present, and how the changing political calculus in the 1880s shaped their religious activism. In his address, Rev. Marshall called the AME Church ministers to holy living and encouraged apolitical piety as black citizens' civil and political rights vanished. While he said he regretted "the spirit of lawlessness in . . . the land," Marshall commended "the arm of Jesus" to save black citizens from mob violence, rather than any legal aid. As a white Southern Methodist who appeared somewhat progressive by comparison to his peers, Rev. Marshall acknowledged the possibility of black Christians' intellectual and religious equality, but he rejected black Christians' argument that they deserved equal civil and political rights including protection from extralegal violence.[28]

Amid the paltry support of white southern Christians, AME ministers and lay leaders knew they remained their own best advocates. In a subsequent speech titled "Dr. Tucker Answered," delivered without white Southern Methodist observers, AME Rev. J. N. Abbey argued forcefully for black equality. Rev. Abbey, a prominent minister in the adjacent AME conference, traveled from Port Gibson, Mississippi, to deliver his address on Tucker. Living in the same town as the aged white Southern Methodist minister Rev. John G. Jones, Rev. Abbey would have known the power of white Christians' paternalistic arguments for Democratic power, and in his address on Episcopal Rev. Dr. Tucker, Rev. Abbey "handled Dr. Tucker without gloves, severely criticized his argument and positions, and insisted that the address . . . was a malicious and willful misrepresentation of a defenseless people." AME leaders in attendance called for the publication of that speech to circulate Abbey's ideas broadly. AME Church ministers recognized that they could not expect aid from northern white officials, and even as they called Marshall a "hero," black Christians showed they did not expect much support from white southern Christians.[29]

Denominational newspapers created a forum through which black Christians critiqued contemporary events and created solidarity among readers across the region. The *Christian Index*, published in Jackson, Tennessee, by the CME Church, and the *Southwestern Christian Advocate*, published in New Orleans, Louisiana, by the northern-affiliated Methodist Episcopal Church, commented on current local and national politics, and published the views of ministers and lay members. Both papers decried white supremacist violence and defended black civil and political rights. The significant overlap between papers run by distinct denominations showed the shared urgency of these matters in the 1880s. The *Southwestern Christian Advocate* published stronger defenses of black civil and political rights and included more articles about the rising scourge of lynching. Despite the CME Church's conservative leadership, *Christian Index* editorials frequently lambasted whites' racial prejudice as unchristian. Southern Methodists pointed to the CME Church as proof of their ongoing paternalism, but the *Christian Index* enumerated examples of white hypocrisy, suggesting the paper enjoyed more editorial freedom than the closely observed CME General Conferences every four years. There, bishops praised white Southern Methodists as their foster mother and friend, but the *Christian Index* showed that many CME Church members and clergy were unsatisfied by white paternalism. The paper pointed out that by 1888, Southern Methodists still had not raised the funds for Paine Institute that they had promised six years earlier. Paine's practice of allowing students and white faculty to eat together bothered white southern would-be donors, and CME Church members praised the much more egalitarian practices of the Methodist Episcopal Church, white Southern Methodists' archrival.[30]

True Christian practice was incompatible with racial prejudice and violence, black Christians argued. The *Christian Index* exclaimed: "How a man can be a possessor of true religion" yet support "all the wrongs perpetrated upon a down-trodden race" and "hold prejudice against his fellow man . . . is a wonder to us." The power of white Christians' racial prejudice "almost made" black Christians "doubt the power of Christianity" as presented by its white adherents. White Christians simply must not be converted Christians because "all persons who profess to have Christ dwelling within them" yet "retain any ill-will . . . against their brother in black, are surely in need of the Savior." Reversing white claims about the deficiencies of black Christianity, black Christians warned that whites "may have a great deal of religion, but possess none of Christ, be they clergy or laity."[31] White Christians who "always preach and argue that God is no respecter of persons" should not "claim to be his followers and act so very different." Being fellow Christians meant that "no matter how black, white, red, blue or any other color, we are all brethren." Since religion "has great power . . . to overcome all things," even to make "a bad man a good man," it was "strange" that it "has thus far failed to break down the prejudice between the races." The article concluded that white southerners were not truly converted Christians.[32] The *Southwestern Christian Advocate* condemned racial prejudice as "a sin, a shame, a huge iniquity, an undeniable sign of complicity with the iniquitous sin of slavery." Nothing could be called "a Christian society" unless its "work is to bring all redeemed souls into one fold," and "there can be no fraternity and unity without equality." To the white southerners who claimed to be Christians, their fellow Christians "entreat our brethren to . . . put on the only Christ[ian] robe of brother love." Both denominations saw racial prejudice as sin that must be denounced.[33]

Black Christians worked to claim their political and civil rights, including access to education, as citizens. They defended their legal rights, such as publicly funded schools that the Reconstruction state constitutions guaranteed but Democrats were undermining. In doing so, they challenged white southerners' claims of historical continuity from the antebellum period and assertions that white southerners sought black communities' best interests. When quoting a standard white line that white southerners were black people's best allies, the *Christian Index* turned to sarcasm. "Hold on, sir," the article began. "We have heard that racket before and don't believe a word of it." White southerners might claim to do more for black citizens than Republicans had done during Reconstruction, yet it was not, the article insisted, for good. The white South "lynches his brethren by the wholesale" and "will either keep them from voting or 'cast his vote out' after it has been 'put in.' Oh, yes; the South does a great deal for the negro." White southerners' claims that they respected black rights were an outright lie. Black Christians knew that for the South to become a safe place for their rights, it would take "a revolution . . . in the government affairs and in hearts of the bourbon democrats." Such editorials showed that not all CME members thought much of white paternalism. Christian and legal truth demanded that revolution, even as black southerners knew it was an uphill battle.[34]

Education lay at heart of Christian progress for black Christians, who believed that "God has a hand in the work of bringing about better things for the colored people of this country." Even when "some enemy will rise and give vent to his feelings," such as a white minister who used a racial slur in a recent sermon, "the hand of the great Creator can be seen ever and anon working mightily in the elevation of the race." Increasingly, it should then follow that "No man clothed in his right mind will oppose the education of the Negro."[35] When a white observer praised a black man's character as "good for a darkey," the paper pointed out that "the expression" revealed "that he considered the 'darkies' to be . . . inferior to the whites." Drawing upon the opportunity to defend racial equality, the article insisted that black men possessed equal attributes "making up a man and a gentleman," including being "a good and quiet citizen, one who has great respect for the laws that be, and who loves his country, his people and his God." Indeed, black citizens' "respect for the truth, right and justice, for religion, morality, intelligence, temperance, etc." exceeded that of whites. Their desire for education demonstrated these superior qualities, and education strengthened moral and religious commitments.[36]

Black Christians seized many local events or the opinions of other newspapers as occasions to insist that racial segregation and Christian practice were mutually exclusive. When the famous evangelist Rev. Dwight L. Moody preached nearby to white and black audiences separately, CME Church authors criticized his capitulation to local norms. Although Moody was one of the most respected Christian ministers in his day, his black critics insisted that they had "no faith in any man's religion who will carry or encourage prejudices against a race on account of their color." Moody and many of his followers "could learn some very important things respecting the religion of our

Lord Jesus" by recognizing the hypocrisy of their racial prejudice. Criticizing such a prominent figure showed the strength of black Christian arguments that "white professors of religion [who] hate their brother in black . . . have not the true religion." Moody's travels, which received much attention from many religious periodicals and local papers, became another occasion to criticize white Christians' hypocrisy.[37]

To counter white southerners' new historical narratives, black Christians created corrective histories. CME Church minister Rev. E. W. Moseley defended black civil and political rights by insisting that "the negro is an American citizen," yet "the colored people are mistreated" in both "north and south." Such mistreatment of "citizens be they red, black or white" was "a farce, a failure, a stench before the nostrils of high heaven." Black American loyalty and sacrifice stretched back to the Boston Massacre of 1770, where the first casualty of the American Revolution was the enslaved Crispus Attucks, who "fought for the establishment of this great republic." Attucks's memory "speaks up from the dust" to proclaim black citizens' loyalty. Later, in the War of 1812, "the colored man fought bravely," earning the praise of General Andrew Jackson, who "acknowledged their work and complemented their bravery" in the Battle of New Orleans, saying, "My colored countrymen, you made good and loyal soldiers." Taking on whites' historical narratives, Moseley repurposed a popular, albeit apocryphal, narrative of white southerners that enslaved people remained loyal to the Confederacy throughout the Civil War. During the war, "when the old 'masters' and the young ones, too, shouldered their muskets and went out and fought to uphold slavery, their servants remained at home, worked, fed and protected old 'miss' and the little ones." This long history of black patriotism had "alas, . . . been forgotten" by southern whites who think "the negro is a thief and a worthless scamp." Yet Moseley used this myth to defend black political rights because "southern whites know something about negro loyalty," and should recognize that black Christians belonged as peaceable citizens in the 1880s.[38]

Like many black Christians, Rev. Moseley argued that black southerners must exercise their political rights, not simply wait for divine deliverance. God "will be the leader" of righteous defenses of civil and political rights, but that did "not mean . . . the colored man should not vote. Yes, vote every time you can." Self-help, through voting, gaining wealth, and pursuing education, was compatible with praying for God's help, especially after the Supreme Court's 1883 decision overturning the Civil Rights Act, a decision one *Southwestern Christian Advocate* editorial likened to the *Dred Scott* decision.[39] In efforts to claim "all rights, suffrages and immunities guaranteed to our fellow-

men of the great Anglo-Saxon race," the *Christian Index* urged black southerners to "tak[e] God as their shield" and to demonstrate that they were
"God-fearing [and] loyal to our government." By doing this, and being strate-
gic in their willingness to adopt new approaches to the fight for equal rights,
they could hope to battle against whites' racial prejudice.[40] Although black
men were "citizens of this country . . . their rights are very limited," and "their
privileges at the ballot box are a mere myth in most of the Southern States."
Retaining the right to vote remained of vital importance so that both political
parties would have to respond to the demands of black voters, yet "the surest
road to success is for the negro to labor hard and obtain wealth and intelligence accompanied with good religion and morality." With personal wealth
and education, "no power that is formed against him shall stand." In an increasingly hostile legal and political situation, black Christians argued that
not only were they legally entitled to equal rights but also that their moral
and educational fitness showed that they deserved equal citizenship status.[41]

Black women claimed that they were Christian ladies who expected the
same respect given to pious white women. Because women could not vote,
black women's assertion of equal status did not carry the same political implications as black men doing the same. In the context of white southerners' renewed rhetoric about family order and protecting white women, black
women's assertion that they too were respectable Christian ladies, given the
class and racial implications of the term, was significant. Linking Christian
piety to class and educational status, church women argued that they were
the equals of white women in the Methodist Episcopal Church, South. Describing female students at the CME Church's Lane Institute in western Tennessee as "the young ladies" and reprinting numerous temperance stories,
poems, and essays about the work of ladies linked morally upright, well-
educated black Christian women to similar white ladies. These black ladies
taught children, wrote histories of their church, and supported temperance
work. In newly organized local Woman's Missionary Societies, "the ladies"
showed "a willing spirit to do something for the cause of Christ," although
they were "the weaker sex," much as Southern Methodist women did at the
same time. The *Christian Index* editors endorsed missionary societies and
recommended that "a lady organizer" form such societies in every area. CME
Church missionary societies focused on racial uplift by "raising up the destitute" in their communities and signaling a class divide between the missionary ladies and the people whom they helped, although the overwhelming
majority of black women in voluntary groups like these worked for pay as
cooks, laundresses, or maids, unlike their white missionary counterparts.[42]

The CME Church's rhetoric about women's virtue as Christian ladies mirrored that of other black Christians. At a denominational level, the CME Church and AME Church were distinct in their politics, but their approaches to gender and family norms within Christian citizenship were similar. In Louisiana, AME Bishop Richard H. Cain urged local ministers, as "christian gentlemen" and "the embodiment of christian refinement," to advance the "higher education of our females, that our homes may be refined and exalted by the love of our firesides and the dignity of motherhood." The AME Church's work of racial uplift demanded "the absolute necessity of an educated laity, an educated family circle, an educated ministry and refined christian churches [with] highly cultured Sunday-school children." While CME Church and AME Church statements on racial justice and politics varied widely, both churches placed similar value on gendered Christian virtue and education, and both condemned antiblack racial prejudice as sinful and unjust.[43]

Black Christian men and women showed their Christian piety through their commitment to temperance causes across all denominations. Temperance pledges—commitments that individuals would abstain from alcohol—had long been features of nineteenth-century evangelical piety, and by the 1880s, nearly all denominations had temperance societies to teach the dangers of alcohol. Reconstruction-era black denominations all had such societies and urged temperance sermons on a regular basis in their churches. The longer history of temperance work showed that this Christian temperance work was not merely an effort to demonstrate Christian respectability as the nadir of black political power approached. At the same time that the AME Church denounced white supremacist politics, they condemned "Demon Intemperance" as "maddening the brain, making widows, and worse than orphan children." The *Christian Index* published temperance articles in every issue, and many of these were reprinted from Woman's Christian Temperance Union materials with no direct racial or regional ties. These morality tales and essays about the dangers of alcohol spoke to broad religious concerns, particularly for women, and did not connect to specific local ballot initiatives. Embracing ubiquitous temperance rhetoric suggested that avoiding alcohol sales and consumption formed a central Christian cause for many southern black Christians, not merely a goal through which to signal respectability.[44]

While temperance was not primarily a display of respectability politics, it was the only 1880s political issue where black and white Christians voted for the same goal, so black men used it to demonstrate their fitness to vote as Christian citizens, with mixed results. As prohibition measures appeared on local ballots, black ministers urged members to vote for them, but black

Christians repeatedly complained that "the white temperance element" proved "unwilling to join hands with the negroes to back this law." Yet some white Christians saw black Christians as temperance allies, if not broader political allies. In 1882, Rev. D. A. Williams of the Methodist Episcopal Church and Southern Methodist Rev. Charles B. Galloway created a monthly temperance journal, *The People's Adviser*. The *Southwestern Christian Advocate* praised Galloway for being "a minister . . . who despised caste" and for "preaching *with* and to the colored people." This rare cross-racial collaboration between two Mississippi ministers hopefully promised that "ere long the stain and blotch of other days will be wiped away" and "all hearts and races" would join together in religious work. Such sentiments were premature, as Rev. Galloway became a strong defender of segregation policies and black men's disenfranchisement.[45] When Arkansas voters supported prohibition ballot initiatives in the 1888 election, black voters claimed a victory for their work to restrict alcohol sales. Before the 1888 elections, Southern Methodist Rev. Atticus G. Haygood said that, although he thought black enfranchisement had been hasty and unwise, educated black Christians overwhelmingly voted for prohibition measures, while well-educated whites often sided with alcohol interests. Haygood here echoed part of black Christian claims that black men deserved the right to vote because they were upright Christian citizens. By configuring temperance as a religious and political effort, black Christians argued that they were political allies for white Christians' prohibition goals, but southern white Christians did not see this as a reason to defend black voting rights.[46]

The 1888 national elections drew urgent efforts to defend black men's voting rights. Particularly concerning were reports from Jackson, Mississippi, early that year, that for the first time since Reconstruction, not a single Republican held an elected municipal position after "the negroes abstained from voting" because of threats from local whites, including printed circulars decorated with images of guns warning black men not to vote. In light of these reports, the *Christian Index* editors invoked divine blessing: "God pity our southland, and may He speedily hasten on the day when things shall assume a different phase."[47] Although the CME Church officially prohibited political activism, the *Christian Index* used its editorial page to denounce the Democratic party and endorse Republicans. The editors warned that "the prevailing idea of southern democracy" was "keeping the negroes in a state of serfdom, [and] taking from them their rights." These efforts meant that "the great mass of colored voters in the South are disenfranchised" and that "daily the papers contain the record of lynchings . . . so that the condition of the

Negroes of the south is almost hopeless." Black support of Democrats meant "to kiss the hand that murders their fellow man." Despite what white southerners claimed, the editors knew that "Every negro vote cast for the democratic party is but endorsement of the many wrongs done their brethren." Clearly, "every negro should come boldly to . . . rally around the Republican standard" because "the Democrats—especially those of the south—are unwilling to give the negro his rights. They allow him to be lynched . . . without offering any protection whatever." The CME Church's paper rallied its members against Democratic advances in much the same way other black denominations did, showing how similar black defenses of their Christian citizenship became amid growing white supremacist danger and how many voices in the CME Church differed from the conciliatory General Conferences' statements made before white Christians.[48]

Overall, the 1888 elections proved disappointing for black Christians, who saw growing disenfranchisement on local and national levels and apathy from former northern white Republican allies. After Republicans won control of Congress in 1888, black voters hoped that the party would recognize their support, yet national Republicans had little interest in defending southern black voters.[49] President Harrison, black Christians hoped, would "doubtless . . . see to it" that white southerners' extralegal oppression of them in the name of "so-called states rights" ended.[50] Black Christians insisted that the "only live issues before the American people" were "the temperance question" and the rights due "the Negro [as] a citizen." The Republican Party needed "the moral courage to take these up and solve them"; otherwise, the party did not "deserve future success."[51] Such action did not happen for many reasons, including the fact that black voter rolls were shrinking rapidly across the South. With Mississippi's 1890 constitutional convention, a darker day was to come.[52]

Lynching and the Specter of Social Equality

The new white supremacist paternalism that white Christians re-created in the 1880s relied on the terror of lynching violence to bolster its defense of family and social order. On Sunday evening, July 6, 1885, 400 residents of Oxford, Mississippi, gathered around the Southern Methodist churchyard to witness the lynching of Harrison Tunstal, a black man. Tunstal had been accused of the rape "of a young white lady of the town" in the early morning hours of that day. The woman and her sister had allegedly identified him that morning, and Tunstal did not have a clear alibi for the previous night. A self-appointed "committee of twelve citizens" deliberated over the case for a few hours that Sunday. The sham court believed that "the evidence strongly pointed to his guilt . . . but there existed a reasonable doubt." Their ad hoc deliberations "stayed the hands of violence" for a few hours until the father of the alleged victim gathered supporters to lynch Tunstal. Led by the father, "thirty or forty men went to the jail and brought forth Harrison" to Oxford's Southern Methodist church. There the white mob prepared to hang him on a makeshift gallows constructed between a large oak tree next to the church and churchyard's fence. Rev. Burrell L. Crump, a northern Methodist Episcopal Church minister, witnessed the scene and recorded Tunstal's final moments.[53] Before he was killed, Tunstal addressed the assembled white mob and "said a thing happened last night, and he was accused of it." He continued, "I suppose I will have to suffer for it, but I am not guilty." Turning to Rev. Crump, he "said pray for me, pray for me." Crump then prayed for Tunstal, and Tunstal in turn prayed for Crump. "After prayer he bid them all good by" and readied himself to be killed. Moments later, he was hung and died instantly, his murder witnessed by hundreds of Oxford residents in the yard of one of the most influential white churches.[54]

Harrison Tunstal addressed the lynch mob and spectators with his final words and prayers, mirroring well-known accounts of Christian martyrs. In Rev. Crump's account, Tunstal maintained his innocence, and asked for the assembled crowd's prayers. When Rev. Crump stepped forward to pray for him, Tunstal joined in the prayers, indicating his Christian identity, one that Crump's account confirmed by relating their shared prayers. The desecration of a Sunday evening in a churchyard made this lynching significantly more gruesome, and Crump lamented: "I hope I shall never see anything like it again. Oh, just to think of hanging a man on Sunday." His letter to the *Southwestern Christian Advocate* concluded, "Please pray for us here in Oxford." The paper printed Crump's letter with an editorial condemning the event. Emphasizing that Tunstal deserved a fair trial where he would be given the benefit of "the least doubt of guilt," the editors denounced lynching as white supremacist terror. The clear purpose of this "disregard for the forms of law" was "to impress the Negroes with a sense of their helpless condition, and to inspire them with fear." During the "twenty long years" since the end of the Civil War, "these horrible killings have gone on," but the setting of "the Lord's day and the Lord's house" showed new fearlessness on the part of white mobs. The incident revealed that "unlawful killing" had become "more sacred in the eyes of these actors" than "the influence of the Sabbath and the church." White southerners worshipped white supremacy more faithfully than Christianity.[55]

Black Christians fought the rise of lynching in the 1880s with all the resources of their Christian citizenship. White southern Christians' new paternalistic rhetoric took no responsibility for protecting black lives, and its defense of white supremacist order and opposition to rights-based claims for equality justified lynching to white audiences. White Christians cited their concerns about family order and white men's duty to protect white women to defend lynching as a response to black men's sexual threats to white women. Black Christians argued that lynching was a tool of white supremacist terror. A few victims were accused of raping white women, but many more faced other charges, such as being too politically vocal. While a tiny handful of white Christians cautiously criticized lynching because it violated law and order, their new paternalistic claims meant that most offered tacit, even vocal support, for extralegal measures to advance white power.

Black Christian arguments about the evils of lynching regularly invoked biblical language and denounced the hypocrisy of white Christians' sympathy for lynch mobs. They pointed to obvious evidence in favor of the lynching victim's innocence and stories of white men covering up crimes they had committed by accusing and killing a black man.[56] Yet it was particularly when there were allegations that a black man had raped a white woman that black Christians insisted on white Christians' hypocrisy. The *Southwestern Christian Advocate* decried "the horrible lynching of a poor colored man" in Mississippi who "was *suspected* of committing a criminal assault upon a white woman." "A crowd of white men" murdered him with "no judge, no jury, no trial." No arrests were likely in the case because "the public conscience has been seared, and preachers, teachers, lawyers, officials and people, all sympathize with such outrageous lawlessness." How could southerners, white or black, "pride ourselves upon our Christian" identity under such circumstances, the article asked. Yet if human means of justice failed, white Mississippians must remember they faced divine justice, as the Bible promised "'vengeance is mine. I will repay' saith the Lord."[57] The promise of divine justice served both as a warning to whites and as a recognition of how little black Christian communities could do to stop lynching. With "the daily reports of the lynching and otherwise murdering of Negro men and women, most of whom could, perhaps, not be convicted even by a jury chosen with that intent," the idea that "we live in a civilized Christian land (?)" appeared a farce.[58]

White Christians rarely spoke against lynching because it fit into their new paternalistic order of white supremacist politics. When they did, they merely criticized how it challenged proper law and order, not for its white supremacist terror. One wealthy white man called for the "leading men" of both races to work "to bring about the best feelings" between whites and black. He criticized all "riots and mobs." Without using the word lynching, he obliquely criticized the "unnecessary striving between the two races caused by the actions of the low grade men of our own race." Even in this indirect criticism, the article blamed working-class white men when lynching required the support of elite whites.[59] The strongest white criticisms of lynching came from Southern Methodist Rev. Atticus Haygood, one of the most progressive southern white voices. Haygood insisted that "there is no such thing as 'lynch law'" but that "'lynching' is itself lawlessness." Lynching, he maintained, was "a crime against man and God," similar to "vengeance," "barbarism," and "anarchy." Rather than being justified for white women's protection, "lynching does more to put down law than any crime it takes in hand."[60] Black denominational papers reprinted such statements from Haygood and praised them as "a vigorous and manly blow to the terrible crime." Haygood, though, was an exception who proved the broader rule of white inaction. The vast majority of white Christians were unwilling to condemn lynching. They had too little concern for black lives and too much to gain from white supremacist violence.[61]

Only the most chaotic events of white supremacist violence earned any significant response from southern white Christians. The murder of thirteen black men in the Carrollton, Mississippi, courthouse while the court was in session earned brief outrage. Two black men had brought charges against a white man for assault after he fired his pistol at them. On March 17, 1886, while the case was being tried, a group of white men stormed the courthouse and killed more than a dozen black men and wounded others. The Southern Methodist *New Orleans Christian Advocate* condemned the "butchery" that "fill[ed] every true citizen with horror and sorrow," and many other religious periodicals and local newspapers voiced similar concern. The events forced whites to ask, "Must we surrender to the reign of the mob?" The setting disturbed white southerners most, because "this blood was shed in the county courthouse and while a justice was on the bench trying a criminal cause." Some white southerners argued the event was spontaneous rather than premeditated, but the *New Orleans Christian Advocate* knew that spontaneous impulses could not have "brought a number of men together from scattered houses, on a certain day, organized them, and guided their horses along the public roads for miles to the county town." The law must be defended because "if such outrages are to be condoned and the perpetrators go unpunished, Mississippi ought to pluck from our national flag the star that answers to her

Statehood." However, after the first shocked reports, white southerners ignored the events, and no charges were filed in the murders.[62]

Black Christians were hardly surprised that after the initial "unqualified condemnation from a large portion of the Southern press," no indictments followed for the "deliberately planned murder, executed with military precision" in Carrollton, Mississippi, that "region of crime where the light of liberty does not dispel the darkness."[63] Naming white supremacy in "the failure to indict, arrest and punish any participant in the massacre," black Christians challenged "the peculiar notions" of justice under which "the laws and courts are merely for the protection of white people." Black Christians saw clearly that white supremacy, not justice, was white Christians' goal.[64] Nevertheless, denominational papers urged readers to rely on God's aid against injustice. While "troops of cruel and malignant enemies to their freedom and progressive prosperity" might swarm around them now, "like Gad of old, the Negroes will overcome these foes at the last." Quoting phrases from the Old Testament about Gad, one of the sons of the patriarch Jacob and thus the name of one of the twelve tribes of Israel, black Christians argued that they must stand their ground while they sought divine aid. Insisting that a "silver lining" remained in their present challenges, the editors quoted from a psalm that while "Sorrow is for a night, joy cometh in the morning." Joy, though, would remain elusive.[65]

Faced with the complete absence of prosecution for white lynch mob members, black Christians recommended self-defense. The *Southwestern Christian Advocate* wrote that because even white "clergy say nothing in condemnation of these barbarous acts" that "disgrace the South," black southerners needed to protect themselves. Preventing lynching appeared impossible, so "a Negro . . . had better prepare to fix a price upon his manhood, and see that at least one of his captors shall die before his own life shall be taken." Because he could hope for no other protection, "a Negro is justified in defending himself by all means in his power, under the circumstances."[66] Even the *Christian Index* wrote that "patience has about ceased to be a virtue. . . . LYNCH LAW MUST GO."[67] The paper pointed out the bitter irony that those who lynched black citizens under any pretense were never charged, but when a black father and his neighbors responded to the brutal rape and murder of his daughter by killing the white alleged perpetrator, the black men were arrested, tried, and sentenced to death. Black men could not defend family order through legal or extralegal means. Only white families—and especially rhetoric of white women's virtue—mattered amid the Christian paternalistic claims that defended white supremacy in the 1880s. The *Christian Index* editors lamented: "As we said in our last issue, patience has almost ceased to be a virtue, and since so many Negroes have been lynched by 'unknown parties,' and for nothing . . . it is at least reasonable to suppose they will feel the necessity of taking a hand in the game." Facing lynching, patience, nonviolence, and humility ceased to be laudable elements of black Christian citizenship.[68]

Black Christians rejected the connection white southerners drew between lynching and allegations of sexual violence against white women, and they pointed out that black women never received the same protection from harassment or sexual violence perpetrated by white men. Lynching represented a tool of white supremacist racial terror, not an effort to combat sexual violence or sex across the color line, as newspapers from multiple denominations attested. As Ida B. Wells would show in 1892, allegations of sexual violence against white women did not even appear in two-thirds of lynchings across the South. Nevertheless, black Christians disavowed whites' fears of "social equality," with its implications of sex across the color line, because "the question of social equality is not involved," but only "that spirit of manhood which is inseparable from a God-fearing American citizen." The "prattle of social equality" served only to distract from pressing issues. Indeed, black Christians "respectfully inform our white friends that the Negroes are not begging for social equality." Rather, "the Negroes of this country are asking for social equality about as much as they asked to be brought to this country." Lynching was not about sex across the color line. Yet black Christian citizens knew that myth was one of white supremacy's strongest tools.[69]

While they rejected allegations of black men's sexual pursuit of white women, black Christians were concerned about white men's sexual harassment and assault of black women and black women's lack of recourse against it. The *Christian Index* thought "some of our white colleges," where affluent white men studied to be religious and political leaders, should "warn their students against attempting to form criminal association with the young colored women" who were working "to build for themselves a character worthy of a woman." White men's harassment meant that "our wives and daughters cannot walk the streets of a southern city without being insulted." Black Christians invoked "the heaven-favored white Lord" to make southern white men "let our colored ladies alone."[70] If white southern Christians wanted to argue that sexual discipline and chastity formed vital aspects of Christian identity, then white men should give black women the respect that they claimed to give white women.[71]

Sexual norms undergirded all of these assertions of black Christian women's status as ladies, especially as lynching rose to a national crisis. White southerners defended only white women in their calls for family order. Black Christians pointed to this hypocrisy as rooted in slavery's history, where white men had unfettered sexual access to enslaved women, and to the ongoing sexual abuse of black women by white men. CME Church minister Rev. Elias Cottrell promised black women the same protection that white women enjoyed, because "we colored men have resolved to protect you at the sacrifice of our lives if you will let us." Speaking in Memphis, Tennessee, he addressed ongoing sex across the color line in 1889 as that of white men who coerced black women "for the gratification of basic desires" and continued to have the power to do this because of black women's impossibly low wages as "an honest house girl or cook." Black women needed to earn a living wage and to have the same protection of their sexual virtue as white women enjoyed. Cottrell showed white hypocrisy by asking, "If the white men are such lovers of virtue, why do they not come to the rescue of those working women by paying them more for their work?" Cottrell argued that it was because many men, as they had done during slavery, wanted a "colored mistress" for whom they bought gifts with the money they could have been paying domestic workers fairly. Rev. Cottrell's plan, published with adulation in the *Christian Index*, was full of class-based arguments about gendered Christian norms, but at its core was his effort to declare that black women's sexual virtue was as worthy of protection as white women's. Yet, as black Christian citizens repeatedly found, southern legal systems only permitted extralegal violence to protect white family order.[72]

AS BLACK CHRISTIANS condemned lynching as unchristian and unlawful, they recognized the importance of Christian citizenship claims to construct the future of the Mississippi River Valley. They joined biblical condemnation of racial prejudice with vigorous defenses of their civil and political rights. Not only did black Christians deserve equal rights with white Christians because of Christianity's teachings and Reconstruction's legal promises, but black citizens as devout Christians and loyal Americans had proved their worth to the states and nation from which they now sought equal treatment. Using their religious identity as a chosen marker of their equal status with white citizens, black Christians tried to give the seemingly immutable markers of racial identity less power to determine who deserved civil and political rights. Yet the momentum of social and political change was accelerating in the opposite direction. The final decade of the nineteenth century would bring greater violence and fewer political options for black citizens across the region. The difficult situation of the 1880s would soon be dire. Yet in this moment, black access to Christian arguments would become even more important, as their recourse to civil and political rights would nearly disappear.

The Christian paternalism that white southern Christians re-created in the 1880s justified white supremacy by claiming that it restored the biblical paternalism of the antebellum South. Their new historical narratives of continuity from the antebellum past to their present in the 1880s used the logic of proslavery theology to legitimize white supremacist political power. They imagined an antebellum past of peaceful plantations and dutiful slaves governed by benevolent paternalists, alleging proslavery fantasy as historical fact. As they defended family and social order and discounted rights-based claims, white southern Christians made lynching and mob violence tools of white order, just as they had justified the Democratic political takeovers in the 1870s as efforts to reestablish order by violently overthrowing democratically elected governments. In the 1890s, white Democrats would employ this logic as they created legal segregation.

White Christians claimed a paternalistic duty to oversee the religious, educational, and political life of black southerners in order to undermine black communities' self-determination and their civil and political rights. From this claim, Christian efforts to create legal inequality and white male power followed easily. Paternalism was the rhetoric that legitimized white supremacist power, but white southerners did not hold themselves to fulfilling paternalistic duties. White southerners never funded this work anywhere close to the level of their antebellum missions to enslaved people. They used Christian paternalism as a vehicle to apply the core logic of their antebellum proslavery theology to shape the twentieth century. Because they had transformed their proslavery theological commitments into a new Christian paternalism, white southerners were poised to create the Jim Crow South and to justify it as a system of Christian benevolence.

CHAPTER FIVE

Segregation

Violent Order in a Christian Civilization, 1890–1900

The year 1890 opened on an ominous note. Early months brought devastating flooding along the Mississippi River, displacing thousands of residents. White mobs continued to lynch black citizens with impunity. And then Mississippi convened a state constitutional convention to restrict black civil and political rights. On August 12, 1890, Southern Methodist Bishop Charles Betts Galloway opened the convention by praying for God's blessing on his fellow Mississippians in this task. In the sweltering midday heat inside the state capitol, Bishop Galloway's lengthy prayer thanked God for Mississippi's blessings: "its genial skies, its generous climate, its productive soil, its fruitful seasons, and its growing material prosperity." He prayed for "this Convention, called together by the voice of the whole people to reconstruct their organic law" during a "solemn" time of "crisis in this history of our beloved State." Invoking an honorable legacy of antebellum Mississippi's leaders, he continued "O, God of our fathers, give these, our brethren, strength for this momentous responsibility and grace for this sublime opportunity." Galloway asked for divine blessings of "wisdom," "charity," "pure patriotism, high-born courage, clear discrimination and . . . statesmanship" on the delegates as they undertook this work. He concluded his prayer, "May the organic law here carefully and prayerfully framed stand the test of years" without "moral taint upon any of its provisions, affording the amplest protection to the humblest citizen, [and] preserving the integrity of our traditional liberties . . . to benefit the entire people of this commonwealth."[1]

Although Galloway's prayer insisted that the "whole people" sought a new constitution "to benefit the entire people," Mississippians and outsiders knew that the convention sought to replace the Reconstruction-era 1868 constitution with one that disenfranchised black men without explicitly making race the point of disqualification to avoid entanglement with the Fifteenth Amendment. Before the ratification of the new constitution, black men still constituted a theoretical electoral majority, although violent white supremacist intimidation meant that most had not voted in more than a decade. While issues like flood control on the Mississippi River occupied some of the convention's attention, observers readily commented that black disenfranchisement was the convention's chief goal.[2] The Mississippians whom Galloway considered the "whole people" were white, propertied men. When Galloway imagined black Mississippians, he ignored their efforts for self-determination and equal civil and political rights in favor of the white supremacist view that they welcomed white southerners' benevolent paternalism. A specious claim, to be sure, but one to which white southerners clung as they crafted segregation policies that they believed re-created the benevolence of their slaveholding forebearers. Southern white Christians had created that benevolent Christian paternalism over the previous quarter century by uniting idealized antebellum family order with opposition to rights-based equality as unbiblical. This new white Christian citizenship found its full expression in the Mississippi constitution of 1890.

Bishop Galloway invoked the historical narratives that white southerners had invented in the 1880s in his opening prayer as he asserted unchanging benevolent paternalism toward black southerners. Using these recent historical claims, Galloway showed how widespread these white supremacist narratives had become. Even though he was a somewhat moderate white Christian leader who had earned black Christians' praise for supporting black schools, including the public Alcorn College, Galloway endorsed the constitutional convention, suggesting the strength of white Christians' commitment to white supremacist political power.[3] Before the assembled delegates, all but one of whom were white, Galloway's prayer expressed his joy "in the inheritance of our fathers—in their sturdy virtues, their love of liberty, and their heroic history." He prayed that the convention would "show ourselves worthy of such an ancestry and history, and . . . the heritage of virtue and liberty, they have bequeathed us." Galloway continued, "we pray, O Lord, that a double portion of their spirit may descend upon us all to-day." After invoking antebellum white statesmen's hallowed memory, Galloway asked divine blessing for "the solemn and weighty responsibilities of his hour." To discharge these duties, delegates needed "patriotic citizenship" as they crafted a new state constitution.[4]

White Christian power solidified during the constitutional convention as Jackson's white Protestant churches joined the delegates' work. Each morning, ministers from local churches opened the day's session with prayer.[5] The delegates discussed many strategies for ensuring a white majority of voters, even briefly considering enfranchising white women married to propertied men, before settling on the literacy test and poll tax, which would form two principal tools for black disenfranchisement in Mississippi and throughout the South.[6] As these debates coalesced into settled policy, delegates paused for a "day of special prayer" on Sunday, September 21, to seek "the direction of an All Wise Providence" in addressing "the magnitude of the race problem." They asked local white ministers to "call the attention of their congregation to the subject," so that all of Jackson's white Christian citizens would understand their Christian duty of protecting white Mississippians' political control from black citizens. Politicians and ministers united Christian citizenship and white supremacist political ambition as Mississippi crafted a model that the rest of the South would use to disenfranchise black citizens for decades to come.[7]

Black citizens, too, recognized that the Mississippi constitutional convention had both religious and political significance. In religious gatherings and church newspapers across the region, they decried the efforts of the Mississippi constitutional convention as unchristian and unconstitutional. Reporting from New Orleans, Louisiana, the *Southwestern Christian Advocate* wrote that the convention's "time is almost wholly taken up in devising some plan to insure white supremacy and the round-about disfranchisement of the Negro majority." The paper asked rhetorically, "Will the nation suffer the constitution of the United States to be thus presumptuously nullified?" The next week, the paper updated its readers that "the Mississippi Constitutional Convention . . . as yet has not decided" "how to disfranchise its colored voters," but warned that "its unconstitutional constitution" persisted in that goal. Yet these critiques lacked the force of earlier calls for equal black civil and political rights because black Christians had less electoral power and fewer northern allies. While black Christians could issue powerful criticism of the convention's attacks on the Reconstruction amendments to the U.S. Constitution and on their Christian citizenship, they had little power to interrupt this work.[8]

ARGUING FOR EQUAL civil and political rights became virtually impossible in the Mississippi River Valley after 1890, as Congress, northern public opinion, and northern churches lost interest in defending black rights against new segregation laws. As a result, black Christians shifted Christian citizenship advocacy in two directions: toward education and toward Christian civilization arguments against lynching. Doing so, they defended black families from legal and extralegal white supremacist threats. Most black ministers grew more cautious in their political advocacy, and women increasingly led black advocacy. Instead of equal rights, black churches pursued education both as a prerequisite for civil and political participation and as an alternative to political life. Black Christians could advance education, from children's primary education to higher education for clergy, within black communities despite the growing wave of segregation policies. Black churchwomen took a larger role in education in church and schools. As they celebrated black achievement, black Christian women showed that as Christian wives, mothers, and teachers, they formed the backbone of black Christian communities. With this turn to education and women's work, black Christians narrowed their political advocacy on the evils of lynching. They denounced lynching as an assault on American Christian civilization, not just a violation of black citizens' now-uncertain civil and political rights.[9]

In the 1890s, white southerners created legal segregation and black disenfranchisement across the Mississippi River Valley and justified their work as the orderly re-creation of antebellum Christian paternalism in the "New South." Because they had stripped this paternalistic rhetoric of any duty to care for or protect black lives, this white supremacist paternalism demanded nothing of white Christian citizens in return for their complete political power. Segregation in train cars and public accommodations spread across the South and the nation, and the 1896 Supreme Court decision in *Plessy v. Ferguson* upheld segregation of public facilities through the principle of "separate but equal." White southern Christians celebrated having solved "the Negro problem" so thoroughly that they had secured white Democratic political control for many years to come. Southern whites, after many years of work, believed they had finally undone the religious and political damage wrought by northern religious and political officials during Reconstruction. After 1900, a few white southerners grudgingly accepted black Christian arguments that lynching was an uncivilized practice, but these white Christians launched no organized opposition, nor did they connect white supremacist violence to the increasing number of legal discriminatory practices. Instead, as white southerners reviewed their history and planned their future, they glorified nostalgia for the Christian paternalism of the antebellum and Confederate past.

Black Education and Women's Christian Citizenship

By the 1890s black citizens had effectively lost their battle for equal civil and political rights in the Mississippi River Valley for decades to come. With men's disenfranchisement, black women became more influential advocates as black Christians shifted their focus to pursuing self-improvement through education and to denouncing lynching as a threat to American Christian civilization. Ministers and denominational newspapers become more cautious about political arguments because of the combined threats of extralegal violence and legal disenfranchisement. Their conservatism varied, but ministers across denominational lines were less willing to advocate publicly for civil and political rights or to condemn all racial inequality as sinful. Even the formerly outspoken AME Church turned to matters that they could control more fully as legal segregation took hold. Churchwomen became the face of black Christian citizenship claims because, as women, they did not contest the right to vote, and as mothers, wives, and teachers, they called for education and an end to lynching within their womanly Christian duties. White supremacist family order, which legitimized white men's total political control and mob violence in the name of white womanhood, threatened to destroy black families, and black Christian women fought this menace with their work in families, churches, and black communities.

Black Christians extolled the virtues of education to strengthen religious life, create wealth, and earn white southerners' respect. AME ministers in southern Arkansas called education the key to "religious and social advancement of the negro race" and "the lever of success in every avenue of life."[10] In Baton Rouge, AME Church members pledged $1,500 to build their own high school because education would advance "the negro character for honesty, for truth, and integrity to Christian principles" that black Christians defended. Other congregations rallied to help churches destroyed by Mississippi River floods in the spring of 1890. Many black Christians showed "honesty, integrity, morality," and "self-denial" in their faithful church work, even amid "the cruelty of midnight assassination."[11] AME ministers lamented that "a very considerable majority of whites in this country" refused "to give equal rights to the colored citizens." But where they had previously proposed collective political action, in 1891 the AME Church's lament over "the state of the country" rested "our case into the hands of God Almighty who will do right" and proposed that "while God is solving the problem let us preach a pure gospel, build church and schools and colleges, educate our children, buy . . . property . . . [and] enter all forms of business."[12] Education advanced this good character through "a better type of manhood and womanhood" within black communities. AME ministers preached that "self help is the best kind of help" as they urged that "negro schools should be taught by negro teachers."[13] AME minister and former U.S. senator from Mississippi Hiram Revels preached a politically conservative message that "ignorance and whiskey" among both black and white southerners caused most race conflicts, but "education under the influence of Christianity" promised "the panacea for this evil."[14] Education formed the necessary first step for any major goal that black Christians had.

Denominational newspapers followed this more cautious tone. They noted that black citizens should have political rights, but they devoted more space to encouraging black Christians to pursue education and to gain property. A writer in the *Christian Index* asked that "it be forgotten that he is a Negro and an ex-slave and remembered only that he is a man and a citizen."[15] For every clear statement that "we deplore any and all legislation which aims to abridge and destroy the civil and political rights of the Negro as a class," there were many more that insisted that "the Negro should pay less attention to politics and devote his attention to those things that appertain more directly to his educational and moral interests."[16] As they shifted their rhetoric to reflect the dire state of black political rights in the 1890s, black Christian authors encouraged educational pursuits within their communities.[17]

Black Christians who had previously relied on northern white Christians' support, especially members of the northern-based Methodist Episcopal Church, found that their national denomination was no longer willing to advocate for political rights. In New Orleans, the white and black authors in the *Southwestern Christian Advocate* encouraged black readers to shift their focus inward from politics, toward self-examination and internal community action, warning that "we are too much more anxious about our rights than we are about our duties." While "American prejudice in church and state, in pulpit and pew, in the hall of legislation and in the courts of justice, asserts itself incessantly," black Christians needed to attend to "their own sins and folly" and to improve their education and moral character. In a subsequent editorial, the paper admitted "the completeness of the elimination of the Negro as a political factor in the South," but expressed hope that "as the Negro rises in intelligence, virtue and the acquisition of wealth, the barriers in the way of his progress will give way, and he will become a . . . political factor." These statements showed a new resignation instead of earlier arguments for civil and political rights, and they mirrored the national denomination's shifting focus away from black rights. Black men's loss of the franchise, the newspaper contended, did not signal any inferiority in "the moral and social and intellectual status of the Negro." Instead, black Christians should choose patient self-improvement rather than "throw the bomb of the anarchist." This reference to the Haymarket protests in 1886 called for a Christian patience from mistreated black southerners that northern anarchist labor activists lacked.[18]

During the Mississippi constitutional convention, the CME Church's *Christian Index* editorialized on "The Negro in Politics," suggesting that black men should turn their focus from politics to education and property. While "as a citizen every Negro has a right to cast his vote and have it counted," the article promised that "our real happiness and success" depended on factors outside politics. Black Christians should "devote more time [to] the accumulation of homes, property, education and such things as ... can speak ... louder than any office." Without calling for "the Negro to quit politics altogether," the paper encouraged readers to consider politics "subordinate to other matters of more importance" and to prove their fitness for full rights through greater economic and educational achievement. This call, despite its cautious tone, still pushed beyond the deep conservatism of leaders like Bishops Isaac Lane or Lucius Holsey to echo statements of other black Christian groups, suggesting that these bishops did not represent the views of the whole denomination.[19]

By the late 1890s, the *Christian Index* more emphatically taught that black citizens might eventually appreciate disenfranchisement as a push to self-improvement and educational achievement. New voting restrictions represented "obstacles intentionally thrown in the path of the Negro by ... his brother in white," yet "upon reflection ... these would-be hindrances are blessings in disguise." Noting briefly that "every man should be allowed to cast his ballot untrammeled," the paper hoped that black Christians would use new restrictive laws to "awaken in them a ... determination to educate themselves and their children" and to "work to the best interest of the Negro." The injustice of disenfranchisement, which "strike[s] at the manhood of the Negro," could prove "fruitful" if it could "excite him to shake himself like unto the mighty Samson." Black Christians should pursue disciplined self-improvement to thwart white supremacy, as the supernaturally strong Israelite warrior Samson had done to destroy the ungodly Philistines. Unjust legislation could not stop black self-improvement because, just as "a man cannot be legislated into ignorance, he cannot be legislated out of it." "Despite the present darkness" of white supremacist efforts to "stigmatize our manhood and remand us to a position of inferiority ... forever," black Christians should take charge of their lives through education to strive "to higher planes, to loftier heights and to more responsible positions of affluence and honor." These lofty heights existed outside of politics, and so did not depend on white Christians' support.[20]

Black Christians identified their ministers and the next generation of children as the two central targets of educational efforts. Having an "educated ministry" helped religious and racial development because ministers who were broadly educated could better direct congregants toward religious, moral, and intellectual attainment.[21] Partnerships among families, churches, and local governments should ensure that black children received the education they needed. Parents, especially mothers, needed to offer a moral and religious education at home, yet local white leaders owed black citizens a better public education system than existed after the gutting of Reconstruction educational plans.[22] Any community aiming to be "peaceful and prosperous" needed to awaken "to the importance of religion and education," because "we need education more than we need gold or silver." Education also promised to make people "better qualified to accumulate wealth." Accordingly, black Christians should see that "if any race needs wealth it is our race. If we will educate ourselves we will soon be a wealthy people."[23]

While the power of education appeared universally heralded, the substance of that education varied significantly from local common schools, private high schools, industrial schools, and liberal arts and theological colleges. The CME Church supported its own Lane Institute as well as Paine Institute, which was run by white Southern Methodists to educate CME Church ministers and teachers. AME Church members sent funds to their flagship Wilberforce College in Ohio, while they also created local high schools and required ongoing education of new ministers under established local ministers' supervision. The northern Methodist Episcopal Church sponsored Rust College in Holly Springs, Mississippi, and the American Missionary Association sponsored Straight Normal School in New Orleans, Louisiana; Tugaloo College near Jackson, Mississippi; and Fisk College in Nashville, Tennessee, among other institutions. Quakers' Southland College in Arkansas attracted Baptist and other pupils. Many prominent black ministers and leaders attended these schools or worked to support them in various ways. Beyond these schools, Booker T. Washington's Tuskegee Institute and its model of "industrial education" also earned praise from many black Christians. Recognizing that "there are some who believe he presses industrial education too far . . . at the expense of a more liberal education," the *Christian Index* noted that "we have never said one word of criticism against his teachings" and "congratulate this distinguished educator upon his efforts and wish for him even greater success." The *Southwestern Christian Advocate* heralded Washington as "an apostle of industrial education." This journal's support for both industrial education and education in the liberal arts indicated the value placed on any form of education, but also signaled a growing class divide among black Christians.[24]

Black Christian women used their Christian missionary work, temperance organizing, and roles as mothers and preachers' wives to shape a new form of Christian citizenship under segregation. Susie E. Bailey was a prominent Arkansas Baptist woman who, together with her husband Rev. Isaac Bailey, was a leading force for black Baptists. A trained teacher, she built cross-racial relationships that resembled equality with northern white educators, including Alida Clark, the Quaker cofounder of Arkansas's Southland College. Clark and Bailey worked together from the 1880s on temperance causes and shared an admiration for the Woman's Christian Temperance Union and especially Frances Harper, the black author and advocate for temperance and racial justice. Clark, a generation older than Bailey, regarded the younger woman as "my dear friend," and concluded a letter to her: "I hope to hear from you soon & often."[25] Bailey built on her relationship with Clark, even after Clark's death, as she corresponded with Southland College's new President William Russell about sending her son there in 1895. Bailey introduced herself as an educator in search of the best school for her son, rather than as a black Christian seeking charity. Russell presented Southland College to northern donors as a school that elevated "the simple earnest faith of these poor colored men and women" who lived in "log . . . cabins without paint or whitewash." Yet Susie Bailey, who had attended high school and normal school in St. Louis, and Alida Clark had regarded each other as fellow Christian educators and leaders of women's missionary work, and relationships like these among well-educated black Christian women and northern white women gave black women new avenues for demonstrating their Christian citizenship.[26]

Churchwomen defended their Christian families by celebrating marriage, parenting, and gendered respectability as a counterargument to white supremacist Christian paternalism, which declared that only white families and white women were worthy of protection and celebration. As black Christians focused on education and self-improvement in the face of segregation policy, churchwomen led efforts to celebrate black identity, educate children, and protect families. Women, especially teachers and preachers' wives, argued that racial uplift and traditional gender norms together worked to elevate all black people, not just men who were potential clergy or voters. Women wrote in denominational newspapers for other women and for clergy to appreciate women's work for church and race. Aware that affluent black Christians could illustrate black potential for religious and economic achievement, these papers celebrated elite black women's and men's achievements, from opulent weddings to elegant homes, as a triumph of black Christian self-improvement. Along with celebrating black success, black women, following Ida B. Wells, would argue that lynching black men in the name of white women's protection destroyed black families and threatened Christian civilization to defend a baseless lie.[27]

Black women celebrated their communities' advances since emancipation as proof of black Christians' gendered achievement. Black churches and fraternal organizations held annual emancipation celebrations on the anniversary of the Emancipation Proclamation's taking effect on January 1, 1863. Their newspapers republished Lincoln's proclamation with commentary on their economic, religious, and educational progress since emancipation. These reports celebrated black womanhood and manhood as gendered accomplishments of faithful Christians. Women participated increasingly in this work of celebrating black achievement, and they often used Christian imagery. Mrs. M. L. Halle emphasized the duty of helping other members of the race by enjoining "Christians, one and all, be on your watch; trim up your lamps and let your little lights shine out." When Miss H. B. Hamilton described "Twenty Six Years of Progress" for free black citizens from the end of the Civil War to 1891, she highlighted progress in education and character. These celebrations of black progress omitted the growth and subsequent restriction of civil and political rights. Since women authors had never had the right to vote, they were best positioned to enumerate black advancement outside of politics.[28]

Black Christians used ubiquitous Protestant tropes of women's piety to argue that black Christian women deserved the respect and protection from violence that white women received. Black women and men across denominations praised Christian civilization for valuing women more highly than other historical periods or cultures had done and celebrated black women and black marriages as part of this higher civilization. Numerous articles on womanhood in Christian civilization set the stage for black Christians' condemnation of lynching as an assault not simply on black people but on American Christian civilization. Church leaders celebrated "The Influence of Womanhood" within Victorian gender and sexual norms and echoed international missionaries' claims that Euro-American Christian imperial power elevated the status of women wherever missionaries and colonizers went around the world. By including black women in this elevated, modern Christian womanhood, black Christian authors argued that black women belonged to a virtuous womanhood that deserved men's protection, an assertion that white southern Christians rejected. From these claims, black men's explication of black women's role as men's "helpmeet," with a duty of wifely submission, both supported black men's authority through a traditional Christian interpretation of women's subordination and argued that black marriages and families conformed to respectable white marriage norms from which white supremacist social order excluded them.[29]

Male and female authors praised the Christian behavior of the much discussed "preacher's wife" as exemplifying black Christian refinement across the Mississippi River Valley. A preacher's wife should be "a model of meekness, patience, godliness, temperance and cleanliness," who always appeared "neat and clean but never . . . fancy appareled."[30] One minister's wife wrote that "the work of a Methodist preachers' [*sic*] wife is equally important . . . as that of her husband" and required that she be "a self-denying, sacrificing Christian." Her work in the Sunday school was vital, and she should follow the example of the valorized Susannah Wesley, mother of John and Charles Wesley, "a devoted Christian," full "of meekness and peaceableness." Many Methodists praised Susannah Wesley as an exemplar of female piety, mapping respectable Victorian norms onto this woman raised in the late seventeenth century. Identifying the idealized English mother of Methodism's founders as a model for black preachers' wives connected southern black womanhood in the 1890s to a cross-racial and transatlantic vision of Methodist female piety going back two centuries.[31]

Nevertheless, church leaders agreed that all women, especially wives and mothers, bore responsibilities similar to the preacher's wife. Women's work supported churches in a growing number of Woman's Missionary Societies. This work of raising funds for their churches, leading Sunday schools, and engaging in temperance activity earned the support and recognition of church organizational structures and of the male clergy as a valuable contribution to church and community life.[32] Children's moral training was to begin at home, not in a Sunday school or public school setting, so all mothers must be Christian teachers.[33] Discussions of women's duty as mothers and wives sought to elevate women's domestic labor, and they followed well-established norms for Protestant women's piety across lines of race and denomination. "A Mother's Work," wrote a mother from Lexington, Mississippi, began "at the cradle's side." Because a "mother has no time to idle," she "must be like Mary Magdalene, [and] rise early while it is yet dark" on Sundays to ensure that her children are clean and prepared for Sunday school. The article linking Mary Magdalene's predawn visit to Jesus's tomb, where she became the first witness of the resurrected Christ, to a black mother's preparing her children for Sunday school stretched the biblical story to value all women's domestic work as sacred Christian labor, and praised Mary Magdalene as an exemplary Christian woman against centuries of extrabiblical Christian tradition that described her as a prostitute.[34]

Women writers explained to male and female readers that Christian womanhood stressed literacy and Bible knowledge, homemaking skills, and sexual mores. Central to mothers' Christian duty lay keeping "their entire life . . . clean, for cleanliness is next to Godliness." Within women's domestic and religious duty, cleanliness implied moral and sexual purity as well as the responsibility for keeping a home clean. Joining the theological valences of moral cleanliness to the duties of the home, another woman insisted: "Find a godly person and you have a clean person, for godliness is cleanliness, no person is godly who is not also cleaned."[35] Cleanliness, "that virtue that lies next to godliness," meant more than "dish-washing," extending to "cleanliness of the tongue" in avoiding coarse language or gossip. "Every young couple" setting up their own home should "build there an altar to purity," where their children would learn "high views of morality and honor." Sexual propriety—premarital celibacy and marital monogamy—remained central to this moral cleanliness and to the defense of black Christians' respectability. As women worked to care for their children and home, their sexual behavior, and their shaping children's sexual behavior, proved an essential aspect of their religious duty.[36]

Writers for denominational periodicals celebrated elaborate wedding ceremonies to highlight black marital sexual propriety and the affluence of some black Christians. Regular notices of marriages appeared in earlier decades, but during the 1890s, marriage announcements increasingly showcased conspicuous consumption through discussions of flower arrangements and the many "valuable and useful presents" that the couple received. For a winter wedding, "the church was beautifully lighted up" in the dark evening, and the minister preached "a noble sermon on the marriage relation," allowing one couple's wedding to extol marriage broadly. At the wedding of a minister, "the bride was handsomely dressed in a white silk dress and the groom wore a clerical diagonal suit." At a wedding officiated "with dignity and grace," the "bride and groom looked as two angels." The wedding of a couple who "looked very handsome . . . both of them wearing graceful smiles of delight" drew both white and black guests to a rural western Tennessee town to enjoy "an abundance of refreshments of all kinds." The narrative adapted a biblical reference from the Psalms to relate to marriage: "How pleasant it is for them to dwell together in holy matrimony. It is like the precious ointment upon the head that ran down on the beard, even Aaron's beard; that went down to the skirts of his garments; as the dew of Hermon and as the dew that descended upon the mountains of Zion." Weddings like these gave "a proof positive of the progress the people of the colored race have made in social and intellectual matters." While only a small set of couples could afford white silk wedding gowns, luxurious presents, or lavish feasts, lifting up those who could allowed a broader group of black Christians to celebrate the respectability and affluence of this group.[37]

This small but prosperous group of black southerners strengthened opposition to legalized segregation of train cars. Unlike disenfranchisement, which applied to black men broadly, the creation of "Jim Crow cars" on trains primarily affected those who could afford to buy first-class train tickets or sleeping car berths—affluent passengers. In decrying these new laws, this elite group defended their class status and respectability as deserving seats alongside wealthy white travelers, while avoiding more dangerous defenses of black political rights. Denominational papers rarely protested disenfranchisement, but train car segregation earned condemnation as "rotten to the core." The new laws made "travel in the South, for Colored people . . . more and more intolerable." Numerous articles solicited funds for legal challenges and expressed support for what became the *Plessy v. Ferguson* Supreme Court case. Because the laws did not pertain strictly to political rights, black Christians could oppose them as a legal affront to the respectability of more elite black Christians, rather than as a demand for equal political rights for all black citizens. At the same time, newspapers' decision that opposing train car segregation was less dangerous than opposing disenfranchisement allowed them to publish striking condemnations of legal segregation.[38]

Black Christians made arguments about women's piety, elaborate weddings, and first-class train seating to argue against racial inferiority while sidestepping questions of political rights. Women's arguments that they were exemplary Christian women claimed that they deserved the protections given to white women as ladies. Black women's work as wives, especially preachers' wives, defended black men's status as men whom their families respected. Yet with these claims, black Christians shifted away from the organized defenses of their equal civil and political rights that had formed the centerpiece of earlier Christian citizenship arguments. Collectively, black Christians' work in education, women's organizations, and elite respectability demonstrated ongoing self-improvement despite political losses. Black Christians' advocacy in these areas prepared them to denounce lynching as an attack on American Christian civilization.

Lynching as an Attack on Christian Civilization

Anti-lynching arguments formed the primary activist work for black Christian citizens in the 1890s, and black Christians pushed the full force of their Christian citizenship arguments against the scourge of lynching. Lynching had been a crisis since the 1880s, but with its growth, black Christians shifted from denouncing lynch mobs' denial of black citizens' right to trial by a jury, to a new argument that lynching was a fundamental attack on the rule of law in a Christian civilization. They argued "in the name of Christianity, civilization and humanity" that "government" must "stop this wholesale murder of men." Even white supremacists who denied their other civil and political rights must recognize that protection from mob violence was a civil and human right that black citizens must be granted. Law, even unjust segregation laws, prohibited this uncivilized violence. Black Christians argued that if only white Christian ministers would teach that the Bible opposed lynching, the crisis would end, but southern white Christians had too much to gain to heed that call. Black Christians selectively deployed white Christians' own historical narratives of the antebellum and postemancipation South to argue against lynching. As they fought lynching, black Christians devoted all the energy of their Christian citizenship against this terror.[39]

Ida B. Wells's investigative journalism after the 1892 People's Grocery lynching of her friend Thomas Moss and two other men in Memphis, Tennessee, pioneered this work. She conclusively demonstrated that the overwhelming majority of lynching incidents had no link to the allegation of the rape of a white woman. Knowing that prominent white men led the Memphis lynching to protect white grocers from competition from the black-owned People's Grocery, Wells launched into an investigation of other reported lynchings as white supremacist terror. She published her conclusion that less than a third of recorded southern lynchings related to the allegation of rape as *Southern Horrors* in 1892. She built upon those claims in 1895 with *A Red Record*, which used national data about lynching from 1892 through 1894 to prove that lynching expressed white supremacist rage, not black crime. Wells confirmed Frederick Douglass's claims that white southerners invented successive excuses for murdering black people after emancipation: first false accusations of riots that threatened white lives, then false claims that black men's voting amounted to a criminal "negro domination," and finally, after black men's disenfranchisement, false myths of black men's rape of white women. Following Wells, many black Christians in the South debunked the myth of the black male rapist and argued that lynching was not about black criminality or even due process, but the utter inability of white Christians to maintain the barest requirements of civilized society.[40]

Black Christians believed that recording and denouncing lynching was their duty as Christian citizens. Lynchings occurred so frequently that the weekly *Southwestern Christian Advocate* warned, "if this paper should chronicle all the hellish crimes committed against the colored people of the South, it would have to be a daily and of greatly enlarged size." Still, the paper listed white supremacist crimes, arguing that even if citizenship did not guarantee them equal civil and political rights with white southerners, freedom from such terroristic violence must be "a constitutional and God-given right" of "the Negro citizen." Lynching was the "legitimate fruit of the cry for white supremacy."[41] Lynching's threat "almost" suggested that "an avenging God has turned his all-seeing eye from such scenes." Yet the paper promised that "God *does* witness them, and in his own time and way will stretch forth *his* strong arm to defend," while "pitying, loving Christ also sits at his right hand to plead." Because God could defend black Christians in ways that they could not defend themselves, the editorial called upon "our people to cry mightily to him for help day and night—to live righteously, deal justly with themselves and neighbors, and by good conduct command the respect of friends and foes." At the very least, citizenship and Christianity must, black Christians pled, end lynching.[42]

In the 1890s, black Christians framed lynching as a threat to American civilization and the rule of law, not just to black lives. They argued that the United States' future hung in the balance and asked, "Can the great American nation afford to tolerate one of the greatest horrors of civilization—the crime of lynching?" More pointedly, black Christians queried, "Has the game of American forests become so scarce that the poor unprotected Negro will have to answer as a substitute?" The gross inhumanity of lynching emerged forcefully. Even though local and federal law no longer protected their equal rights, black Christians pled for the rule of law as the only hope of stemming the "barbarism and . . . attack on the rule of law" that threatened lives and terrorized communities. The *Christian Index* echoed similar condemnation of "this diabolical lawlessness" under which "lynching of negroes is becoming more and more a habit." The paper "counsel[ed] peace and submission to the laws of the land" for outraged black citizens. Even if white people ignored the law, black people could not afford to "rise up against the whites" because "they have the Army and the Navy and the ammunitions of war behind them." Black Christians condemned white supremacist lynching as a force that would undo the United States from within because "no civilization can be enduring which permits lawlessness to go unpunished, or which fails to enforce justice in the spirit of absolute impartiality."[43]

White Christians were dangerous hypocrites, black Christians warned, whose white supremacist Christianity was as dangerous as it was heretical. Black Christians connected the American rule of law with a supreme divine law articulated in the Old and New Testaments because any "solution of the race problem in the South" depended "upon the moral law and our Lord's

Sermon on the Mount." Following that biblical law could "give stability to our government ... [and] unadulterated Christianity in our churches and homes." Lynching was fundamentally at odds with morality and Christian teaching. Black Christians connected the inexplicably cruel violence they faced with that of ancient persecuted Christians. An article for children explained the martyrdom of St. Luke as being like a lynching, showing that lynching had become a touchstone for unjust executions in sacred history.[44]

Black Christians argued that white Christians bore direct responsibility for white supremacist violence. Lynching continued only because many white "best citizens," who were "members of the Christian churches," continued to allow it. The deep hypocrisy of "these really good (?) people" showed that white Christians "have consciously or otherwise condoned the great evil" of lynching. Black Christians must "appeal to the patriotism of the South, to her press, to her pulpit, to her Christianity, to her sense of justice, and to all that is dear to human life to help us in our helplessness" and "to do [a]way with the midnight mob and let the law which is supreme have its course." Week after week, black Christians argued that "if Southern pulpits, and the Southern presses should speak out frequently against ... lynchings," then "lynching of Negroes will be impossible, and mob rule and mob law will reign no more." If only "the white pulpits throughout the entire Southland would teach the Siniatic law, 'thou shalt not kill'; and the golden rule and teach the unity of the human race according to ... Christianity," then lynching would end. White Christians' refusal to preach these basic Christian teachings permitted "all mob violence, [and] the harrowing, sickening reports of lynching, burning and drag[g]ing of lifeless bodies of human beings through the streets of a Christian city, town or village." Their "southern white fellow citizens" needed to "espouse the cause of these most defenseless citizens." Indeed, "the good men, the Christians and patriots of the South, must combine" with "the great ecclesiastical bodies, the conferences and presbyteries, as well as the political conventions" so that white southern Christians, as individuals and as denominational bodies, would end lynching.[45]

White Christians needed to recognize that their own country needed the same reforming work they eagerly prescribed for distant lands. Black Christians argued that lynching made white Christians less civilized than the supposedly inferior people to whom they sent missionaries. Lynching was a systemic problem that indicted all white people. The "barbarity" of lynching revealed that there was "great work for Christians to do in this country" to reform uncivilized practices, in much the same way that Western Christians tried to reform cultural practices in Africa or Asia as part of spreading Christian civilization abroad. If white Christians would remove "the cruel barriers which prevent" the black man "from becoming a member of the same spiritual family of the followers of Christ; [and] treat him as one for whom our blessed savior made the sacrifice of his own precious life," then Christianity could rid the nation of lynching. As citizens, black Christians claimed, "we are industrious, patient, law-abiding, eager to conceed [*sic*] and willing to submit." Unlike labor activists in northern cities, "we are not anarchists or dynamiters." Accordingly, "the wholesale lynching of individuals of the race" who maintained this posture of humble citizenship "savors of cowardice." Lynching was "an atrocious crime, in which no life is secured, no man is exempt" when mobs "murder their victims without . . . remorse of conscience." White Americans needed a civilizing mission to reform their barbarity more urgently than any supposedly uncivilized foreign people.[46]

Black Christians rooted white Christians' uncivilized support of lynching in the racial prejudice at the heart of white Christian citizenship, as they used fictions of the antebellum South to condemn lynching. Just as southern whites had discounted Christian critiques of slavery and black Christian citizenship, they refused to make "any progress in the line of humanity or respect for law," and showed "the same disregard for the rights of others, the same brutal, domineering disposition, which prevailed in the days when the Legrees cracked their whips over the bruised and scarred backs of their human chattels."[47] Like the infamously cruel enslaver in Harriet Beecher Stowe's bestselling novel *Uncle Tom's Cabin*, white southerners showed scant concern for black lives. Invoking a different antebellum fiction—white southern Christians' false historical claims of an idyllic antebellum South full of contented enslaved people—black Christians quoted Jefferson Davis's wife's praise of enslaved people's loyalty to the Confederate cause. "Surely" such loyal enslaved people, "who so faithfully guarded the homes and families of their masters during the war . . . and who in every trying hour since have shown heroic devotion to their country," deserve "as citizens" to be free of the violence that plagued the South. Both the famed novel of antebellum slavery's brutality to families and the apocryphal claims of the Confederate president's widow condemned white southerners' support of lynching; there simply was no justification to be made.[48]

Black Christian citizens explained that white southern Christians directly encouraged lynching. Their brutal hypocrisy appeared vividly in a recent account that "the leader of a lynching party . . . stopped the proceedings long enough to offer a fervent prayer that heaven's choicest blessings might descend upon the helpless wretch who was about to be launched into eternity."

The cruelty of a white Christian man who would pray for black man's eternal soul while killing his body illustrated how white Christian citizenship arguments denied black people the most basic human rights while claiming a paternalistic concern for black religious lives. When a Southern Methodist bishop expressed support for a lynch mob, black Christians denounced him for having "disgraced himself and his church by making a speech in defense of lynchers of colored men in the South." A "minister who defends murder, no matter on what ground," was reprehensible because no "man claiming to be a Christian should resort to deliberate misrepresentation in order to make a defense of the barbarism that exists in the South to-day." White southern Christians' support for white supremacist violence lay behind every aspect of lynching's cruelty.[49]

Black Christians wove appeals to divine judgment into their attacks on southern white Christians' hypocrisy. Believing that God would judge whites' evil actions and that God could intervene in human affairs motivated black Christian citizenship, but also revealed how few options black citizens had to attempt to stem this rising tide of mob killings. Black Christians in Louisiana called for a day of fasting and prayer, "that we may thereby invoke God's continued help and favor until the last vestige of oppression and wrong" should end. They gathered in churches to "solemnly and earnestly offer up thanksgiving to Almighty God for the mercies of the past, [and] implore his divine protection and guidance in the midst of the crisis through which we are passing."[50] Praying that "the public sentiment of this Christian nation might be roused on behalf of their brethren in the great South-land," the day of prayer sought to remind white Americans that white and black Christians together were "descendants of one Father, the redeemed children of one God, citizens of one nation, neighbors with common interests." Afterward, black Christians resolved "to exercise that patience and forbearance which has already won many friends to our cause, and which in the good providence of God will surely bring deliverance." God would judge white southerners' hypocrisy because "as slavery . . . brought a terrible visitation from Almighty God upon the white people" in the Civil War's destruction, "so will the p[r]actice of allowing mobs to overrule just and equal law." With the growing violence, "the people who are committing these outrages are 'piling up wrath against the day of wrath,' and 'more terrible than an army with banners' will be the visitation of God's vengeance," black Christians warned in the language of the Old and New Testaments.[51]

Despite all of these arguments, black Christians had few practical means to awaken southern whites to the urgent need to oppose lynching, and they drew on biblical language to lament the suffering that they faced. In their "time of outrage, lamentation, and sorrow," black Christians asked, in the words of psalmists, "Oh Lord! How long?"[52] With the prophetic tradition of the Old Testament, they cried: "O God! Open the eyes of the people that they may see; that they may turn from evil-doing and deal justly with all mankind."[53] On Thanksgiving Day 1895, black communities reasonably wondered, "Why should we be thankful?" They fought against the terror of lynching, white northern apathy, legal disenfranchisement, "odious and discriminating laws," and "the downright opposition of . . . Christian people." Yet, despite "this baptism of blood, [and] this unparalleled . . . race hatred," black Christians on Thanksgiving Day "should be thankful for the privilege of being persecuted for righteousness sake, and for the proud honor of contributing the blood of martyrs as a libation upon the altar of outraged justice." Invoking Matthew's Sermon on the Mount, where Jesus praised the meek and righteous, brought little promise of change for black Christians in the 1890s, but such claims showed how black Christians used Christian language to try to make sense of their suffering.[54]

As the nineteenth century closed, black Christians faced deep suffering in the American South. The promises of emancipation and Reconstruction had dwindled as local, state, and national leaders curtailed black civil and political rights. Extralegal violence continued to rise. Yet their arguments for their Christian citizenship had linked their religious and political lives together in ways that allowed them to argue against the evils of segregation and to demand justice and equal rights. Those arguments would be important in black Christian claims through the civil rights movement, as would black Christians' clear understanding of the depths of white Christians' sanctification of white supremacy as a Christian goal through their reinvented paternalism.[55]

White Southerners Memorialize Their Christian Paternalism

With the creation of legal segregation and black disenfranchisement, white southern Christians had succeeded in implementing white Christian citizenship as a religious and political justification for white supremacy. The Christian paternalism that white southerners reconfigured from the logic of proslavery theology defended hierarchical white family order, opposed rights-based arguments, discounted black self-determination, and justified white supremacist violence as necessary to protect white families. White southern Christians celebrated their success in giving white supremacist segregation the same legitimacy that they believed the antebellum South had held. After 1890, white southern Christians believed that after decades of argument, they had finally dismantled black Christian citizenship claims. They worked to memorialize their newly constructed history in white churches and Confederate memorial groups, and they ignored black Christians' charges that lynching was an affront to Christian civilization. The rare white criticisms of lynching at the turn of the twentieth century did not denounce the white supremacy of extralegal terror, but merely expressed discomfort with its attack on legal order.

White southern Christians believed that the best proof of their faithful paternalistic Christian citizenship lay in their antebellum missions to enslaved people, and they continued to celebrate that work long after they had abandoned it in the Civil War. They had used these missions to argue in the 1880s that their ongoing antebellum paternalism justified their white supremacist political power after they "redeemed" southern white Democratic rule. In 1893, Southern Methodist Rev. William P. Harrison published *The Gospel Among the Slaves: A Short Account of Missionary Operations Among the African Slaves of the Southern States*, a four-hundred-page celebration of white southern Christians' missions to enslaved people as the cornerstone of postemancipation white claims of Christian paternalism. Harrison quoted many antebellum ministers, missionaries, and other white Christians who gave portraits of docile enslaved people whom Christianity made content in their duties to their masters. This book illustrated proslavery theology's depiction of slavery as an orderly household hierarchy, like marriage or parenting. From the outset, Harrison reminded readers that "the inherent sinfulness of human slavery is not taught in" the Bible. Instead, the "most illustrious men in sacred history" were "owners of slaves." From Abraham in Genesis, who formed "a considerable army among the slaves born in his own house," to the Apostle Paul, who, "unlike the Garrisons, Gerritt Smiths, and Henry Ward Beechers," returned the escaped slave Onesimus to his owner in the New Testament epistle to Philemon, the Bible supported slavery. It was "the conduct and spirit of the abolitionists of fifty years ago" who abandoned "the conduct and spirit of St. Paul" with their anti-biblical arguments against slavery. Proslavery white southerners had remained faithful.[56]

Harrison's book read like a religious complement to the Confederate memorials that white southerners erected in these years. He memorialized an invented past when faithful white southern Christians devoted themselves to saving black souls, and enslaved people gratefully responded with loyal affection that left them eager to continue to serve their former enslavers long after emancipation. Harrison insisted that only Northern Methodist antislavery agitation challenged this work, as he ignored black self-determination. Free of antislavery pressures after 1844, Southern Methodists maintained Christian order in slavery, as shown by the total absence of "the heinous offenses" such as the "assault committed by a negro upon the person of a white woman," which Harrison believed to be widespread in the 1890s. Reiterating myths of black male rapists, Harrison warned that "the fearful outbreakings of lawlessness in these latter days are eloquent proofs of the degeneracy" of black people deprived of the benevolent control of Christian slavery. Black journalists like Ida B. Wells recognized the sudden emergence in the 1880s of the image of a black male rapist who attacked white women and showed that it was an invention of white supremacists. Harrison argued that this new fear added further proof that antebellum Christian slavery was the best form of government for black southerners. Slavery had not only been scriptural and benevolent; it had been necessary.[57]

Rev. Harrison celebrated white Christian benevolence as slavery's central legacy. Harrison reveled in the idea that "the fidelity of the white people of the South to the religious welfare of the African slaves" was "one of the most remarkable facts . . . in modern history." From his research as Southern Methodist book editor, he concluded that white Methodists had spent nearly two million dollars in missions to enslaved people over several decades. Yet Harrison valued personal testimonies more than this quantitative data, and he included dozens of white accounts of the faithful Christian missions they had performed or witnessed as children in slaveholding households. Harrison added "testimonies of gratitude from the members of a race formerly held in bondage" to his "record of toil, hardship, and self-denial on the part of the missionaries of the cross." Most of these accounts were from CME bishops whose autobiographies Harrison quoted selectively to describe their conversion in antebellum Southern Methodist churches. Harrison especially praised Lucius Holsey (though he identified him consistently as Lewis Holsey) because "this brother has been eminently conservative, and . . . has proved himself an able and trustworthy counselor of his race." With his carefully curated praise of a small group of black Christians, Harrison rested his case.[58]

Harrison found CME Church leaders to quote for his book because their bishops often published autobiographies to sell to white Southern Methodists as fundraisers for CME education. In that context, the authors framed their lives to avoid challenging white readers' Christian paternalism. To raise funds for Paine Institute, a school for teachers and ministers run by Southern Methodists, Lucius Holsey published an autobiography with sermons. He situated his life within white southerners' imagined version of antebellum history as a peaceful paternalistic order. About his enslaved childhood and youth, Holsey wrote, "I have no complaint against American slavery. It was a blessing in disguise to me and to many." After emancipation, Holsey continued to find "in slavery a providential blessing to both white and black—a harsh measure to bring the ignorant Negro in contact with the educated Caucassian [sic]." To showcase the benefits of this education, his sermons were full of literary allusions to Milton and other British authors and made no demands for political or civil rights. In a glowing introduction to the book, Southern Methodist Rev. George W. Walker lauded Holsey as a living testimony to white Christians' benevolent paternalism and "a faithful product of . . . the missions to the slaves." For his willingness to ignore political rights in favor of Christian education at a school still managed by white southerners, Holsey earned praise and some funding from white Christians.[59]

However, most white churches were happy to ignore black religious lives after segregation, rather than support them as fellow Christians. In the first years after emancipation, white churches lamented black members' desire for independence and tried to create paternalistic structures to control black Christians, but by the 1890s, they were content as white-only communities. Some denominations had maintained racially distinct rolls, noting members as "white" or "colored," but as the membership became entirely white, such practices disappeared. Louisiana's Southern Methodists had nearly 30,000 members statewide, but after the "colored" roll dropped below ten members by the late 1890s, they dropped the racial distinction when noting members. Most regional church assemblies collected a modest sum for missions to black people, just as they did for foreign missions and Indian missions in the American West, suggesting that rather than viewing black Christians as their neighbors and fellow Christian citizens, white southerners viewed them as distant groups who needed white missionary intervention, albeit at far lower levels than in antebellum missions.[60]

Southern white Christians wrote denominational histories in the 1890s that placed these specific denominations squarely within the narrative frameworks of white Christian citizenship. They began with churches' antebellum prosperity and piety, followed by the parallel disasters of the Civil War and Reconstruction, and finally a new, hopeful present in which black Christians had been forced to the margins. A history of Mississippi Baptists noted "the disturbed condition of our land" during "the years of the Civil War," but spoke more strongly about the damage wrought by Reconstruction, when "strong churches seemed then to be on the decline." For Baptists and other

Christians, "reconstruction was ominous" and "disastrous to spirituality all over our State." A history of Methodists in Arkansas took pride in their avoidance of all political questions, unlike their northern counterparts who had been deeply involved in opposing slavery, yet the author praised antebellum missions to enslaved people, where white ministers were "held in great esteem by the negroes." Black Methodists in Arkansas appeared an unthreatening, marginal group with whom white Methodists had very little interaction. Where white Christians had lambasted black churches' political activism and impiety before segregation, they now nearly ignored black Christians.[61]

In the 1890s, the United Daughters of the Confederacy became a major force for celebrating the new fictions about Confederate honor and history. Like southern denominational histories, white women's memorials marginalized enslaved and free black accounts. White Christian women memorialized their antebellum vision of the Confederate South as a place of biblical household order. As a young woman in Natchez, Mississippi, during the Civil War, Kate Foster had encountered numerous challenges to Confederate Christianity, including the 1863 intrusion of a freedman wanting a seat among white congregants in her church. Foster reflected on the event, not as a sign of emancipation amid Union occupation, but as a transitory trial from God before his ultimate vindication of the Confederate cause. She lambasted formerly enslaved people for emancipating themselves as proof they lacked proper duty. Foster faced a series of personal challenges, starting with emancipation and her brothers' deaths in the war. Together with two older unmarried sisters, she cared for her aging father and managed his two large farms, one where they lived in Mississippi and another across the Mississippi River in Louisiana. After her father died and they had lost most of their land, the Foster sisters opened a Natchez hotel as they led Confederate women's memorial work. By her death, Foster had almost no money to her name, but she had filled Natchez with memorials to the time she had been a carefree, wealthy young woman with living brothers, potential suitors, and a life made easy by the daily enslaved labor of black women and men. While she could not stop the radical change that emancipation and Confederate defeat brought, Foster developed an alternative religious and historical world through the United Daughters of the Confederacy.[62]

Confederate veteran and Cumberland Presbyterian minister Fontaine Richard Earle rehearsed these standard white Christian lines when he spoke in 1897 at Park's Grove, an Arkansas site that had been a Confederate camp. He recognized that "African Slavery was the cause" of the Civil War but maintained that "the northern people opposed slavery and thus were the aggressors." Along with other former Confederates, Earle insisted, "we do not confess a wrong. We retract nothing." As he outlined the history of the Civil War, he reiterated common narratives of Confederate bravery despite limited resources and claimed that the Confederate army had very few deserters, even near the end of the war. These oft-repeated narratives were false, just as claims of antebellum tranquility had been, but Earle's repeating these claims as a Confederate veteran and Presbyterian minister, then in his late sixties, used his religious authority to preserve an invented history of Confederate honor and valor. This speech represented the maturing of his earlier efforts to defend the white supremacist political takeover of the 1870s, when he had compared ousted Republicans to the biblical villain Haman. By the late 1890s, white supremacist power had been firmly established, so Earle simply argued that white southerners had done "no wrong."[63]

By the turn of the twentieth century, white southern Christians expressed pride in restoring a white supremacist religious, social, and racial order from the chaos of emancipation and the misguided interference of Reconstruction. After emancipation, white southerners had only slightly modified the biblical defenses of orderly hierarchies headed by white men that undergirded proslavery Christianity's defense of family order. In this celebration of white identity, white southerners presented the segregated South as a peaceful, harmonious region, like the benevolent order of the antebellum South. This portrait of the allegedly tranquil New South hid the growing terror of lynching, just as the pastoral descriptions in antebellum proslavery theology obscured the violence endemic to slavery. From their accounts of a peaceful, orderly antebellum South, white southern Christians found models for describing the orderliness of segregation without mentioning racialized violence. White Christians presented the violent inequality and systematic discrimination of segregation, as they had slavery, as a benevolent, orderly, paternalistic structure.

Freed from political concerns about black rights because they had succeeded in creating legal disenfranchisement and segregation, white southern Christians turned to other issues. They argued that the most urgent moral issue facing churches and the nation was alcohol. Methodists and Baptists, especially, argued that late nineteenth-century Christian citizenship demanded that the faithful do all in their power to press for the legal restriction of alcohol sales and for complete abstinence among those in their churches or families. Just as black churches had done for years, white Christians used regularly scheduled temperance sermons, annual denominational conferences, and religious periodicals to warn that alcohol corrupted young people, caused domestic violence, and impoverished families. Although black churches had supported temperance work in these same ways since Reconstruction, white Christian groups claimed they alone were the standard bearers for this cause. Ignoring black Christians' temperance activism was another way to dismiss black Christian citizenship and to proclaim that southern whites alone could govern their region with Christian moral order.

Lynching earned almost no mention from southern white Christians in these years. Only after the turn of the twentieth century did a few prominent white ministers cautiously criticize lynching. Southern Methodist Bishop Charles B. Galloway, who offered the opening prayer at the 1890 Mississippi constitutional convention, appeared to his white friends as a moderate of sorts on racial issues. He firmly defended white-only political power, but he had urged Mississippi's state legislature to keep open Alcorn College, a black public college, when its closure had been threatened. In a 1904 speech on "The South and the Negro" at a conference of mostly white leaders gathered to discuss education, he insisted that lynching must end and that black Americans, like "every American citizen," must have access to "the equal protection of the law." In a rare statement for a southern white Christian leader, Galloway insisted, "I give it as my deliberate judgment that there is never an occasion when the resort to lynch law can be justified," no matter how "dark and dreadful the crime," such as the alleged rape of a white woman. As proof that a "better day" had arrived, he cited a gathering of Confederate veterans who had condemned mob violence as proof that public opinion was changing among southern whites. When these former Confederates, "who feared not the wild shock of battle in contending for what they believed to be right," condemned lynching, they were, Galloway argued, "loving justice, hating wrong and despising unfairness." Citing these Confederate veterans allowed Galloway to place the critique of lynching in the paternalistic context of the slaveholding South and to show that even stalwart defenders of a slaveholders' republic recognized the full legal safety of white Democratic power.[64]

Galloway singled out lynching as an injustice to be opposed, while he upheld the legal structures of segregation as essential for social order. Indeed, he thought lynching was unnecessary precisely because white supremacist political structures were so strong that white Democrats did not need terroristic violence to stay in power. "The old cry that 'white supremacy' may be imperiled is a travesty," Galloway maintained, because "with every executive, judicial and legislative office of the State in the hands of white people," white supremacy rested on a sure foundation. The "suffrage qualifications that have practically eliminated the negro from political affairs" would continue indefinitely, he thought, but lynching must end. Recognizing, as black Christians had done, that lynching's terror strengthened white supremacy, Galloway argued that white political control, especially in his native Mississippi, was secure without extralegal violence. Segregation would last forever because "in the South there will never be any social mingling of the races." Ending lynching would not weaken whites' political control; its terror had already secured white supremacist power.[65]

Although Galloway ignored black Christians' arguments that lynching was antithetical to Christianity and civilization, Episcopal priest Rev. Quincy Ewell in the Mississippi Delta town of Greenville addressed precisely this point in a 1901 sermon. His sermon condemned lynching and suggested legislative steps to end the practice. When excerpts from his sermon were published nationally, he followed with an editorial that warned, "Not much longer can the Christian preachers of the Southern States afford to keep silent on the crime of negro lynching; they must speak out" to be "true to the spirit of Jesus Christ," or face charges "that their ministry is a mockery of the spirit of Jesus Christ." Ewell insisted that southern ministers were hypocritical to ignore lynching. In his claims, he echoed black Christians' laments that lynching was a serious affront to America's Christian civilization. Still, Ewell's claims were sufficiently rare that they attracted the attention of a northern Christian periodical, which reprinted his remarks with much praise. Amid efforts to protect white women against the alleged dangers of black rapists, criticism of lynching would remain infrequent among southern whites until Jessie Daniel Ames organized the Association of Southern Women for the Prevention of Lynching in the 1930s. Denouncing lynching as evil and unchristian remained a provocative claim for white southerners at the start of the twentieth century.[66]

ACROSS THE POSTEMANCIPATION SOUTH, Christian citizenship was the language of political negotiation. When black communities argued that they deserved civil and political rights as fellow Christians and fellow citizens with white southerners, or when white southerners prayed for God to help them to craft policies for disenfranchisement, all sides recognized the Bible and Christian theology as shared cultural touchstones through which to debate the best path toward a better society. After white southerners legislated away black civil and political rights, black communities argued that as Christian citizens, they deserved greater respect from white southerners. In the 1890s, black Christians shifted their Christian citizenship arguments to support education and women's religious work and to denounce lynching as an attack on Christian civilization. Their condemnation of racial prejudice as deeply unchristian and hypocritical would reemerge strongly in twentieth-century battles for racial equality.

White southern Christians, by the turn of the twentieth century, celebrated their own Christian citizenship as they disenfranchised black men and created a segregated society based, they claimed, on the biblical logic of the antebellum South. They memorialized their antebellum proslavery paternalism alongside the Christian heroism of Confederate soldiers. In their ongoing commitment to hierarchy and inequality, white southern Christians claimed that they followed the Bible more faithfully than those who imposed liberal political ideas of equal rights onto their readings of scripture. This supposedly strict biblicism that had supported theological defenses of slavery would find echoes across the twentieth century.

Conclusion
Family Values and Racial Order

Speaking to the Women's Interracial Conference in Memphis, Tennessee, in October 1920, Charlotte Hawkins Brown, a nationally known black educator, addressed a novel gathering of mostly white Protestant women concerned about racial injustice. Brown told the assembled white women that they held responsibility for the crisis of lynching and the injustices of segregation as she indicted the paternalistic family order that protected white families at the expense of nonwhite families. She relayed the indignities she experienced that week traveling on segregated trains to Memphis for the conference. In full view of other passengers, including "southern white women passing for Christians," she had been forced out of a sleeping car by a mob of white men who boarded the train in Alabama. Accusing white women of "passing" as Christians linked racial passing with Brown's insistence that Christian behavior must oppose racial injustice. Brown reminded the white women in her audience that they benefited from the white supremacist paternalism that oppressed black women, saying that "The Negro women of the South lay everything that happens to the members of her race at the door of the Southern white woman," because "we all feel that you can control your men." Black women could not successfully oppose lynching alone, and Brown charged: "We feel so far as lynching is concerned that, if the white woman would take hold of the situation that lynching would be stopped, and mob violence stamped." If white women read occasional stories of black men's insulting white women, they should "just multiply that by one thousand and you have some idea of the number of colored women insulted by white men." She pressed her audience, urging, "I want you as Christian women, to ask yourself, 'What would Jesus do if he were in my place?'" Brown did not give the white women in her audience any space to identify themselves as Christian women unless they worked to oppose lynching and to see that black women had the same gendered protections they did. White women were hypocrites if they welcomed the paternalistic protection of white men and ignored the violence that undergirded that so-called protection.[1]

The language that Charlotte Brown used to argue for shared Christian identity across a rigid color line and to articulate a prophetic critique of white supremacist Christianity built upon the work of black Christians throughout the postemancipation South. Black and white Christian citizenship claims constructed competing racial and theological agendas in the tumultuous decades after the Civil War. Religious and racial identities shaped each other as these contrasting Christian imaginations set the boundaries of what seemed possible in these years. White southerners transformed proslavery theology into a postemancipation paternalistic argument for a male-led white supremacist society, while for black Christian citizens, Christianity and the U.S. Constitution denounced all racial prejudice. Black communities consistently forced white southerners to address their claims for justice, even though they could not ultimately prevent the destruction of their civil and political rights. While many histories of this period focus on either white or black communities, this study brings these groups together to show how, even as they established separate churches in an increasingly segregated society, they were responding to one another's claims to authentic Christian citizenship.

With each major change from emancipation to segregation, southern Christians remade their political framework with religious arguments that defended the social order they found most familiar. Southerners from many backgrounds drew on biblical stories as they debated what true Christian behavior demanded. Freedpeople prayed to the God of Abraham, Isaac, Jacob, and Abraham Lincoln. Black voters invited Republican politicians to speak in their churches, and politicians in turn praised black citizens for being like the persecuted Christians in the Roman Empire. White southerners legitimized insurgent Democratic Redeemers as defenders of paternalistic Christian families. When Mississippi's constitutional convention disenfranchised black voters, they paused deliberations for a day of prayer to seek God's blessing on their work.

Christian claims about how politics and society should operate proved powerful visions both for advocates for black citizens' equal rights and for segregation's architects. Black communities argued for civil and political rights as fellow Christians as well as fellow citizens with white southerners. They drew on black abolitionist claims to denounce all racial prejudice as sin. Their biblical and political arguments condemned white southerners' hypocrisy in the face of segregation policy and racial violence. White southern Christians used biblical arguments, crafted from antebellum proslavery claims, to congratulate themselves for resisting federal incursions in Reconstruction and black efforts at self-determination and equality. They insisted that they alone maintained the strict biblicism that true Christian faith demanded, while their northern counterparts polluted Christianity by believing fashionable extrabiblical notions of human rights and political activism over biblical truth. White southerners crafted a new paternalistic rhetoric that transformed antebellum proslavery paternalism into a white supremacist social hierarchy that had lost all concern for black lives. Across lines of race and denomination, Christian claims diverged sharply, yet the arguments that white and black Christians developed in these years would reverberate across the South and the nation.

White Christians showed how arbitrary the distinctions of race were in the late nineteenth century as they strengthened whiteness. Yet even when working for clearly white supremacist aims, they were forced to acknowledge the impossibility of whiteness and blackness as distinct categories. Amid emancipation in Mississippi, antislavery northern white missionaries in 1864 hired Eustis Beady, a *"nearly white"* formerly enslaved man with "gifts as a preacher," "until we can do better." Describing formerly enslaved Beady as "far more intelligent than the most of them," missionaries linked Beady's racial, intellectual, and religious ability. When Southern Methodists praised CME Bishop Isaac Lane for preaching on personal moral responsibility rather than political activism to his black congregation in the late 1870s, they linked his religious message to his body, which was "tall, erect, and showing in his general appearance a preponderance of the Anglo-Saxon blood." Because Lane did not urge political activism, but instead personal religious piety, his physical body—marked, as Lane acknowledged himself, as the son of his white enslaver father and his enslaved mother—testified to the sexual power of white men and reaffirmed an increasingly rigid color line. Southern Democrats voiced fears of social equality, namely sex between black men and white women, to justify lynching, yet they ignored white men's past and present sexual violence toward black women. Later, white Mississippians added to their 1890 state constitution a prohibition of marriage between "a white person" and "a negro or mulatto, or person who shall have one-eighth or more of negro blood." That white lawmakers needed various qualified terms for the nonwhite category showed the difficulty of defining race even for white supremacist lawmakers. Their legal and extralegal work preserved whiteness, strengthened white families, and protected white women's supposed sexual purity at the expense of nonwhite families and communities, and particularly black women's lives and bodies.[2]

The history of the late nineteenth-century South shows that progress—whether economic, political, or social—does not proceed in a linear forward march through time. Many of the civil and political rights that black southerners achieved during Reconstruction disappeared as white southern Democrats gained power. White Christians worked to erase even the memory of these rights. Yet this book's trajectory is not merely one of tragedy. Black churches had grown explosively across the region, with dozens of Christian periodicals, thousands of new church buildings, and hundreds of thousands of new church members. From one-room primary schools to university-level seminaries, black educational institutions covered the region, with more black educators administering institutions that had been run earlier by white Christians. Many more black families owned property and businesses by the end of the century. Throughout these years, black Christians sometimes disagreed sharply with each other over different strategies for political activism and religious devotion. They never operated as a unified bloc, and in the range of attitudes they advocated—whether directly defending equal civil and political rights, demonstrating black competence through erudite sermons, or emphasizing gendered Christian piety—black Christians laid out many of the religious arguments that would appear in twentieth-century movements for social and political justice. No universal black church or single strategy for resistance existed in these years, even as black Christian communities marshaled religious and political arguments against the violence of new paternalistic rhetoric.

As black and white Christians wrestled with the often-intimate relationship between Protestant Christianity and white supremacy, they set the stage for national religious and political conflicts that reverberate to our day. White Christians in the postemancipation South argued against black civil and political rights, saying that they must follow biblical teachings against new cultural innovations, much as later white Christians would resist movements for racial and gender equality as challenges to their Christian fundamentals. In both cases, conservative white Christians resisted rights-based claims for justice by citing biblical teachings about proper family values. Defending the white family against various challenges—real and imagined—became a primary religious and political goal. Because white southerners argued that antislavery northern Christians held heretical views and that black Christians were racially and religiously inferior, they rejected dialogue with those who disagreed with them and isolated their communities from all who might challenge their views of Christianity, history, and politics.

New Histories of the Present

Controlling historical narratives allowed southern communities to advance their version of Christian citizenship and to commemorate the elements of the past that they wanted to celebrate. White and black Christians created new historical narratives to make powerful theological and social arguments by linking their nineteenth-century lives to millennia-old conflicts where God's chosen people navigated challenges. No longer were postemancipation Christians improvising amid a chaotic historical transformation; they were living faithfully, following the example of sacred biblical figures. Black Christians recounted dramatic changes and hard-won progress in their narratives, while white southerners argued that they replicated antebellum slaveholders' biblical paternalism in a white-controlled political order. Both sets of histories cited biblical precedents along with recent events to support their mutually exclusive goals for the tumultuous region. Even as they created incompatible histories, these stories responded to each other's claims as black Christians decried racial prejudice as sin and white Christians defended paternalism as an afterlife of proslavery theology. The incommensurability rested on their opposing views of slavery and Christian theology.

These two sets of histories described slavery in entirely opposite ways. Whether slavery was an inhuman exploitation of fundamental human rights or a benevolent paternalistic arrangement mattered greatly for these postemancipation historical debates. Black Christians narrated slavery as an evil system that destroyed human dignity and assaulted families. Slavery ended thanks to the combined efforts of enslaved people's resistance, the Union army's power, and divine aid. Emancipation radically and irrevocably altered history, as God's intervention to aid enslaved people's pursuit of freedom. Defending their Christian citizenship after emancipation, black Christians insisted that racial prejudice was unchristian and that God would judge those who allowed racial violence. The Bible and the U.S. Constitution together promised the fulfillment of black hopes with equal rights and freedom from racial prejudice, and black Christians argued that all Christians and citizens must oppose racial hierarchy in all its forms. By contrast, white southern Christians elevated slavery as the historical ideal on which their Christian paternalism drew. Their histories minimized emancipation's impact by describing enslaved people as happy recipients of their white owners' generous benevolence in orderly household and family structures. Northern interlopers rudely disrupted the peace of these idyllic households and forced emancipation on people who had not sought it. Despite this unwanted change, many formerly enslaved people chose to remain loyal servants of their previous enslavers once made free. White southerners rejoiced when God allowed them to reinstate a modified form of the godly rule of the antebellum plantation with the abrupt end of Reconstruction. The long afterlife of proslavery theology

allowed the white supremacist account to persist with powerful claims to authenticity, even though its historical basis was in antebellum white rhetoric,
not historical fact.

Black Christians, unlike their white antislavery allies, saw the danger of
white proslavery theology after emancipation. In late 1865, Colored Convention members such as Arkansas's William H. Grey argued that the "corner-
stone of a bastard republic" was Confederate Christians' belief that "slavery
was divine, and . . . that God had abandoned the negro to the tender mercies
of the . . . Christians of the nineteenth century." In opposition to that white
supremacist lie, black Christians celebrated their achievements in education,
business, politics, and religion to show that their national loyalty, to the nation that had denied civil and political rights, mirrored their evangelical piety.
Black Christians celebrated their Christian citizenship against the ascension
of hypocritical white supremacy, and they lambasted white southerners as
unchristian for their treatment of black citizens. Challenging white southerners' claims of historical continuity between the antebellum South and the late
nineteenth century, black southerners denounced the only continuity that
that they saw: white southerners' lack of humanity or respect for justice.

Yet white Christians undercut black narratives at every turn by arguing for
paternalistic order against rights-based claims of equality and justice. They reinvented a narrative of slavery and emancipation that turned antebellum proslavery theology's idealized image of slavery into an authoritative history. White
southerners' histories gave the antebellum myth of benevolent household
paternalism new life as a definitive history of the Old South. Black self-
determination evaporated in white histories even as white southerners' legal
and extralegal violence targeted black leaders. Faced with black voters and their
federal allies, southern white Christians during Reconstruction could not have
made these historical claims, but the logic of proslavery theology allowed white
southerners to resurrect new afterlives of proslavery paternalism in the years
after they destroyed Reconstruction. Doing so ignored slavery's physical, sexual, and psychological violence and discounted the voices of enslaved and
free African Americans. Armed with these histories, white Christians defended white supremacist politics as an outgrowth of the duties demanded of
faithful Christians: submission to God's and white men's authority to create
family and social order.[3]

White southerners lost the Civil War, but they won the postwar battle over
southern history. The Lost Cause was not simply its own civil religion, but
the core of orthodox white southern Protestantism. By the 1890s, white
southern Christians mobilized their moral and political authority to legislate

legal segregation, encourage extralegal violence, and erect monuments to an invented Confederate past. These white Christian claims, shared by distinct southern denominations, justified the violent transformations of the Mississippi River Valley from a seat of black political power during Reconstruction to a pioneering arena of white supremacist power that would serve as a model for the South and the nation. Historians have stressed the reunion of northern and southern whites in the late nineteenth century, but this history of Christian citizenship in a particularly tumultuous region of the South shows that any national reunion amounted to northern whites' capitulation to southern white views. White southerners demanded acquiescence to their version of Christian citizenship from anyone with whom they might partner. Amid acrimonious denominational divisions that preserved slavery-era divides well into the twentieth century, members of southern Methodist, Baptist, and Presbyterian groups believed that they alone, not their northern counterparts, remained true to the Bible's teachings of organic social hierarchy over rights-based claims. Southern Protestantism remained the intellectual and moral bulwark of white supremacy for the South, and the nation.[4]

White southern paternalism's greatest power lay in its ability to justify grotesque violence as a defense of Christian family order. Paternalism allowed a seemingly race-blind ideology—of fidelity to the paternalistic hierarchy that a plain sense reading of the Bible clearly outlined—to legitimize white supremacist power amid some of the worst violence in U.S. history. White Christians legitimized all manner of racial and gender violence against black bodies by proclaiming white men's power as God's orderly social vision and denying black Christians' claims of equal rights as a refusal to submit to God's design. Antebellum slavery relied on the constant threat of physical, sexual, and psychological violence, but ignoring that violence allowed white southerners to imagine the idyllic benevolent paternalism that the proslavery theological texts had described as a true picture of the antebellum period. As white southern Christians lobbied to restore a modified antebellum paternalism through legal segregation, they deliberately ignored the violence of slavery in order not to confront the violence of the white supremacist Democratic power that made segregation policy possible.

Black and white Christians narrated mutually incompatible accounts of southern history that created separate echo chambers in which distinct views of the world reverberated. These histories drew on opposing models of Christian citizenship to describe rival understandings of racial identity, family order, historical fact, and political rights. They diagnosed contemporary problems, their historical origins, and their optimal solutions differently. In short, they baptized contradictory views of the world as Christian truth. Black Christians argued that racial prejudice was unchristian and that lynching had no place in a Christian civilization. Yet white Christians claimed that paternalistic hierarchy, modeled on the slaveholding household, was God's design for human flourishing, and they defended white family order even to the point of justifying mob violence.

Although they adapted their claims in response to each other's arguments, black and white Christians spoke to distinct audiences who shared their view of the world. White southerners refused to consider their black neighbors to be equal Christians whose theological and political claims deserved attention. Even experiments in paternalism, such as those led by the bishops of the CME Church, ultimately failed to convince white southerners to heed black voices. The Confederate monuments that white southern Christians created in the late nineteenth century still dot twenty-first-century American landscapes, memorializing a false history of the antebellum South. These post-emancipation visions of white supremacy and of racial equality, each supported as faithful Christian approaches for American citizens, would be transformed over the twentieth century, yet studying how competing Christian citizens created these models in the late nineteenth-century South might help us understand the stark religious and political divides of our own time. How we narrate our complex and often violent history—and whose voices we include as we do—shapes our priorities for our present and our collective understanding of which lives matter today.

Gender and Christian Family Order

Christian citizenship rhetoric consistently fixated on families and gender norms. Black and white Christians worked to defend families as a religious and social good, but they diagnosed the challenges facing families very differently, rooted in their opposing views of slavery's legacy. They suggested distinct relationships between gender and sexual norms and Christian citizenship. Black Christians defended families as a critical element of black autonomy. Slavery prohibited marriage among enslaved people and separated parents from children, so black Christians saw the ability to marry and to create a better future for their children as crucial elements of freedom.[5] They argued that equal civil and political rights would protect black families. White Christians defended the family order of the slaveholding white household as the ideal family, a model that defended only white families. They used this antebellum model to justify white supremacist violence in the name of family protection, most notoriously by citing white women's protection as a justification for lynching. Black and white Christians adapted their discussions on family values over the decades after emancipation, setting up arguments that would extend well into the twentieth century. Amid their incompatible defenses of family, both black and white southern Christians saw Christian marriage as a rallying point, as women and men debated what proper families entailed and how to encourage family development.

Black Christians fought for their families' independence to demonstrate their freedom from the legacy of slavery. During emancipation and Reconstruction, defending black manhood meant gaining access to the same civil and political rights as white men, and black families sought the legal protections that enslavement had denied them. Black men defended their manhood by pointing to their Civil War service in the Union army and their Christian identity to bolster their claim to the franchise. They welcomed the federal government's intervention and new U.S. constitutional amendments as allies for black autonomy. Both children and adults attended day and night schools to learn to read because they saw literacy as a sign of autonomy and a key to religious, political, and social advancement. Black Christians saw Christian identity as inextricably connected to equal political rights and to gendered manhood and womanhood. Through the mid-1870s, many northern whites considered themselves allies to black families, although black Christians remained their own best advocates even at the height of national support for black autonomy. As they condemned all racial hierarchy as unchristian, black Christians sought to elevate their families as equal to white families.

Amid national support for black rights during Reconstruction, white southerners defended white family order as a sphere over which they could wield influence during their relatively brief loss of political power. Believing that they alone took the Bible's paternalistic instructions seriously, they praised the antebellum slaveholding household as the best model of family order. In doing so, they excluded black families entirely from the Christian family order they imagined and resurrected an afterlife of proslavery theology as a defense of Christian paternalism. Surrounded by the explosive growth of black churches, black voting power, and black elected officials, white southerners refused to see black families or black women as worthy of the family and gendered protections they defended vigorously as the biblical norm. White Christian family theology sanctified racial and gender hierarchy as biblical. This work claimed to be an internal, apolitical religious conversation, but it laid the ideological foundation for white supremacist politics after Reconstruction. White Christian paternalism protected white women and white families even if it meant destroying black ones.

As they overturned Reconstruction with the "Redemption" of white supremacy, white southerners claimed that voting rights required adherence to gender and sexual norms, yet they defined these norms to exclude black families. Black Christians argued that they needed equal civil and political rights to protect their families, but white Christians flipped the script, making family order according to antebellum white models a prerequisite for rights. Lambasting black churches as chaotic Republican political organizations, white newspapers published waves of stories alleging sexual impropriety and crime among ministers. When they vilified ministers' sexual conduct and raised the specter of black male sexual power, white southern Christians rewrote antebellum history. The deep ironies of white southerners' reliance on accounts of antebellum intimacies between enslaved people and their white enslavers in order to create segregation emerged most strikingly here. The sex across the color line that concerned white southern Christians was not the long history of white men's sexual power over enslaved women, but the myth of black men's sexual threats to white women. As white southern Christians articulated concerns about black sexuality, they showed their willingness to use partial or invented histories to justify violence in the name of family order.

Black Christians denounced Democratic Redemption as an illegal and unchristian assault on their families and communities. They defended black men's and women's gendered norms, but they insisted into the 1880s that black citizens deserved equal civil and political rights without regard to their conformity to gendered or educational norms. Black Christians reminded white critics that slavery's legacy, not racial inferiority, accounted for any perceived racial differences, and they celebrated their achievement in the short years since emancipation. Fighting for black self-determination united their family, religious, economic, and political goals. Yet the total loss of federal legal support and the rise of lynching forced a different calculus for black Christian arguments by the 1890s. They denounced extralegal violence as an assault on Christian civilization, as they lost the legal grounds to defend their civil and political rights. Most ministers grew more cautious, and black women became more influential as they used denominational periodicals to celebrate black accomplishments and advance economic and educational achievement. Because black women had not had the right to vote, women writers more easily sidestepped black men's loss of political rights as they defended their families' religious lives. Ida B. Wells's transition from writing women's advice columns to becoming one of the nation's most outspoken critics of lynching illustrated the strong links between women's gendered religious work and courageous efforts to end mob violence.[6]

White women amplified Christian defenses of white family order as lynching showed white citizens' willingness to sacrifice black bodies and terrorize black families to bolster white supremacist fictions. Women built monuments to this imagined order as the self-appointed guardians of new historical narratives through Confederate memorial work. In church and club groups, white women celebrated the Christian past of orderly antebellum households. They celebrated virtuous antebellum slave-owning women as model southern ladies and as an inspiration for white women's ongoing voluntary work. Women like Kate Foster, who never regained the status she enjoyed in antebellum Natchez, Mississippi, created monuments to a past they wished they could restore fully. The myth of white women's virtuous but vulnerable ladyhood strengthened women's claims to moral authority in defending invented memories of the Confederate past.

In the early twentieth century, the paternalistic family order that white southern Christians imagined after emancipation became a national mythology. White family order vaulted onto a stunning visual stage in D. W. Griffith's 1915 film *The Birth of a Nation*, based on Thomas Dixon's 1905 novel *The Clansman*. The film's portrayal of white female vulnerability to black male sexual aggression celebrated extralegal mob violence and portrayed black men as criminal and incapable of family order. The heroism of Ku Klux Klan members and their Christian patriotism blazed on the silver screen with the burning crosses that Griffith imagined. Griffith portrayed Klan members as Christian defenders of white supremacy and inspired the second Klan of the 1920s, whose white Protestant nativism reached well beyond the South. Black leaders across the nation worked to counter the film's power through the press and alternative narratives, such as Angelina Weld Grimké's *Rachel*. Grimké's 1916 play, commissioned by the still-new NAACP, portrayed the multigenerational violence and grief that lynching wrought on surviving wives, mothers, and children, even years after the killings. Echoing late nineteenth-century Christian arguments, *Rachel* invoked biblical arguments about the injustice and cruelty of such terroristic violence. Yet the play hardly diminished the national adulation of Griffith's cinematic masterpiece of white supremacist Christianity.[7]

Defending white womanhood would cost many black lives in the twentieth century. White women would not reject the shibboleths of vulnerable white womanhood until the 1930s, when the first sizable group of white women joined with Jessie Daniel Ames in the Association of Southern Women for the

Prevention of Lynching. Even then, many more white women embraced idealizations of the antebellum South, as the overwhelming popularity of Margaret Mitchell's 1936 novel *Gone with the Wind* would demonstrate. In these valorizations of antebellum southern womanhood, white women repurposed white supremacist historical narratives to celebrate slaveholding paternalism as the ideal model for a Christian society.[8]

White Christian men appealed to antebellum slaveholding mastery as the religious and gender ideal that God designed for benevolent social order, yet they voiced nostalgia for a past that had never existed. The vast majority of antebellum white men had only aspired to slaveholding mastery; few had the wealth to become enslavers. Yet inventing a past of mastery over white women and children and all people of African descent comforted those who felt threatened by the changes that emancipation and Reconstruction wrought, especially with black political rights. Fearful of their lost privilege, they backed a white supremacist fantasy of good old times that God wanted them to re-create. Their imagined past obscured the violence of the nineteenth-century South and continued to justify assaults against racial and religious minorities, as well as women, immigrants, and others. White Christians enshrined this Christian paternalistic social order as the only faithful, plain sense reading of the Bible, and doing so preserved a white male supremacist ideology as Christian orthodoxy. Their twentieth- and twenty-first-century legacy would continue to uphold visions of family and social order that elevated certain white Christian families over all others.

Family values still rally religious communities to political action. Conservative religious and political arguments claim that biblical teaching and natural family order necessitate urgent action. Debates about biblical authority turn to schism most often around gender equality and sexual orientation, and the ordination of women and of LGBTQ+ clergy continues to divide American and global Christian groups. Scholars of the religious right's power over the past half century have debated whether that movement grew in response primarily to the civil rights movement's push for racial inclusion or to the feminist movement's demands for gender equality. Yet the history of post-emancipation Christian citizenship shows it was the intersection of racial equality and gender norms that created the most powerful claims for conservative political power. These seemingly race-blind and nonviolent calls to protect families have justified much violence. White southerners praised the gender and racial order of the antebellum slaveholding household when they destroyed Reconstruction and created segregation. Southern white women joined these defenses of white male power because of the gendered and racial protection they enjoyed. Understanding this history of Christianity in the postemancipation South reframes religious and political debate over family values.[9]

The Long Echoes of White Supremacist Christianity

If the problem of the twentieth century was the problem of the color line, as W. E. B. Du Bois famously diagnosed in 1903, then American Christianity defined the contours of that line and the problems it delineated. The theological arguments that white and black Christians developed in the postemancipation South drove conflicts over American religion and politics long past that era. As they debated Christian citizenship, southern Protestants across lines of race, class, and denomination used theological principles and biblical narratives to sketch competing plans of action in a rapidly changing society. Whether in black Christians' claims that racial prejudice was sinful hypocrisy that must end to guarantee equal civil and political rights, or in white southerners' appeals to restore biblical Christian order by re-creating the idyllic antebellum benevolent paternalism of slavery, Christian arguments powerfully shaped how race and politics would be debated. In the Mississippi River Valley, political changes took place more quickly than in other parts of the South, and the dominant evangelical populism proved agile amid these new conditions, accelerating the creation of ideas that would shape the rest of the South and the nation. These mutually exclusive visions of Christian activism guided political strategies through the civil rights movement and beyond.[10]

Black Christian citizenship arguments about Christianity, race, and politics echoed the antebellum antislavery arguments of David Walker and Frederick Douglass and foreshadowed the powerful theological claims of the civil rights movement. Yet these claims also demonstrated tremendous flexibility and diversity throughout the postemancipation period. Different strategies, from powerful demands for equal civil and political rights to seemingly cautious appeals to personal piety, could operate simultaneously, in concert with or in opposition to one another. There was no single black Christian approach to the urgent crises of segregation and lynching, nor would there be unified black Protestant strategies in the twentieth century. Black activists would invoke these claims as they pushed twentieth- and twenty-first-century movements to claim the promise that Reconstruction-era black Christians had envisioned—a nation where both law and religion recognized that racial prejudice was evil and allowed for equal rights and protections for all people to flourish.

When they refused to disavow proslavery theology after emancipation, white Christians argued that they alone had been faithful to the Bible during a time of theological confusion. Postemancipation southern white Christians rejected the possibility of national reunion of denominations severed by fights over slavery as they accused northern Presbyterians, Methodists, and Baptists of having abandoned biblical truth for fashionable extrabiblical ideas of human equality and inalienable rights. The survival of proslavery theology's logic—and the denominational schisms that it drove—long after emancipation shaped future Protestant theology by preserving those Bible-reading strategies and by keeping the largest southern denominations from any meaningful contact with those who might challenge southern white theology's comfort with white supremacy. Yet this theology would find a broader audience in twentieth-century fundamentalism. A leading northern Christian architect of early twentieth-century fundamentalism, Presbyterian Rev. J. Gresham Machen, grew up in a Southern Presbyterian Church in Baltimore, where his Georgia-born mother was active in the United Daughters of the Confederacy. When Machen fought growing Christian liberalism at Princeton Theological Seminary, he deployed white southern Christians' anti-innovation arguments. The Bible-reading strategies that southern white Christians developed after emancipation aided the rise of fundamentalism, and American Christian fundamentalism would give the Christianity of white supremacy a national stage.[11]

White Christians would resist rights-based claims for equality as modern heresy in successive movements for social reform throughout the twentieth century. By 1900, white southerners' conservatism was an innovative, activist conservatism that adapted new strategies and rewrote its own history to obscure these changes in arguments of timeless Christian piety and family values. As postemancipation white Christians sought to re-create an older order, they reinvented the past they venerated and transformed it in their restoration. Their religious heirs in the fundamentalist movement of the early twentieth century claimed that fidelity to the Bible meant rejecting all new ideas of reform, modernism, and innovation. Yet in their rejection of so-called modern innovations, fundamentalists too proved to be innovators, employing new technologies to broaden their appeal. Christian conservatives would renew these practices in their twentieth-century fights against movements for equal rights and protections for Americans across lines of race, gender, and sexual orientation. As each major movement for equality and freedom achieved new gains, white conservatives would answer with a powerful call to restore family order by undoing the changes that threatened their perpetually refashioned traditional goals. When they did so, white Christian conservatives from the fundamentalist movement, to the Christian right, to the present would invoke proslavery Christianity's persistent logic.

Notes

Abbreviations

MANUSCRIPT AND ARCHIVAL COLLECTIONS

BAP   Benjamin Arnett Papers, Wilberforce University, Wilberforce, Ohio
JDWL   Special Collections, J. D. Williams Library, University of Mississippi, Oxford,
       Mississippi
JGJ   John Griffing Jones Papers, McCain Archives of Mississippi Methodism,
       Millsaps College, Jackson, Mississippi
MDAH   Mississippi Department of Archives and History, Jackson, Mississippi
SHC   Southern Historical Collection, Wilson Library, University of North Carolina
       at Chapel Hill

PERIODICALS

NOCA   *New Orleans Christian Advocate*, published by the Methodist Episcopal Church,
       South, in New Orleans
SWCA   *Southwestern Christian Advocate*, published by the Methodist Episcopal Church
       in New Orleans. The paper was called *Southwestern Advocate* before 1877, but I
       have used a consistent abbreviation for both titles.

ORGANIZATIONS

AMA   American Missionary Association
AME   African Methodist Episcopal Church
CME   Colored Methodist Episcopal Church in America

Introduction

1. Charles Burch, Chairman, "Committee on the State of the Country," *Minutes of the Tenth Annual Conference of the African Methodist Episcopal Church . . . Baton Rouge, Louisiana, 1875*, 17–18. Benjamin Arnett Papers, Wilberforce University, Wilberforce, Ohio. Burch was listed as the presiding elder for Baton Rouge District, 30. Burch was a delegate from Louisiana to the 1872 and 1876 AME General Conferences. AME Church historian Charles S. Smith praised him for his work building the AME Church in Louisiana. *Minutes of the Fifteenth Quadrennial Session of the General Conference of the African Methodist Episcopal, 1872*, Benjamin Arnett Papers, Wilberforce University, Wilberforce, Ohio; *Minutes of the Sixteenth Session of the Louisiana Annual Conference of the African Methodist Episcopal Church, 1876*, 3. Benjamin Arnett Papers, Wilberforce University, Wilberforce, Ohio; Smith, *A History of the African Methodist Episcopal Church*, 97–98.

2. Palmer, *The Family*, 166, 133–34, 116.

3. On the power of the "color line" to protect whiteness, and the lie of a clear distinction of blackness and whiteness, see Hodes, *White Women, Black Men*.

4. The end of Reconstruction, black disenfranchisement, and the creation of segregation unfolded more gradually in other parts of the South. Jane Dailey has shown that segregation began in 1902 in Virginia. Glenda Gilmore has shown that black women and men were active in public life in North Carolina even after the late 1890s, when white supremacist policies took hold in the state. South Carolina's political history was similar to that of the Mississippi Valley, with a Reconstruction black voter majority, violent overthrow of Reconstruction, and the 1895 state constitution designed to disenfranchise black voters, but it had a significantly different religious landscape along its Atlantic Coast, with both Anglican and Episcopalian dominance and African-derived black religion. Dailey, *Before Jim Crow*, 14; Gilmore, *Gender and Jim Crow*; Kantrowitz, *Ben Tillman and the Reconstruction of White Supremacy*; Lippy, ed., *Religion in South Carolina*.

5. Mark Noll argues that plain sense readings of the Bible diverged sharply in antebellum slavery debates, fracturing national consensus. I show that these fractures long endured. Noll, *America's God*.

6. Among works on religion in the postemancipation South, I have especially drawn upon Blum, *Reforging the White Republic*; Giggie, *After Redemption*; Harper, *The End of Days*; Harvey, *Christianity and Race in the American South*; Harvey, *Redeeming the South*; Stowell, *Rebuilding Zion*. On violence in the postemancipation Mississippi River Valley, see Ash, *A Massacre in Memphis*; Hogue, *Uncivil War*; Rable, *But There Was No Peace*; Rosen, *Terror in the Heart of Freedom*.

7. In keeping with my sources, I use "Southern Methodist" and "Methodist Episcopal Church, South," interchangeably. On the founding and early history of independent black denominations in the South, see Angell, *Bishop Henry McNeal Turner and African-American Religion in the South*; Dvorak, *An African-American Exodus*; Evans, *The Burden of Black Religion*; Giggie, *After Redemption*; Harper, *The End of Days*; Hildebrand, *The Times Were Strange and Stirring*; Maffly-Kipp, *Setting Down the Sacred Past*; Martin, *For God and Race*; Miller, *Elevating the Race*; Montgomery, *Under Their Own Vine and Fig Tree*; Rivers and Brown, *Laborers in the Vineyard of the Lord*; Sommerville, *An Ex-Colored Church*; Walker, *A Rock in a Weary Land*.

8. Among Presbyterians, I primarily study the Presbyterian Church in the United States (known commonly as the Southern Presbyterians), the main southern Presbyterian denomination, which was initially formed in 1861 as the Presbyterian Church in the Confederate States of America by a union of southern Old School and New School Presbyterian denominations. A few individuals who belonged to the Cumberland Presbyterian Church or the Associate Reformed Presbyterian Church appear in some chapters, and I have indicated these affiliations and their significance where relevant. While Baptists formed a very large group of southern Christians, their decentralized congregational organization and often less educated ministers and members mean that there are fewer archival sources available about Baptists than about other denominations. Additionally, the National Baptist Convention, the largest black Baptist denomination, was not organized until 1896, so most black Baptist churches in these years operated independently and did not have central record-keeping systems. Other Methodist denominations, including the African Method-

ist Episcopal Zion Church or the Methodist Protestant Church, did not have a significant influence in this region during this period.

9. Roman Catholics constituted a significant religious group, particularly in southern Louisiana, but they lacked wide political influence across the region and had a distinct history of theology and slavery. As John McGreevy has noted, American Catholics in the antebellum period had inherited a long history of Catholic engagement with slave societies that meant that Catholics adopted neither the religiously motivated antislavery sentiment of many northern Protestant reformers nor the southern Protestant defenses of slavery as a positive good. Bennett, *Religion and the Rise of Jim Crow in New Orleans*; McGreevy, *Catholicism and American Freedom*; Stern, *Southern Cross, Southern Crucifix*; Woods, *A History of the Catholic Church in the American South*.

10. Irons offers an exception to this trend among works on southern evangelicals in the antebellum period. Irons, *The Origins of Proslavery Christianity*; Carwardine, *Evangelicals and Politics in Antebellum America*; Mathews, *Religion in the Old South*; Noll, *America's God*.

11. The CME Church, because of its entanglement with white Southern Methodist paternalism throughout its nineteenth-century history, has a vexed historiography. Most histories come from ministers in the denomination, much of which is hagiographic: Cade, *Holsey—The Incomparable*; Lakey, *The History of the CME Church (Revised)*; Phillips, *The History of the Colored Methodist Episcopal Church in America*; Sommerville, *An Ex-Colored Church*; Spragin, *The History of the Christian Methodist Episcopal Church*. Other scholars have illustrated CME Church leaders' varying, if limited, success navigating white paternalism: Eskew, "Black Elitism and the Failure of Paternalism in Postbellum Georgia"; Gravely, "The Social, Political and Religious Significance of the Formation of the Colored Methodist Episcopal Church"; Jackson, "The Colored Methodist Episcopal Church."

12. Women's citizenship, particularly married women's citizenship, remained tenuous through the nineteenth century. Cott, "Marriage and Women's Citizenship in the United States, 1830–1934"; Cott, *Public Vows*, 56–104; Gardner, *The Qualities of a Citizen*; Kerber, "The Meaning of Citizenship"; Kerber, "The Paradox of Women's Citizenship in the Early Republic"; Pascoe, *What Comes Naturally*.

13. Churches were the primary voluntary organizations in the antebellum South; missionary societies, temperance groups, and the like developed slowly after the Civil War. McCurry, *Masters of Small Worlds*; Friedman, *The Enclosed Garden*; Varon, *We Mean to Be Counted*.

14. Martha Jones has uncovered the antebellum legal history of black citizenship claims and advocacy for what became the Fourteenth Amendment's birthright citizenship clause. Jones, *Birthright Citizens*.

15. The earlier definition had two parts: "In a *general sense*, a native or permanent resident in a city or country; as, the *citizens* of London or Philadelphia; the *citizens* of the United States," and "In *the United States*, a person, native or naturalized who has the privilege of exercising the elective franchise, or the qualifications which enable him to vote for rulers, and to purchase and hold real estate." Webster, *An American Dictionary of the English Language* (1850 and 1853), 208; Webster, *An American Dictionary of the English Language* (1864 and 1866), 234.

16. Walker, *Appeal to the Colored Citizens of the World*.

17. On Christianity, race, and late nineteenth-century American citizenship, see Blum, *Reforging the White Republic*; Chang, *Citizens of a Christian Nation*; Paddison, *American Heathens*.

18. Katharine Gerbner argues that before white supremacy took hold in early modern slave societies, Protestant supremacy served to distinguish Protestant, free elites from enslaved heathen people who were not allowed access to Christianity. Her work makes major contributions to the important conversation about race, religion, and freedom in the early modern world. Gerbner, *Christian Slavery*; Jordan, *White over Black*; Kidd, *The Forging of Races*; Goetz, *The Baptism of Early Virginia*. The phrase "romantic racialism" was coined by George Fredrickson, and Curtis Evans has expanded its analysis. Fredrickson, *The Black Image in the White Mind*, 97–129; Evans, *The Burden of Black Religion*, 17–104.

19. Rosen, *Terror in the Heart of Freedom*; Edwards, *Gendered Strife and Confusion*; Foner, *Reconstruction*; Hahn, *A Nation Under Our Feet*.

20. Savage, *Your Spirits Walk Beside Us*; Evans, *The Burden of Black Religion*.

21. Histories of religion and the Civil War by George Rable and Harry Stout presume that Confederate belief in the proslavery cause disappeared with Confederate defeat. Mark Noll argued the Civil War was a theological crisis, but concluded that "military coercion determined that, at least for the purposes of American public policy, the Bible did not support slavery." Luke Harlow's work is the important exception to this trend as he has shown that southern white denominations continued to shape their Bible reading strategies around proslavery theology's plain sense interpretation. This book expands his analysis by demonstrating how white Christians adapted proslavery claims for the postemancipation period by relying on gendered family order, and how black Christians' arguments countered white claims at every step. Rable, *God's Almost Chosen People*; Stout, *Upon the Altar of the Nation*; Noll, *The Civil War as a Theological Crisis*, 160; Harlow, *Religion, Race, and the Making of Confederate Kentucky*; Harlow, "The Long Life of Proslavery Theology," in Downs and Masur, eds., *The World the Civil War Made*; Harlow, "Slavery, Race, and Political Ideology"; Harlow, "The Civil War."

22. Rather than northern and southern white reunion in the late nineteenth century at the expense of black rights, I argue that southern Protestants, including Methodists, Baptists, and Presbyterians, maintained a distinctive paternalistic racial and gender hierarchy. They appreciated northern apathy about black rights as an aid to their white supremacist paternalism, but until their newly created southern histories and segregation policies gained national acceptance, they resisted reunion. Blight, *Race and Reunion*; Blum, *Reforging the White Republic*.

23. White southern Christians pointed out that the four New Testament instructions for slaves to obey masters appeared alongside instructions for wives to obey their husbands. Ephesians 5:22, 6:5; Colossians 3:18, 22; Titus 2:3–5, 9–10; I Peter 2:18, 31.

24. I draw especially on Stephanie McCurry's analysis of antebellum proslavery ideology's reliance on gender hierarchy, among several influential treatments of proslavery theological argument. Stephanie E. Jones-Rogers has shown that married slave-owning women used their power over enslaved people ruthlessly, proving the lie that slavery was at all like white marriage. McCurry, *Masters of Small Worlds*; Jones-Rogers, *They Were Her Property*; Fox-Genovese and Genovese, "Divine Sanction of Social Order"; Holifield, *The Gentlemen Theologians*; Faust, *The Creation of Confederate Nationalism*.

25. Stewart, *Meditations from the Pen*; Douglass, *Narrative of the Life*; Noll, *God and Race in American Politics*; Fredrickson, *The Black Image in the White Mind*, 97–129; Evans, *The Burden of Black Religion*, 17–104.

26. When southern Christians accused their northern counterparts of taking the Bible less seriously and introducing new ideas into their religious arguments, they were right to a certain extent, because antislavery white Christians sought to criticize slavery but not racial hierarchy. Molly Oshatz has shown how antislavery arguments that slavery as an institution was sinful gave rise to new liberal ideas among northern Protestants. Oshatz, *Slavery and Sin*; Noll, *America's God*, 386–438; Carwardine, *Evangelicals and Politics*.

27. "Report of the Select Committee on the Condition of the South," January 15, 1875. House of Representatives, Report no. 101. *Index to Reports of Committees of the House of Representatives for the Second Session of the Forty-Third Congress*, 194–95.

28. Raboteau, *Slave Religion*.

Chapter One

1. July 28, 1863, entry, Kate Foster Diary, Rubenstein Library, Duke University. Subsequent references to the diary are noted as "[date] entry, Foster Diary, Rubenstein." As historians have noted, women's diary keeping often gave a record for their children. Foster, who was unmarried, mentioned her nieces and nephews as possible future readers of her diary. Diaries also created spaces in which women (and men) sought to reconcile their religious beliefs and their lived experience. For these reasons, diaries should not be read as wholly private, personal spaces, but as sites for ongoing individual formation within the confines of religious doctrine and as texts written for the edification of future generations. Brekus, "Writing as a Protestant Practice"; Brekus, *Sarah Osborn's World*; Kerrison, *Claiming the Pen*.

2. The first quote, "war of Independence," is from June 25, 1863. The discussion of Vicksburg's fall is from July 9 and 13, 1863, the rest from July 28, 1863. Foster Diary, Rubenstein. For Foster's later life and work with the United Daughters of the Confederacy, see Broussard, *Stepping Living in Place*, 185–87.

3. Mark Noll has noted that few critics of proslavery theology argued that New Testament discussions of slavery did not refer to race-based enslavement of people of African descent because doing so would be an indictment of their racial prejudice. Molly Oshatz also notes that most white antislavery Christians did not criticize the unbiblical racism justifying slavery as they created new theological ideas of slavery as a sinful institution. Noll, *The Civil War as a Theological Crisis*; Noll, *God and Race in American Politics*, 39–42; Oshatz, *Slavery and Sin*, 61–80.

4. Stephanie McCurry was the first to note that ministers wrote the majority of all proslavery writings, and I draw significantly on her analysis of gender and marital hierarchies in defenses of slavery. April Holm has shown the intense conflict these denominational divides prompted in border states. McCurry, *Masters of Small Worlds*; Holm, *A Kingdom Divided*; Carwardine, *Evangelicals and Politics in Antebellum America*; Noll, *America's God*.

5. Ephesians 5:22, 6:5: "Wives, submit yourselves unto your own husbands, as unto the Lord. . . . Servants, be obedient to them that are your masters according to the flesh, with fear and trembling, in singleness of your heart, as unto Christ"; Colossians 3:18, 22: "Wives, submit yourselves unto your own husbands, as it is fit in the Lord. . . . Servants, obey in all things your masters according to the flesh; not with eyeservice, as menpleasers; but in singleness of heart, fearing God"; Titus 2:3–5, 9–10: "The aged women likewise, that they be in

behaviour as becometh holiness, not false accusers, not given to much wine, teachers of good things; That they may teach the young women to be sober, to love their husbands, to love their children, To be discreet, chaste, keepers at home, good, obedient to their own husbands, that the word of God be not blasphemed. . . . Exhort servants to be obedient unto their own masters, and to please them well in all things; not answering again; Not purloining, but shewing all good fidelity; that they may adorn the doctrine of God our Saviour in all things"; I Peter 2:18, 3:1: "Servants, be subject to your masters with all fear; not only to the good and gentle, but also to the froward. . . . Likewise, ye wives, be in subjection to your own husbands; that, if any obey not the word, they also may without the word be won by the conversation of the wives" (King James Version).

6. Elizabeth Fox-Genovese, Eugene Genovese, Drew Gilpin Faust, Charles Irons, and Stephanie McCurry have argued that defenders of slavery situated their defense in an organic, hierarchical view of society that offered a critique of rights-based, individualistic arguments. A prominent body of recent scholars including Edward Baptist, Sven Beckert, and Walter Johnson have argued that slavery relied on brutal capitalist calculations. In light of the capitalist brutality of slavery, I examine the stark difference between white southerners' justification of slavery as benevolent hierarchy and slavery's dehumanizing violence. Fox-Genovese and Genovese, "Divine Sanction of Social Order Religious Foundations of the Southern Slaveholders' World View"; Faust, *The Creation of Confederate Nationalism*; Irons, *The Origins of Proslavery Christianity*; Scully, *Religion and the Making of Nat Turner's Virginia*; Johnson, *River of Dark Dreams*; Beckert, *Empire of Cotton*; Baptist, *The Half Has Never Been Told*.

7. Furman, *Exposition of the Views of the Baptists*, 12; Ross, *Slavery Ordained of God*, 53 (emphasis in originals). Mark Noll has written that Ross's text "made the conventional defense of slavery." Noll, *The Civil War as a Theological Crisis*, 83.

8. July 25, 1863, Foster Diary, Rubenstein. Stephanie Jones-Rogers has built on the work of Thavolia Glymph and Deborah Gray White to show that white slaveholding women benefited from and defended the power they had over the bodies and labor of enslaved people. Earlier women's historians who focused on white women as ladies and "mistresses" perpetuated white southerners' statements about white women's retiring, delicate ladyhood. Clinton, *The Plantation Mistress*; Fox-Genovese, *Within the Plantation Household*; Glymph, *Out of the House of Bondage*; Jones-Rogers, *They Were Her Property*; Scott, *The Southern Lady*; White, *Ar'n't I a Woman?*; Wood, *Masterful Women*.

9. Douglass, *Narrative of the Life*; Jacobs, *Incident in the Life of a Slave Girl*; Brown, *Good Wives*; Painter, "Of *Lily*, Linda Brent and Freud"; Hodes, *White Women, Black Men*.

10. Palmer, *Thanksgiving Sermon*, 19. "Report of the Committee on the Religious Instruction of the Colored People," *Southern Presbyterian Review* 16, no. 2 (October 1863): 191, 192.

11. Obadiah 1:7: "All the men of thy confederacy have brought thee even to the border: men that were at peace with thee have deceived thee, and prevailed against thee" (King James Version). "The War of the South Vindicated," *Southern Presbyterian Review* 15, no. 4 (April 1863): 483.

12. In a later autobiographical manuscript written for his children, "A Brief Autobiography of John G. Jones, Written for His Children," Jones said he had been unable to pray for Confederate victory, but only for the safety of his sons and nephews fighting in the war. While retrospective accounts of individuals' attitudes during the Civil War are notoriously dubious, I think this particular claim fits well with Jones's extant sermon notes from the

Civil War, which list secession as a violation of the U.S. Constitution. Jones recorded a one- or two-page outline and then preached from it for fifty to fifty-five minutes, according to his autobiographical manuscript. The first of these fast day sermons is not dated, but plausible dates include: June 13, 1861; November 15, 1861; February 20, 1862; March 27, 1863; and (less likely) August 21, 1863, boxes 1–2, JGJ Papers, Millsaps College.

13. James A. Lyon, "Slavery, and the Duties Growing," *Southern Presbyterian Review* 16, no. 1 (July 1863): 7, 26. This rebuttal came from "A Slave Marriage Law," *Southern Presbyterian Review* 16, no. 2 (October 1863): 147, 149, 151.

14. June 25, 1863, and July 13, 1863, Foster Diary, Rubenstein.

15. February 28, 1864; January 2, 1864; March 28, 1864; May 21, 1864; March 28, 1864; and May 2, 1864, entries. All spelling and capitalization are original to Edmondson's diary. Punctuation has been standardized for clarity. Belle Edmondson Diary #1707-z, Southern Historical Collection, Wilson Library, University of North Carolina at Chapel Hill.

16. Sermon preached on November 16, 1864. Box 2, JGJ Papers, Millsaps College. See II Chronicles 20 for the story of Jehoshaphat's prayer and its miraculous results.

17. Samuel Agnew was a minister in the Associate Reformed Presbyterian Church, a small denomination closely related to Old School Presbyterianism. Entries for 1865 dated April 17, April 19, April 22, May 8, May 15, May 25, and May 29. Samuel Agnew Diary. Southern Historical Collection, Wilson Library, University of North Carolina at Chapel Hill. Scanned and transcribed portions of the diary are available at http://www2.lib.unc.edu /mss/inv/a/Agnew,Samuel_A.html, and http://docsouth.unc.edu/imls/agnew/menu .html. Subsequent references to the diary are noted as "[date] entry, Samuel Agnew Diary, SHC."

18. Rev. G. N. Carruthers to Simeon S. Jocelyn, Corinth, Mississippi, June 12, 1863, AMA 71552–53; Rev. Phineas Mixer to Rev. Simeon S. Jocelyn, Natchez, Mississippi, February 29, 1864, AMA 70601. American Missionary Association Archives, Amistad Research Center, Tulane University, New Orleans, Louisiana. Hereafter cited as "Author to Recipient, Place of Writing, Date, AMA #."

19. Rev. George N. Carruthers to Simeon S. Jocelyn, Corinth, Mississippi, June 12, 1863, AMA 71552–53 (emphasis in original). Carruthers's language here parallels biblical passages. See Psalm 107:44, Psalm 116:16, and especially Isaiah 58:6 (King James Version).

20. A. O. Howell, Natchez, Mississippi, January 19, 1864, AMA 71594. The latter quote came from Psalm 118:23. "This is the LORD'S doing; it is marvellous in our eyes" (emphasis in original).

21. Among other examples of contrasting "citizens" to "freedmen," see S. G. Wright to George Whipple, Natchez, Mississippi, November 18, 1865, AMA 71841; S. G. Wright to George Whipple, Natchez, Mississippi, March 28, 1865, AMA 71748; J. P. Bardwell to M. E. Strieby, Natchez, Mississippi, November 4, 1865, AMA 71829–30; J. P. Bardwell to George Whipple, Grenada, Mississippi, April 28, 1866, AMA 72059–60.

22. Blanche Harris to George Whipple, Natchez, Mississippi, March 16, 1866, AMA 71971. For other perspectives on the conflict between Harris and her white AMA supervisors, see J. P. Bardwell to George Whipple, Jackson, Mississippi, March 2, 1866, AMA 71961; Palmer Litts to S. G. Wright, Natchez, Mississippi, March 7, 1866, AMA 71970; J. P. Bardwell to George Whipple, Natchez, Mississippi, March 20, 1866, AMA 71992.

23. S. G. Wright, Natchez, Mississippi, March 9, 1864, AMA 71610 (emphasis in original); Ms. Elsie Spies, School Report, Natchez, Mississippi, February 1864, AMA 71604.

24. Rev. S. G. Wright to Rev. Henry Cowles, Natchez, Mississippi, March 15, 1864 (emphasis in original).

25. This statement nearly quotes Romans 8:38–39: "For I am persuaded, that neither death, nor life, nor angels, nor principalities, nor powers, nor things present, nor things to come, Nor height, nor depth, nor any other creature, shall be able to separate us from the love of God, which is in Christ Jesus our Lord" (King James Version); Unidentified newspaper clipping of Andrew Tait et al. to the Union Convention of Tennessee, January 9, 1865, enclosed in Col. R. D. Mussey to Capt. C. P. Brown, January 23, 1865, Letters Received, Series 925, Department of the Cumberland, U.S. Army Continental Commands, Record Group 393, pt. 1, National Archives. Published in Berlin et al., eds., *Free at Last*, 497–505, and available at http://www.freedmen.umd.edu/tenncon.htm.

26. Berlin et al., eds., *Free at Last*, 497–505.

27. L. A. Eberhart to Rev. C. H. Fowler, Vicksburg, Mississippi, February 1, 1864, AMA 71588.

28. Rev. S. G. Wright to Rev. Henry Cowles, Natchez, Mississippi, March 15, 1864; Rev. Phineas Mixer to Rev. Simeon S. Jocelyn, Natchez, Mississippi, February 29, 1864, AMA 70601.

29. Rev. Phineas Mixer to Rev. Simeon S. Jocelyn, Natchez, Mississippi, February 29, 1864, AMA 70601.

30. "Proceedings of the Convention of Colored Citizens of the State of Arkansas, Held in Little Rock, Thursday, Friday, and Saturday, Nov. 30, Dec. 1 and 2, 1865," in Foner and Walker, eds., *Proceedings of the Black National and State Conventions*, 191, 193, 192.

31. "Pastoral Address of the Southern Methodist Bishops," *New York Times*, September 10, 1865. Letter signed by J. O. Andrew, R. Paine, and G. F. Pierce in Columbia, Georgia, on August 17, 1865.

32. "Pastoral Address of the Southern Methodist Bishops."

33. May 28, 1865; May 27, 1875; May 29, 1865; Samuel Agnew Diary, SHC.

34. June 21, 1865; July 20, 1865; December 15, 1865. Samuel Agnew Diary, SHC. Eric Foner quotes a portion of this last entry in *Reconstruction*, but Agnew is mentioned simply as a planter rather than a minister. Foner, *Reconstruction*, 134.

35. Minutes of the Memphis Conference of the Methodist Episcopal Church, South, Twenty-Sixth Session Held in Covington, Tennessee, October 4–10, 1865, *Minutes of the Memphis Conference*, 100–101. *Laws of the State of Mississippi*, 165. I have found no evidence of this restriction on preaching without a license being enforced. The 1868 Mississippi constitution, which was passed under Congressional Reconstruction and guaranteed black men's voting rights, promised full religious freedom.

36. November 1865 sermons, box 2, JGJ Papers, Millsaps College.

37. "Memphis Riots and Massacres," *Reports of the Committees of the House of Representatives*, 12–13.

38. Rosen, *Terror in the Heart of Freedom*.

39. *The Reports of the Committees of the House of Representatives, Made During the First Session of the Thirty-Ninth Congress 1865–1866*, vol. 3 (Washington: Government Printing Office, 1866), 4.

40. May 5, 1866, entry, Samuel Agnew Diary, SHC. On sexual violence and citizenship in the Memphis Massacre, see Rosen, *Terror in the Heart of Freedom*, 23–86.

41. Rable, *But There Was No Peace*, 57; Hollandsworth, *An Absolute Massacre*.

Chapter Two

1. "Episcopal Address," *Minutes of the Fifteenth Quadrennial Session of the General Conference of the African Methodist Episcopal*, 35, 41. Benjamin Arnett Papers, Wilberforce University, Wilberforce, Ohio (BAP). Brown here quoted I Corinthians 13.

2. "Resolution on Civil Rights," *Minutes of the Fifteenth Quadrennial Session of the General Conference of the African Methodist Episcopal*, 74–75; BAP.

3. "Resolution on Civil Rights." *Minutes of the Fifteenth Quadrennial Session of the General Conference of the African Methodist Episcopal*, 74–75; BAP. The resolution passed unanimously.

4. Among classic histories of Reconstruction, see Du Bois, *Black Reconstruction*; Foner, *Reconstruction*.

5. L. D. Barnett to George Whipple, Memphis, Tennessee, December 25, 1867, AMA H9266; *Minutes of the First Session of the Tennessee Annual Conference of the African Methodist E. Church*, 12–13. For 1871 statistics, see State Convention of the Colored Citizens, *Proceedings of the State Convention of the Colored Citizens of Tennessee*, 5.

6. *Minutes of the Third Session of the Tennessee Annual Conference of the African M.E. Church*, 30; BAP. *Third Session of the Arkansas Annual Conference of the African M.E.*, 10; BAP. *Minutes of the Seventh Annual Session of Louisiana Conference African Methodist Episcopal Church*, 16; BAP.

7. E[dmonia] G. Highgate to M. E. Strieby, Enterprise, Mississippi, January 30, 1868, AMA 72261. For more on Highgate, see Catalog of the American Missionary Association Archives, Amistad Research Center.

8. James Scoville to Jacob Shipherd, Camden, Arkansas, May 21, 1868, AMA 4120.

9. H. C. Bullard to E. P. Smith, Raymond, Mississippi, January 23, 1868, AMA 72260.

10. Anna M. Keen to J. R. Shipherd, Brookhaven, Mississippi, February 4, 1868, AMA 72263–63A.

11. *Minutes of the Third Session of the Tennessee Annual Conference of the African M.E. Church*, 30; BAP.

12. State Convention of the Colored Citizens of Tennessee, *Proceedings of the Colored State Convention*, 14–15, 5.

13. State Convention of the Colored Citizens of Tennessee, 11, 3, 5.

14. State Convention of the Colored Citizens of Tennessee.

15. *Minutes of the Third Session of the Arkansas Annual Conference of the African M.E. Church*, 13; BAP.

16. *Minutes of the Third Session of the Arkansas Annual Conference*, 13–14; BAP. Black Christian temperance pledges were not merely signals of black Christian respectability or political ambition, which supports the claims that historian Matthew Harper has made recently about black Protestant temperance work in this period. Harper, *End of Days*, 98–127.

17. "Episcopal Address," *Minutes of the Fifteenth Quadrennial Session of the General Conference of the African Methodist Episcopal*, 1872, 37; BAP.

18. Harris referenced Acts 16. Blanche Harris to George Whipple, Natchez, Mississippi, February 28, 1867, AMA 72245–46.

19. McDonald, "Mississippi and Its Future," 1, 2, 10. Special Collections, J. D. Williams Library, University of Mississippi (JDWL). On A. C. McDonald's founding Shaw University (later Rust College) in Holly Springs, Mississippi, see Giddings, *Ida,* 28–29.

20. McDonald, "Mississippi and Its Future," 9, 13; JDWL.

21. McDonald, 13, 12; JDWL.

22. McDonald, 10, 17, 19–20; JDWL (emphasis in original).

23. McDonald, 4, 16; JDWL.

24. McDonald, 15–16, 19; JDWL. McDonald referred to the conflict between Peter and Paul recorded in Galatians 2. McDonald used the text to argue that Peter's prejudice against uncircumcised Greek Christians represented a prejudice against fellow Christians and against changing social norms similar to white southerners' hostility to black citizens' full citizenship. Black Christians since David Walker had used the story of Peter's recognition that Jewish and Gentile Christians should be viewed equally, recorded in Acts 10, to show that true Christians eschew racial bias. Walker, *Appeal to the Colored Citizens.*

25. Adelbert Ames to Blanche Butler Ames, September 30, 1873, in Ames, *Chronicles from the Nineteenth Century,* 583.

26. Adelbert Ames to Blanche Butler Ames, October 1, 1873, in Ames, *Chronicles from the Nineteenth Century,* 585.

27. Adelbert Ames to Blanche Butler Ames, October 1, 1873, in Ames, *Chronicles from the Nineteenth Century,* 585.

28. Relying on central organizational statements and northern editorials, Richardson claimed that the AMA fought for black southerners' full citizenship rights in these years, but records from AMA teachers in the Mississippi River Valley suggest that most AMA teachers did not support equal civil and political rights for black citizens. Richardson, *Christian Reconstruction,* 20–22.

29. Anna M. Keen to J. R. Shipherd, Brookhaven, Mississippi, February 4, 1868, AMA 72263-63A.

30. Allen Huggins to E. P. Smith, Jackson, Mississippi, January 15, 1869, AMA 72282.

31. H. S. Beals to E. P. Smith, Tugaloo, Mississippi, [n.d.] [late October] 1869, AMA 72336. See also "Rip Van Winkle," in *The Works of Washington Irving,* vol. 2, *The Sketch-Book,* 44–67.

32. Edward P. Smith to [?], Jackson, Mississippi, April 2, 1870, AMA 72358–60 (emphasis in original).

33. State Convention of the Colored Citizens of Tennessee, *Proceedings of the Colored State Convention,* 3–4; *Minutes of the Eleventh Annual Conference of the African Methodist Episcopal Church in Louisiana,* 1876, 23; BAP. See also *Minutes of the Eighth Session of the Tennessee Conference,* 1875, 32; BAP.

34. Dabney, *A Defence of Virginia;* "Book Notices," *Daily Arkansas Gazette,* December 17, 1867; Summers, ed., *Journal of the General Conference of the Methodist Episcopal Church,* 1874, 542.

35. "Bishop's Address," *Journal of the Forty-First Annual Convention of the Protestant Episcopal Church in the Diocese of Mississippi,* 29; JDWL. *Journal of the Forty-Fourth Annual Council of the Protestant Episcopal Church of the Diocese of Mississippi,* 22; JDWL.

36. [Benjamin] P[almer], "Servants, Obey in All Things Your Masters According to the Flesh," *South-Western Presbyterian*, March 19, 1874. Palmer quoted Colossians 3:22: "Servants, obey in all things your masters according to the flesh; not with eyeservice, as men-pleasers; but in singleness of heart, fearing God." See also [Benjamin] P[almer], "Fathers," *South-Western Presbyterian*, February 26, 1874; Palmer, *The Family*.

37. Dedication Sermon at Fayetteville Confederate Cemetery, June 1873, Fontaine Richard Earle Papers, box 1, folder 2, University of Arkansas–Fayetteville.

38. Octavia Otey Diary, 1864–88, MS 1608, Southern Historical Collection (SHC) (emphasis in original).

39. "A Brief Autobiography of John G. Jones, Written for His Children," box 1, vol. 2, JGJ papers, Millsaps College.

40. "Ouachita District Meeting," *New Orleans Christian Advocate* (*NOCA*), October 17, 1868; "Negro Riot in Jefferson," *NOCA*, October 17, 1868. First quote referenced in "New Orleans Christian Advocate," Walter M. Lowrey Papers, Centenary College of Louisiana.

41. "Bishop's Address," *Journal of the Forty-First Annual Convention of the Protestant Episcopal Church in the Diocese of Mississippi*, 29; JDWL. "Parochial Reports," *Journal of the Forty-First Annual Convention of the Protestant Episcopal Church in the Diocese of Mississippi*, 62; JDWL. Douglas, *Christian Priest Taken from Among Men*, 12; MDAH. On George Jackson's religious leadership, see the letters to William Douglas from his wife Sarah and their children recounting Jackson's leading service during Douglas' absence, box 1, folders 8–9, MS 01918, William Kirtland Douglas Papers, SHC.

42. In addition to the manuscript General Conference minutes cited below, I have drawn upon Phillips, *History of the Colored Methodist Church in America*; Lakey, *The History of the CME Church (Revised)*; Sommerville, *An Ex-Colored Church*; Jackson, "The Colored Methodist Episcopal Church and Their Struggle for Autonomy and Reform in the New South."

43. Lane, *Autobiography of Bishop Isaac Lane*, 47, 51, 147–48; Holsey et al., *Sketch of the Life of Richard H. Vanderhorst*, Pitts Library, Emory University. This biographical sketch, written shortly after Vanderhorst's death by CME ministers, was published after the death of Bishop Lucius Holsey in 1922, when it was found amid Holsey's papers. The pamphlet emphasized Vanderhorst's exemplary Methodist piety in language that echoed biographical sketches of hundreds of other Methodist ministers. Incorporating common Methodist tropes allowed CME leaders in 1872 and 1929 to insist on the Methodist purity of the early CME Church. When he faced his final illness in 1872, "Brother Vanderhorst bore his affliction with great patience and Christian fortitude" (12). David Hempton has analyzed Methodist conventions of life-writing as a triptych of spiritual birth, pious life, and good death. Hempton, *Methodism*, 55–85. This relationship between the two Reverends McTyeire appears in the biography of Bishop Holland McTyeire. Tigert, *Bishop Holland Nimmons McTyeire*, 158. I have not located additional biographical material on Charles McTyeire beyond this brief mention in Holland McTyeire's biography. Several early CME leaders wrote that they were the sons of their former enslavers and enslaved mothers. I have no evidence that this was the case for Charles McTyeire, only that Holland McTyeire's biography named Charles's mother but said nothing about his father. Still, the possibility would lend a whole other set of meanings to this interaction.

44. Rivers, *The Life of Robert Paine D.D.*, 77–80. Noll and Carwardine wrote definitive histories of Methodist schisms in their major works on antebellum Protestant history. Noll, *America's God*, 367–401; Carwardine, *Evangelicals and Politics in Antebellum America*.

45. Manuscript CME Church General Conference Minutes 1870, 6. Christian Methodist Episcopal Church Archives. April Holm examined claims of the spirituality of churches in border state church disputes. Holm, *A Kingdom Divided*.

46. Manuscript CME Church General Conference Minutes 1870, 4–5. Laurie Maffly-Kipp has shown how different African American Methodist denominations claimed unique identities through distinct origin narratives. Maffly-Kipp, *Setting Down the Sacred Past*, 93–98.

47. Manuscript CME Church General Conference Minutes 1870, 22.

48. Manuscript CME Church General Conference Minutes 1873, 56–57. Among others, Sara McAfee's 1945 history of CME women's work acknowledged that the denomination had long been seen as an "Uncle Tom" organization. McAfee, *History of the Woman's Missionary Society*, 35. See also Eskew, "Black Elitism."

49. Summers, ed., *Journal of the General Conference of the Methodist Episcopal Church, South, 1874*, 460–61.

Chapter Three

1. Psalm 147:1, 3, 6 (King James Version). Jones read the entire psalm.

2. Box 2, JGJ. For more on Jones's life and work during these years, see box 1, vol. 2. See chapter 1 for Jones's 1865 sermon that linked emancipation with Civil War casualties as afflictions sent by God. The vast majority of Jones's hundreds of sermon outlines focused on ubiquitous Protestant topics of personal piety, faithful living, and religious discipline. Most outlines were used repeatedly. Only a few sermons were written for specific dates with reference to political or social events. JGJ.

3. Box 2, JGJ.

4. The term "redemption" also has economic meanings related to redeeming a debt or redeeming a person from slavery.

5. During Reconstruction, the AMA had worked to hand off its primary schools to local officials and to concentrate on its normal schools and colleges. Eager to protect these colleges amid a changing political environment, AMA officials did not protest Democratic political takeovers. Richardson, *Christian Reconstruction*, 250–55.

6. The phrase "spiritual manhood" comes from an obituary for an AME minister. "Appendices," *Minutes of the Eleventh Annual Conference of the African Methodist Episcopal Church, 1876*, 26; BAP.

7. "Alleged Frauds in the Recent Election in Mississippi," *Mississippi in 1875*, xiii.

8. "Riot in Mississippi," *NOCA*, September 16, 1875; "A Terrible Bereavement," *NOCA*, September 16, 1875. According to John H. Estell, a white lawyer from Jackson, Frank Thompson frequently drank whisky and was the leader of a group of white Democratic men in their early twenties. E. B. Welborne, a sworn witness and state representative, recalled that Thompson was taking frequent sips from a whisky bottle in the time before the political meeting erupted in violence. "Testimony of John H. Estell," *Mississippi in 1875*, 318–22; "Testimony of E. S. Welborne," *Mississippi in 1875*, 492–94. Several white Democratic leaders said Thompson's pistol fired by accident into the ground, after which many black men fired delib-

erately, killing Thompson and others. "The Clinton Riot: A True Statement Showing Who Originated It," *Weekly Clarion* (Jackson, MS), September 29, 1875.

9. "Political Disturbances," *NOCA*, September 16, 1875; "News of the Week," *NOCA*, November 11, 1875.

10. "Testimony of E. S. Welborne," *Mississippi in 1875*, 494; "Testimony of Ann Hodge," *Mississippi in 1875*, 420–22; "Testimony of John Jones," *Mississippi in 1875*, 422–24.

11. "Testimony of Ann Hodge," *Mississippi in 1875*, 420–22.

12. October 28, 1875, entry; November 7, 1875, entry. Samuel Agnew Diary, SHC. No record is left of Agnew's weekly sermons, except occasional comments that he made in his daily diary entries. For more on this manuscript source, including links to digitized portions, see chapter 1.

13. Proverbs 29:2 (King James Version). As is common in these sources, Earle wrote out a one-page outline for a sermon that likely lasted almost an hour. This sermon outline is undated, but because it references "the last eight years" of Reconstruction and Republican politics, it seems reasonable to assume that it was preached at some point in 1874, when the Brooks-Baxter War, the passage and ratification of a new Arkansas state constitution, and the election of a Democratic governor took place. Box 1, folder 9, series 2, Fontaine Richard Earle Papers, University of Arkansas–Fayetteville. See also Fontaine Richard Earle et al., "The Earle-Buchanan Letters of 1861–1876." The Cumberland Presbyterian Church was a distinct Presbyterian denomination with origins in early nineteenth-century revivals in the Cumberland Plateau region of Tennessee and Kentucky. It was distinguished from other Presbyterian denominations by its lower educational requirements for clergy, which enabled the church to spread more quickly into newer communities in the Trans-Mississippi West. Earle, however, did earn a college degree from Cumberland University in Lebanon, Tennessee, before he moved to Arkansas in 1859. See "Finding Aid," Fontaine Richard Earle Papers, University of Arkansas–Fayetteville.

14. Palmer, *The Family*, 128, 187, 186.

15. Palmer, 102, 51–52, 107, 105, 124–25, 137. Recent scholars of the history of capitalism and of slavery have shown that slavery's central role in the development of capitalism, especially through cotton, made slavery far more brutal than most accounts have recognized. See Beckert, *Empire of Cotton*; Johnson, *River of Dark Dreams*; Baptist, *The Half Has Never Been Told*.

16. Historians of emancipation and Reconstruction have noted the priority of marriage in Freedmen's Bureau policies, including blanket declarations that all cohabiting couples be declared legally married, a move that tried to address enslaved people's lack of access to marriage. The Freedmen's Bureau, as well as local and state governments, sought households headed by a man who controlled the labor of his wife and children. Cott, *Public Vows*, 77–104; Bercaw, *Gendered Freedoms*, 117–34; Frankel, *Freedom's Women*, 79–122; O'Donovan, *Becoming Free*, 193–98.

17. "The Negro at the South," *Hinds County Gazette*, June 9, 1875; [Untitled article], *Hinds County Gazette*, July 19, 1876. The *Hinds County Gazette* reprinted the latter article from the *Meridian Mercury*.

18. J. G. Johnson, "Appeal of an Able Colored Minister to His Race," *Hinds County Gazette*, September 29, 1875. Whatever the circumstances behind this letter's publication, the fact that its authorship was listed as that of Methodist Episcopal Church minister Rev.

J. G. Johnson from Jackson, Mississippi, demonstrated the important place that ministers occupied in social and political debates. In 1887, Rev. J. G. Johnson was involved in founding Campbell College for black students in Jackson, Mississippi. Perhaps his acquiescence to white Democratic interests in the 1875 election helped him to earn the support of the white donors and friends who would assist in the creation of the college. Hawkins, *Centennial Encyclopedia*, 295–96. I presume this is the same J. G. Johnson, as both would have been influential black Methodist ministers in Jackson, Mississippi, in 1875 and 1887. Records of the Methodist Episcopal Church list Rev. J. G. Johnson in 1880 as a presiding elder of the Holly Springs District of the Mississippi Conference, but noted that he lived in Jackson, Mississippi. *Minutes of the Annual Conferences of the Methodist Episcopal Church, Spring Conferences 1880*, 6.

19. [Untitled], *The Times* (Shreveport, LA), April 30, 1875; "News Items," *Donaldson Chief* (Donaldson, LA), May 8, 1875; *Louisiana Sugar-Bowl* (New Iberia, LA), May 6, 1875; "Double Murder," *Memphis Daily Appeal* (Memphis, TN), April 29, 1875; "Democratic," *Memphis Daily Appeal*, April 29, 1875. A follow-up article on the preachers' conspiracy to murder two black children appeared in another white local newspaper: "Ledger Lines," *Public Ledger* (Memphis, TN), July 1, 1875.

20. "Attempt to Commit Rape," *Memphis Daily Appeal*, May 2, 1877; "A Rambunctious Preacher," *New Orleans Daily Democrat*, April 18, 1877; "Execution of Wife-Murderer," *Daily Arkansas Gazette* (Little Rock, AR), July 28, 1877; same incident reported in [untitled article], *The Milan Exchange* (Milan, TN), August 9, 1877; "Texas Items," *The Times* (Shreveport, LA), April 6, 1876; "The Knife: How a Colored Preacher Used That Style of Weapon Near Mabelvale," *Little Rock Daily Gazette*, November 21, 1876; "The Clark County Tragedy," *Ouachita Telegraph* (Monroe, LA), December 21, 1877; "Southern News," *Times-Democrat* (New Orleans, LA), April 8, 1879; *Clarion Ledger* (Jackson, MS), April 2, 1879.

21. "'Sturbing a Meetin,'" *Little Rock Daily Gazette*, February 14, 1877.

22. "Badly Treated," *Daily Arkansas Gazette*, September 16, 1880; "Why a Colored Preacher Sold His Mule," *Little Rock Daily Gazette*, March 5, 1880; "A Brutal Preacher," *Daily Arkansas Gazette*, August 17, 1880.

23. This quote comes from a report defending the AME Church against charges made by the AMA about black character. M. R. Johnson, C. Burch, and George W. Bryant, "Report on the State of the Church," *Minutes of the Eleventh Annual Conference of the African Methodist Church in Louisiana*, 23; BAP.

24. *Minutes of the Eleventh Annual Conference of the African Methodist Church in Louisiana*, 7; BAP.

25. Johnston, ed., *Louisiana Conference Annual Consisting of Sermons Preached*, i; BAP.

26. "Appendices," *Minutes of the Eleventh Annual Conference of the African Methodist Church in Louisiana*, 20–21; BAP. The American Bible Society is not named, but the references to a Bible distribution organization founded in 1816 clearly indicates the American Bible Society.

27. *Minutes of the Fourth Session of the West Tennessee Conference of the African Methodist Episcopal Church*, 12; BAP. *Minutes of the State and Sunday-School Convention Held with the Paradise Baptist Church*, 18, published in African-American Baptist Annual Reports, Microfilm Reel 14; Manuscript CME General Conference Minutes 1878, 205, 221–22.

28. "The White League," *SWCA*, July 16, 1874. The paper was called the *Southwestern Advocate* until 1877, when it changed its name to the *Southwestern Christian Advocate*. George Rable has studied the founding of White Leagues in 1874 and their growth through the state. Rable, *But There Was No Peace*, 132–42; Hogue, *Uncivil War*, 116–43.

29. "The White Leagues," *SWCA*, August 27, 1874.

30. "A Few of the Things the White Leagues Are Responsible For," *SWCA*, August 27, 1874. Additional articles about the White League and white supremacist paramilitary violence continued to appear in the *SWCA*: "Immigration and White Leagues," *SWCA*, August 27, 1874; Emerson Bentley, "The Catholic Attitude in Louisiana," *SWCA*, December 30, 1875; "Friends of the Negro," *SWCA*, March 20, 1879; "A White League Hymn," *SWCA*, February 12, 1880.

31. [Untitled editorials], *SWCA*, November 18, 1875. These quotations come from adjacent untitled editorials. The *SWCA* continued to decry violence and inequality and to raise alarm about the growth of southern exceptionalist language that smacked of Confederate ideology. "The Situation in Louisiana," *SWCA*, January 4, 1877; "The Africo-American," *SWCA*, December 12, 1878; "Mr. Blaine's Speech," *SWCA*, January 2, 1879; "Those Murdered Witnesses," *SWCA*, January 9, 1879; A. E. P. Albert, "The Negro," *SWCA*, February 13, 1879; "Friends of the Negro," *SWCA*, March 20, 1879; "The Negro Nemesis," *SWCA*, April 3, 1879; "The Belt of Danger," *SWCA*, September 18, 1879; "The Late Elections," *SWCA*, November 13, 1879; "The Color Bearers," *SWCA*, December 4, 1879; "Politics in the Pulpit," *SWCA*, January 15, 1880; "Louisiana Conference," *SWCA*, February 12, 1880; "A White League Hymn," *SWCA*, February 12, 1880; Isaac G. Pollard, "Letter from Arkansas," *SWCA*, March 24, 1881.

32. *Minutes of the Eleventh Annual Conference of the African Methodist Church in Louisiana*, 26; BAP.

33. *Minutes of the Eleventh Annual Conference of the African Methodist Church in Louisiana*, 23; BAP (emphasis in original).

34. *Minutes of the Fourth Session of the West Tennessee Conference of the African Methodist Episcopal Church*, 17–18.

35. Manuscript CME General Conference Minutes 1878, 147.

36. Manuscript CME General Conference Minutes 1878, 144, 149–50.

37. Manuscript CME General Conference Minutes 1878, 221.

38. Manuscript CME General Conference Minutes 1878, 213. On Thomas Taylor's work in the CME Church's founding, see Phillips, *The History of the Colored Methodist Church in America*, 27; William Gravely, "Christian Methodist Episcopal Church," in Hill et al., eds., *Encyclopedia of Religion in the South*, 189–91.

39. Manuscript CME General Conference Minutes 1882, 244, 246. Summers's proslavery publishing included being editor of the *Nashville Christian Advocate* and editing William Smith's lectures in 1856. Smith, *Lectures on the Philosophy and Practice of Slavery*.

40. "The Colored Methodist Episcopal Church in America," *NOCA*, May 8, 1879.

41. J. W. Medlock, "Notes from the South Bossier Circuit," *NOCA*, July 25, 1878.

42. J. W. McNeil, "The Colored Methodist Episcopal Church of America," *NOCA*, December 6, 1877.

43. "The Colored Bishop and His Spiritual Father," *NOCA*, January 8, 1880. The article was originally published in the *Wesleyan Advocate*.

44. "Bishop Holsey's Address," *NOCA*, June 8, 1882. Holsey's planned visit to the General Conference of the Methodist Episcopal Church, South, had been discussed at the May 1882 General Conference of the Colored Methodist Episcopal Church in America, and Holsey had strategized with other CME leaders to identify the areas where they most wanted aid from the MECS. Manuscript CME General Conference Minutes 1882, 256. Holsey paraphrased Ephesians 2:19–20: "Now therefore ye are no more strangers and foreigners, but fellow-citizens with the saints, and of the household of God; And are built upon the foundation of the apostles and prophets, Jesus Christ himself being the chief corner stone" (King James Version). Because the term "citizen" originated in the text, Holsey's choice to use this verse could have been a careful way to introduce black citizenship into the opening of his address. Alternatively, the term citizen here could have connoted shared religious identity independent of political or social status.

Chapter Four

1. "Iola's Corner," *Christian Index*, June 29, 1889. The *Christian Index* was published beginning in 1869, but no issues are extant until 1885, when the paper was published monthly. No issues are extant from 1886; the paper was published weekly beginning in 1887. All citations are from microfilm copies in the author's collection, duplicated from microfilm held at the Tennessee State Library and Archives, Nashville, Tennessee.

2. For an example of Wells linking women's gendered religious practice to broader issues of civil and political rights, see "Iola's Corner,'" *Christian Index*, March 2, 1889. On her Memphis activism, see Wells-Barnett, *Crusade for Justice*; Giddings, *Ida*; Schechter, *Ida B. Wells-Barnett*, 37–79.

3. "The Negro Problem Solved," *Christian Index*, February 16, 1889.

4. "Multiple News Items," *SWCA*, December 3, 1889.

5. The only references here from white southern Christians to slaveholders' sexual power over enslaved women were accounts of CME Church ministers who appeared less threatening to the racial order because they had white fathers. "Anglo-Saxon blood" is seen as carrying with it a certain measure of respectability, even though it represented the nonmarital sexual activity of white men. See chapter 3. Holsey, *Autobiography, Sermons, Addresses, and Essays*. The phrase "sex across the color line" borrows from Martha Hodes's analysis. Hodes has shown that the term "interracial," when applied to sex or marriage, wrongly rarifies putative white and black racial difference. Hodes, *White Women, Black Men*.

6. "Our Work Among the Negroes," *NOCA*, February 16, 1882; "Southern Methodism and the Negro," *NOCA*, April 8, 1886; A. B. Nicholson, "Something Ought to Be Done," *NOCA*, November 22, 1888.

7. C. K. Marshall, "The Education of Freedmen," *NOCA*, January 18, 1883.

8. W. W. Bennett, "Southern Methodism and Six Millions of Negroes," *NOCA*, March 2, 1882; "Our Work Among the Negroes," *NOCA*, February 16, 1882.

9. W. T. J. Sullivan, "Have We Failed in Our Duty to the Colored People," *NOCA*, March 16, 1882. Sullivan, a prominent Mississippi Methodist, was a trustee for Sardis Female College, chartered in 1876 by the Mississippi legislature and, along with Bishop

Charles B. Galloway, helped to found the Mississippi Methodist Historical Society in 1892. Du Bose, *A History of Methodism*, 418.

10. "Southern Methodism and the Negro," *NOCA*, April 8, 1886.

11. T. J. Upton, "Report of Special Committee on Paine Institute," *NOCA*, February 9, 1888.

12. "To Be Preserved," *NOCA*, January 29, 1880.

13. B[enjamin] M[organ] Palmer, "Fraternal Relations," *Southern Presbyterian Review* 34, no. 2 (April 1883): 318, 329, 328; James A. Waddell, "Political Religion," *Southern Presbyterian Review* 34, no. 2 (April 1883): 373. Palmer had forcefully reiterated the substance of proslavery theology in his defense of organic family and social order with wifely submission, filial obedience, and servants' subjection in Palmer, *The Family*.

14. J. E. Evans, "Paine Institute, Augusta, Ga.," *NOCA*, January 25, 1883. For more fundraising appeals to white donors for Paine Institute (later Paine College), see W. C. Dunlap, "A Statement and Plea to Southern Methodists," *NOCA*, February 19, 1885; W. C. Dunlap, "Paine Institute," *NOCA*, January 28, 1886.

15. C. K. Marshall, "The Education of Freedmen," *NOCA*, January 18, 1883.

16. Tucker, *The Relations of the Church to the Colored Race*, 1–3, 17.

17. Tucker, *The Relations of the Church to the Colored Race*, 29–70; Marshall, *The Colored Race Weighed in the Balance*.

18. "Paine Institute, Augusta, Georgia: Under the Auspice of The Methodist Episcopal Church, South, and the Colored Methodist Episcopal Church in America." Manuscript, Archives, and Rare Book Library, Emory University.

19. T. J. Upton, "Report of Special Committee on Paine Institute, Appointed by Louisiana Conference," *NOCA*, February 9, 1888. See also W. C. Dunlap, "A Statement and Plea to Southern Methodists," *NOCA*, February 19, 1885; "Paine Institute," *NOCA*, January 28, 1886.

20. Haygood, *Our Brother in Black*, 129. On critiques of black enfranchisement amid positive statements of black Christians' voting record on temperance, see A. G. Haygood, "Educate the Voter," *Christian Index*, January 21, 1888.

21. Christian Keener, "The Negro Bonanza-Extravaganza," *NOCA*, February 23, 1882.

22. J. W. Medlock, "'Extravaganza,'" *NOCA*, March 16, 1882; Haygood, *Our Brother in Black*.

23. Gilderoy [Robert Gilderoy Porter], "Educating the Negro," *NOCA*, January 25, 1883. Porter quoted Acts 10:34–35 (King James Version).

24. Gilderoy, "Educating the Negro"; Haygood, *Our Brother in Black*; Charles Galloway, quoted in P. A. Johnston, "The Race Problem," *NOCA*, September 26, 1889. I first found these *NOCA* citations in Walter M. Lowrey Papers, Centenary College of Louisiana. On teaching in black schools as a solution to white unemployment, see C. K. Marshall, "The Education of Freedmen," *NOCA*, January 18, 1883.

25. T. J. Upton, "Report of Special Committee on Paine Institute, Appointed by Louisiana Conference," *NOCA*, February 9, 1888.

26. *Minutes of the Seventh Session of the North Mississippi Annual Conference*, 26, 54–55; BAP.

27. *Minutes of the Seventh Session of the North Mississippi Annual Conference*, 26, 12, 63; BAP.

28. *Minutes of the Seventh Session of the North Mississippi Annual Conference*, 7; BAP.

29. *Minutes of the Seventh Session of the North Mississippi Annual Conference*, 18; BAP. For Abbey's biographical information (and the spelling of his name as Abbey, rather than Abby), see *Journal of the Sixteenth Annual Session of the Mississippi Annual Conference*, 4–6; BAP.

30. [Untitled editorial], *Christian Index*, January 28, 1888.

31. [Untitled editorial], *Christian Index*, January 21, 1888. For similar claims, see below; also [Untitled editorial], *Christian Index*, August 13, 1887. The use of the phrase "brother in black" referred to Haygood, *Our Brother in Black*, 1881.

32. [Untitled editorial], *Christian Index*, May 28, 1887.

33. "Color and Christ," *SWCA*, August 31, 1882.

34. "A Few Words About the Race," *Christian Index*, July 28, 1888. The article began with an extended quotation from an article in the *Gallatin Examiner*. For a similar critique of a white newspaper editorial, this time in the *Nashville Daily American*, see "Let Justice Be Rendered," *Christian Index*, January 26, 1889. The Mississippi state constitution of 1868 promised that all children ages five to twenty-one must be provided free education at least four months of the year. A similar provision in the 1870 Tennessee state constitution specified racial segregation in the state-funded schools: Article XI, Section 12: "No school . . . shall allow white and negro children to be received as scholars together in the same school." *Constitution of the State of Tennessee*.

35. "How Is This?" *Christian Index*, April 6, 1889.

36. "Good for a Darkey," *Christian Index*, January 21, 1888.

37. [Untitled editorial], *Christian Index*, February 4, 1888. The use of the phrase "brother in black" referred to Haygood, *Our Brother in Black*. The editorial was unsigned, but Ida B. Wells criticized Moody on this point; see Giddings, *Ida*, 94–96.

38. E. W. Moseley, "The New Exodus Scheme," *Christian Index*, February 4, 1888. This depiction of enslaved people during the Civil War was popular, but false. See chapter 1.

39. "Civil Rights," *SWCA*, November 1, 1883.

40. John N. Daniel, "Our Only Hope," *Christian Index*, February 26, 1887.

41. E. W. Moseley, "The New Exodus Scheme," *Christian Index*, February 4, 1888; "The Negro," *Christian Index*, August 6, 1887.

42. "Young People's Literary Society," *Christian Index*, February 4, 1888; Mrs. A. C. Mc-Neely, "W.M.S. in Arkansas," *Christian Index*, July 20, 1889; "Our Woman's Missionary Society," *Christian Index*, February 11, 1888; Jennie E. Lane, "The Woman's Missionary Society," *Christian Index*, March 24, 1888. On black women in missionary societies and their employments, see Deborah Gray White, "The Cost of Club Work, the Price of Black Feminism," in Hewitt and Lebsock, eds., *Visible Women*, 247–69. On the shibboleths of the "lady" and its class and racial connotations, see Higginbotham, "African-American Women's History." On women's historical writing, see Mrs. J. R. Rogers, "An Essay Read on Children's," *Christian Index*, August 6, 1887; Mary J. Gary, "A Glance at the History of the C.M.E. Church," *Christian Index*, September 17, 1887. On black women's historical writing, especially that designed for children, see Maffly-Kipp, *Setting Down the Sacred Past*, 234–75.

43. *Minutes of the Sixteenth Annual Session of the Louisiana Conference*, 8–9; BAP. Julius Bailey has explored the role of family devotion and women's religious work in the home within the AME Church. Bailey, *Around the Family Altar*.

44. *Minutes of the Seventh Session of the North Mississippi Annual Conference,* 59; BAP. Temperance societies were ubiquitous in most Methodist and Baptist groups in these years. Matthew Harper has argued that for many black Protestants, temperance and prohibition should not be seen primarily as a project of respectability, but as a deeply pious effort. Harper, *The End of Days,* 98–127. On black Christian women's respectability, see Higginbotham, *Righteous Discontent. Christian Index* was full of articles on the evils of alcohol and the importance of abstaining from drink and of supporting temperance and prohibition efforts. These articles included poems, songs, short stories, scientific literature, and more. Many were copied directly from other religious periodicals or WCTU materials with little reference to racial or regional specificity. Among others, see "Miss Willard's Centennial Address," *Christian Index,* November 1, 1885; "Alcohol and Health," *Christian Index,* January 7, 1887; H. R. Smith, "The Evils of Strong Drink," *Christian Index,* January 15, 1887; Rebecca M. Gray, "Temperance," *Christian Index,* March 19, 1887; "Why She Refused," *Christian Index,* September 10, 1887; "Alcohol's Latitudes," *Christian Index,* September 17, 1887; "Women and Drink," *Christian Index,* September 24, 1887; "Temperance in Africa," *Christian Index,* October 1, 1887; "Baby's Shoes," *Christian Index,* October 22, 1887; "Woman Workers," *Christian Index,* October 22, 1887; "True Heroism," *Christian Index,* November 5, 1887; "The Saloon in Politics," *Christian Index,* November 12, 1887; "A Mother's Influence," *Christian Index,* November 26, 1887; "A Veritable Leech," *Christian Index,* December 5, 1887; "From the Standpoint of Labor," *Christian Index,* December 3, 1887; "Drunkenness and Lying," *Christian Index,* December 10, 1887; "Can Whisky Talk?" *Christian Index,* December 10, 1887; "The Captain's Pledge," *Christian Index,* January 14, 1888; "It Is Prohibition," *Christian Index,* June 9, 1888; "God and the Liquor Traffic," *Christian Index,* December 15, 1888.

45. "The Colored People and Moral Reforms," *SWCA,* January 19, 1882; [Untitled editorial], *SWCA,* October 5, 1882; "What Are We Coming To?" *SWCA,* August 31, 1882. There are no extant copies of *The People's Adviser,* published monthly in Jackson, Mississippi.

46. "News and Notes," *Christian Index,* February 2, 1889; A. G. Haygood, "Educate the Voter," *Christian Index,* January 21, 1888. The former article pointed out that South Carolina's voter rolls had shrunk, suggesting increased disenfranchisement of black men. See also "Prohibition in Tennessee," *Christian Index,* April 2, 1887; W. G. Foster, "Bartlett, Tenn.," *Christian Index,* July 8, 1887; "A Glorious Resurrection," *Christian Index,* May 21, 1887.

47. "Election at Jackson, Miss.: A Significant Election," *Christian Index,* January 21, 1887; [Untitled editorial], *Christian Index,* January 21, 1888.

48. [Untitled editorial], *Christian Index,* July 28, 1888; [Untitled editorials], *Christian Index,* August 18, 1888.

49. "Shall They Be Forgotten or Left Out," *Christian Index,* February 2, 1889; "Clippings About the Negro," *Christian Index,* February 9, 1889. These articles both called for Republicans to include black men in appointed positions.

50. [Untitled editorial], *Christian Index,* April 13, 1889.

51. "Multiple New Items," *SWCA,* December 5, 1889.

52. As an editorial indicated, "The Southern Negro is beginning to ask, 'What became of my vote. [*sic*] Why was it not counted?' A voice whispers, 'it was not for the right party.'" [Untitled editorial], *Christian Index,* November 17, 1888.

53. The Methodist Episcopal Church did not identify ministers by race on principle. I have no written statement of Rev. Burrell L. Crump's racial identity, but given his access to this scene, he must have been white. Various Methodist Episcopal Church conference reports indicate that Crump was a minister (and, after 1891, a presiding elder) in Mississippi from at least 1879 to 1900. *Minutes of the Annual Conferences of the Methodist Episcopal Church, Spring Conference 1879,* 7; *Report of the Board of Education of the Methodist Episcopal Church to the General Conference of 1880,* 86; *Minutes of the Annual Conferences of the Methodist Episcopal Church, Spring Conference 1899,* 11; *Minutes of the Annual Conferences of the Methodist Episcopal Church, Spring Conference 1889,* 14; *Minutes of the Annual Conferences of the Methodist Episcopal Church, Spring Conference 1891,* 9; *Minutes of the Annual Conferences of the Methodist Episcopal Church, Spring Conference 1899,* 14; *Minutes of the Annual Conferences of the Methodist Episcopal Church, Spring Conference 1900,* 25.

54. B. L. Crump, "Lynching in a Churchyard on Sunday," *SWCA,* August 6, 1885. His letter was dated July 12, 1885, and referred to the events that happened "last Sunday evening," from which I conclude that the events happened on Sunday, July 6, 1885. Amy Louise Wood opened her chapter on lynching and religion with the story of this lynching, as narrated in the Memphis *Commercial Appeal.* The victim is named Harris Tunstal in her account, and the timing of his lynching is the morning rather than the evening. Nevertheless, all the pertinent details match, including Tunstal's request for prayer. Wood, *Lynching and Spectacle,* 45–47.

55. B. L. Crump, "Lynching in a Churchyard on Sunday," *SWCA,* August 6, 1885; "The Oxford Lynching," *SWCA,* August 6, 1885. The portrait of a soon-to-be martyred Christian speaking to the assembled crowd drew upon the sermon delivered by Stephen in Acts 7. Protestant martyrs had long been a celebrated part of American religious culture, especially in the memory of England's Protestant martyrs recorded in Foxe's *Book of Martyrs.* Weimer, *The Martyr's Mirror.*

56. "A Few Days Ago Dispatches from Mississippi," *SWCA,* April 21, 1881; "Birmingham, Alabama Has Been the Scene," *SWCA,* December 13, 1883; "Political Review," *SWCA,* March 4, 1886.

57. "A Correspondent from Sturges Station," *SWCA,* August 22, 1880. All emphasis original.

58. "The Year Closes as It Began," *SWCA,* December 30, 1886.

59. W. W. Thompson, "Feeling That Should Exist Between the Two Races," *Christian Index,* July 20, 1889.

60. Haygood, "The Crime of Lynching," *Christian Index,* June 9, 1888.

61. "Is the Pulpit Afraid?" *SWCA,* February 14, 1889. Much of this article reprinted portions of an article by Atticus Haygood published by the *Wesleyan.*

62. "The Carrollton Tragedy," *NOCA,* March 25, 1886. See also "The Carrollton Tragedy Again," *NOCA,* April 1, 1886. The latter article quoted from the Jackson, Mississippi, *Clarion* as evidence that many white-run local papers in Mississippi also condemned the actions.

63. "Political Review," *SWCA,* April 1, 1886. See also "Political Review," *SWCA,* April 8, 1886; "The Carrollton Tragedy," *SWCA,* April 22, 1886. This last article quoted the *Atlanta Constitution*'s condemnation of the Carrollton massacre.

64. "Political Review," *SWCA,* April 22, 1888.

65. "These Clouds Have Silver Linings," *SWCA*, April 22, 1888. Gad was one of the sons that Jacob conceived with Zilpah, the servant of his first wife Leah, with whom Leah encouraged Jacob to have additional children. Leah named the son Gad, which could mean "troop" or "good fortune." See Genesis 30:9–11 (King James Version). In the Hebrew Bible, there are plays on the name Gad as a term meaning troop and good fortune, and as a term that sounds like the word for raiders or enemies, such as the final patriarchal blessing that Jacob gives before his death. See Genesis 49:19 (King James Version). The final biblical quote comes from Psalm 30:5 (King James Version). The quote was not attributed, but the use of the archaic verb form "cometh" would have indicated to the reader that it was a quote from the King James Version of the Bible.

66. [Untitled editorial], *Christian Index*, May 24, 1888.

67. "Lynch Law," *Christian Index*, January 21, 1888.

68. "Here It Comes Again," *Christian Index*, January 28, 1888. See also "Southern Justice," *Christian Index*, March 9, 1889; [Untitled editorial], *Christian Index*, March 30, 1889.

69. "A Talk with a Man Who Laughs," *SWCA*, April 20, 1882; "Color and Christ," *SWCA*, August 31, 1882; [Untitled editorial], *Christian Index*, January 28, 1888.

70. [Untitled editorial], *Christian Index*, January 28, 1888.

71. Both the *Christian Index* and *SWCA* published marriage announcements. Some listed only the names of the couple, but others described elegant ceremonies attended by guests bearing fine gifts for the newly married couple. For the latter style of announcement, see, among others, "Social," *SWCA*, April 22, 1886; "Wedding Bells," *Christian Index*, September 3, 1887; "A Fashionable Wedding," *Christian Index*, July 7, 1888; [Untitled editorial], *Christian Index*, June 8, 1889.

72. E[lias] Cottrell, "An Address, Delivered by Rev. E. Cottrell," *Christian Index*, August 10, 1889.

Chapter Five

1. *Journal of the Proceedings of the Constitutional Convention, of the State of Mississippi*, 3.

2. Among many newspaper accounts showing widespread understanding of the constitutional convention's goal of legal black disenfranchisement, see "The Negroes," *New Mississippian* (Jackson, MS), June 25, 1890; "Suffrage Problem in Mississippi," *Daily Picayune* (New Orleans, LA), August 23, 1890; "Mississippi's Constitution," *New Mississippian*, September 10, 1890; "The Suffrage Question," *Daily Picayune*, September 15, 1890; "The Franchise," *New Mississippian*, October 8, 1890.

3. Charles B. Galloway was seen as a moderate on issues of race and an advocate of black education, for which he earned praise from disparate groups. He worked with black ministers to advance temperance and prohibition work and eventually opposed lynching, yet he steadfastly opposed black franchise and advocated for legal segregation. See chapter 4 and below. Wilson, *Baptized in Blood*.

4. *Journal of the Proceedings of the Constitutional Convention, of the State of Mississippi*, 3–4.

5. On the second day, the convention approved a resolution inviting "the clergymen of the city" to offer an opening prayer each day. While the record did not state this explicitly, only white Protestants would have been included in this cadre of ministers. *Journal of the Proceedings of the Constitutional Convention, of the State of Mississippi*, 18. The subsequent

prayers were not recorded in the convention journal, but the name of the minister who opened the proceedings in prayer appeared in each day's minutes. They were W. C. Black, J. E. Gore, John Hunter, D. A. Little, and Irvin Miller. Hunter was a Southern Presbyterian minister and Black was a Southern Methodist, but there were not extant any biographical details for the other ministers.

6. Article XII: Franchise, Sections 243 and 244 contained the primary tools that would be used to disenfranchise black voters, but other sections of the article also made registering to vote more difficult, particularly if one had moved from another state or another part of the state. "Sec. 243. A uniform poll tax of two dollars, to be used in aid of the common schools, and for no other purpose, is hereby imposed on every male inhabitant of this State between the ages of twenty-one and sixty years. . . . Sec. 244. On and after the first day of January, A.D., 1892, every elector shall, in addition to the foregoing qualifications, be able to read any section of the constitution of this State; or he shall be able to understand the same when read to him, or give a reasonable interpretation thereof. A new registration shall be made before the next ensuing election after January the first, A.D., 1892." *Constitution of the State of Mississippi, Adopted November 1, 1890*, 37–38.

7. *Journal of the Proceedings of the Constitutional Convention, of the State of Mississippi*, 228.

8. "Political Review," *SWCA*, August 21, 1890; "Political Review," *SWCA*, August 28, 1890. The eventual resolution of this issue with poll taxes and literacy tests appeared in "Political Review," *SWCA*, September 25, 1890, only days after the delegates' day of prayer.

9. On northern white citizens' acquiescence to white supremacist policies and their abandoning earlier defense of black rights, see Blum, *Reforging the White Republic*; Blight, *Race and Reunion*.

10. *Minutes of the Fifteenth Session of the South Arkansas Annual Conference*, 26; BAP. Among other AME Church voices on education, see *Journal and Reports of the Ninth Session of the North Louisiana Annual Conference*, 28; BAP.

11. *Minutes of the Twenty-Sixth Annual Session*, 18, 20; BAP.

12. *Minutes of the Twenty-Sixth Annual Session*, 47–48; BAP.

13. *Minutes of the Twenty-Sixth Annual Session*, 44; BAP.

14. H. R. Revels, "Race Problem," *SWCA*, April 24, 1890. On Revels's evolution, see Thompson, *Black Life in Mississippi*.

15. O. C. R. Strayer, "A Letter from a Southerner to a Southerner: Proposed Solution of the Race Problem," *Christian Index*, February 6, 1892. Other defenses of black political rights or criticisms of their deprivation of rights include the following selected articles from a much smaller group than were found in these papers in the 1880s. "Our Political Leader," *Christian Index*, July 2, 1892; "Mississippi Plan," *Christian Index*, August 20, 1892; Frederick Douglass and Ida B. Wells, "To the Friends of Equal Rights," *Christian Index*, May 20, 1893; R. T. Brown, "The Negroes' Equal Rights," *Christian Index*, April 21, 1894; "In League with Evil," *SWCA*, October 31, 1895; "Our Thanksgiving," *SWCA*, November 28, 1895; H. M. Murphy, "Our Contributors," *SWCA*, April 13, 1899.

16. "A Halt Is Called in Alabama," *SWCA*, May 25, 1899; "Race Gleanings," *Christian Index*, October 6, 1894.

17. H. T. Moss, "Influence of Intellectual Pursuits," *Christian Index*, May 3, 1890; "Less Politics," *Christian Index*, August 27, 1892; W. D. Godman, "Education," *SWCA*, August 24, 1893.

18. "Obstacles to Race Progress," *SWCA*, June 11, 1891; "Ex-Senator Ingalls on 'The Negro Question,'" *SWCA*, April 20, 1893.

19. "The Negro in Politics," *Christian Index*, August 16, 1890. A later article defended the Tennessee Republican Party's efforts to organize black voters for the upcoming election. In doing so, the article avoided any broader defense of readers' political rights. "What Is There Wrong About It?" *Christian Index*, October 25, 1890. When describing the work of Baptist ministers in Louisiana throughout the nineteenth century, slavery and freedom were mentioned repeatedly, but none of Hicks's many biographical portraits indicate that any minister had been involved in political activities. Hicks, *History of Louisiana Negro Baptists*.

20. "Blessings to the Negro in Disguise," *Christian Index*, February 19, 1898.

21. H. T. Moss, "The Educated Minister a Failure?" *Christian Index*, June 26, 1890; C. H. Phillips, "The Signs of the Times," *Christian Index*, August 16, 1890; W. S. Rollins, "The Minister," *SWCA*, April 7, 1892; M. C. Nisbet, "Education," *Christian Index*, April 1, 1893; "Bishop Galloway," *Christian Index*, August 25, 1894.

22. Iola, "The Place for Training," *Christian Index*, February 1, 1890; G. W. Spearman, "We Agree with Iola," *Christian Index*, February 22, 1890; "Our Young People," *Christian Index*, March 15, 1890; "Educate Your Children," *Christian Index*, March 22, 1890; A. H. Campbell, "Home Education," *SWCA*, September 25, 1890; Mrs. W. H. Keller, "Shall We Educate?" *SWCA*, June 8, 1893; G. W. Sprallman, "Educate Your Girls," *Christian Index*, January 6, 1894. (The last name of this author is obscured by damage to the page; I have re-created it as best I could.) On the need for public education and thus white support of black education, see "The Needs of a More Thorough System of Public Education," *Christian Index*, July 26, 1890; "Tired of Being Made a Catspaw," *SWCA*, July 3, 1890; T. A. Burkhalter, "Why Is the Education of the Negro Impossible?" *Christian Index*, January 24, 1891; "Negro Education," *Christian Index*, January 27, 1894; "Southern Education," *SWCA*, February 21, 1895; "Education for the Negro," *SWCA*, January 9, 1896.

23. "Education," *SWCA*, October 20, 1892; "The Importance of Education," *SWCA*, May 4, 1893.

24. "Booker T. Washington," *Christian Index*, January 29, 1898. See also "Industrial Education," *SWCA*, July 23, 1891; "An Apostle of Industrial Education," *SWCA*, April 18, 1895; "The Tuskegee Negro Conference," *SWCA*, March 12, 1896; "Booker T. Washington," *Christian Index*, July 16, 1898.

25. William Russell to Susie Ford Bailey, Helena, Arkansas, September 2, 1895. Bailey Family Papers, box 1, folder 5, MARBL, Emory University; Alida Clark to Susie Ford Bailey, Helena, Arkansas, March 7, 1887. Bailey Family Papers, box 1, folder 5, MARBL, Emory University.

26. "Southland College: 1864–1895, Brief Sketch of Thirty Years of Missionary Labor at Southland College," 1895, 13, 11. Brochure contained in Lives Transformed: The People of Southland College, Digital Collection of University of Arkansas Library, Fayetteville, http://digitalcollections.uark.edu/cdm/ref/collection/Southland/id/17.

27. W. E. B. Du Bois first publicized the concept of the "Talented Tenth" of black elites and leaders. W. E. B. Du Bois, "The Talented Tenth," in Washington et al., *The Negro Problem*. Women's creation of a "politics of respectability," especially by a "female talented tenth," has been a major area of focus for histories of African American women and religion since the publication of Evelyn B. Higginbotham's influential work on women in the

National Baptist Convention. Victoria Wolcott built on these ideas in a later period. Higginbotham, *Righteous Discontent*; Wolcott, *Remaking Respectability.*

28. Mrs. M. L. Halle, "Progress of the Race," *Christian Index*, July 2, 1892. The discussion of trimming lamps invokes a New Testament parable in which wise women kept their lamps ready, and foolish women let their lamps burn out; Matthew 25:1–13. A. E. P. Albert, "Emancipation Address," *SWCA*, January 16, 1890; "Echoes from the January 1 Emancipation Celebration," *SWCA*, January 23, 1890; "Whence and Whither?" *Christian Index*, February 10, 1894; Miss H. B. Hamilton, "Twenty Six Years of Progress," *Christian Index*, October 24, 1891; "The Progress and Ambition," *Christian Index*, May 6, 1893; [Untitled editorial], *Christian Index*, May 13, 1893; "Two Southern Witnesses," *SWCA*, June 16, 1898. Laurie Maffly-Kipp has described black churchwomen's work in constructing race histories in this period through novels, church pageants, and children's literature. Maffly-Kipp, *Setting Down the Sacred Past*, 234–75.

29. "Influence of Woman," *Christian Index*, April 26, 1890; "Womanhood," *Christian Index*, July 18, 1891; Mary M. Jackson, "Women's Work and Worth," *Christian Index*, January 6, 1894; Clara A. Teague, "Woman's Dominion," *SWCA*, November 11, 1897; "Man's Helpmeet," *Christian Index*, February 12, 1898; H. W. Madison, "Marriage Relations," *Christian Index*, September 15, 1894. From the context, the latter two articles appear to be authored by men.

30. A. Brown, "The Preacher's Wife," *SWCA*, October 8, 1891. This article was reprinted from a speech Rev. Brown delivered to his district conference, making it one written by a minister for other ministers.

31. Mrs. L. A. Winbush, "The Preacher's Wife on the Work," *SWCA*, December 22, 1892; Mrs. Laura Hamilton, "The Preacher's Wife in the Sunday School, and Her Duty," *SWCA*, November 16, 1893.

32. E. M. Carter, "Woman's Missionary Society of the C.M.E. Church," *Christian Index*, July 5, 1890; "To the Woman's Missionary Society," *Christian Index*, February 26, 1898.

33. Iola, "The Place for Training," *Christian Index*, February 1, 1890; G. W. Spearman, "We Agree with Iola," *Christian Index*, February 22, 1890; "Our Young People," *Christian Index*, March 15, 1890. The *SWCA* published a weekly "Woman's Dominion" column from 1897 to 1899 that included a variety of topics, often reprinted from national publications. Additionally, an "About Women" column appeared weekly through most of 1898 in the *Christian Index*. It reprinted discussions of national groups like the Woman's Christian Temperance Union as well as instructions for women's duties to their families and churches.

34. Mary B. Mullin, "A Mother's Work," *SWCA*, November 15, 1894. See Mark 16:1–8 and John 20:1–18 (King James Version).

35. Mary B. Mullin, "A Mother's Work," *SWCA*, November 15, 1894; "Cleanliness and Godliness," *Christian Index*, March 4, 1893.

36. "Clean Topics in the Home," *SWCA*, January 7, 1897. This focus on household and religious cleanliness resonates with Anthea Butler's work on Baptist and Holiness women of a similar period. Butler, "'Only a Woman Would Do'"; Butler, *Women in the Church of God in Christ.*

37. J. C., "The Hepler-Mebane Wedding," *SWCA*, July 8, 1897; "Married," *Christian Index*, January 18, 1890; F. Parker, "Lewis-Jones Wedding," *Christian Index*, July 2, 1898; "Marriages," *SWCA*, June 19, 1890; "The Wedding Bells," *Christian Index*, May 28, 1898. The adapted biblical passage came from Psalm 133:1ff: "Behold! How good and pleasant it is for

brethren to dwell together in unity." The remainder of the psalm was quoted verbatim in the article, "Hymenial," *SWCA*, July 5, 1894. The phrase "conspicuous consumption" comes from the 1899 social analysis, Veblen, *The Theory of the Leisure Class*. See also "Marriage in High Circles," *Christian Index*, October 3, 1891; "Marriages," *SWCA*, December 22, 1892; "Marriages," *SWCA*, November 1, 1894; "Marriages," *SWCA*, July 12, 1894.

38. [Untitled editorial], *Christian Index*, March 14, 1891; "Travel in the South," *SWCA*, November 19, 1891. See also "Our People Protest Against the 'Jim Crow' Car," *SWCA*, May 29, 1890; "The Jim Crow Car Must Go," *SWCA*, October 29, 1891; W. H. Strickland and I. E. Stearnes, "The 'Jim Crow' Car Must Go," *SWCA*, January 7, 1892; C. H. Phillips, "Fighting the Separate Coach System," *Christian Index*, February 13, 1892; [Untitled editorial], *Christian Index*, May 14, 1892; "Separate Coach Law," *Christian Index*, January 15, 1898; "Race Discrimination on Railroads," *SWCA*, November 14, 1889.

39. "Horrible Crimes!" *SWCA*, September 21, 1893.

40. Wells's strong denunciation of lynching in 1892 forced her to flee Memphis to live the rest of her life in the urban North. Gail Bederman has argued that Wells reframed lynching as a demonstration of white men's uncivilized lack of restraint, so that northern journalists came to view lynching not as a justified attack on black criminals but as a sign of the failure of white civilization. As I build on her work, I show that many other black Christians besides Wells denounced lynching in this way in the southern religious press, including the often-conservative *Christian Index*. Jacqueline Hall showed that no large group of southern whites would oppose lynching until white southern women led by Jessie Daniel Ames did so in the 1930s. Other historians have stressed the modernity of these public displays of racial terror, including the consumer trade in photographs of lynched bodies and even body parts from those killed. Wells, *Southern Horrors*; Wells, *A Red Record*; Bederman, *Manliness and Civilization*, 45–76; Hall, *Revolt Against Chivalry*; Hale, *Making Whiteness*, 199–240; Carrigan, ed., *Lynching Reconsidered*; Feimster, *Southern Horrors*; Wood, *Lynching and Spectacle*; Rushdy, *American Lynching*.

41. E. S. Foreman, "Shall Lynching Be Stopped?" *SWCA*, December 20, 1894; [Untitled editorial], *SWCA*, April 7, 1892.

42. "Crimes Against a Race," *SWCA*, September 15, 1892. Numerous articles listed details of mob violence that occurred around the region: "Negro Lynching," *Christian Index*, July 9, 1892; "Mob Violence," *Christian Index*, July 16, 1892; "Another Burning," *SWCA*, April 20, 1893; "White Caps Sentenced," *Christian Index*, May 13, 1893; "As to the So-Called Investigation in Jefferson Parish," *SWCA*, October 26, 1893; "The Gallant March of the Posse," *SWCA*, November 9, 1893; "White Caps Murder a Negro in Tennessee," *SWCA*, April 5, 1894; "A Fearful Arraignment," *SWCA*, June 28, 1894; "Race Gleanings," *Christian Index*, July 7, 1894; "Oh, Lord! How Long?" *SWCA*, August 2, 1894; "Race Gleanings," *Christian Index*, August 25, 1894; "Lynchings Must Stop," *SWCA*, September 13, 1894; W. R. Patterson, "Appeals to the Manhood of Southern White People," *SWCA*, September 13, 1894; "Lynching Redivivus," *SWCA*, October 25, 1894; "Our Nation's Disgrace," *SWCA*, January 17, 1895; "More Lynching," *SWCA*, June 13, 1895; "Lynchings North and South," *Christian Index*, June 19, 1897; [Untitled editorial], *Christian Index*, January 22, 1898.

43. J. C. Lewis, "The Crime of Lynching," *SWCA*, April 20, 1899; "Lynch Law in the South," *SWCA*, July 28, 1892; "That Great Lynching Near Memphis," *Christian Index*, September 15, 1894; "The Jefferson Parish Lynching," *SWCA*, September 28, 1893.

44. J. B. Middleton, "The Present Aspects of the Race Question," *SWCA*, June 8, 1893; "Children's Watch Tower" *SWCA*, September 21, 1893. See also "In Our Defense," *SWCA*, December 12, 1895; H. M. Murphy, "How Shall We Hold On?" *SWCA*, April 13, 1899.

45. "The Half Not Told," *SWCA*, August 31, 1893; "A Clerical Slanderer," *SWCA*, August 16, 1894; "That Great Lynching Near Memphis," *Christian Index*, September 15, 1894; "That Lynching Again," *Christian Index*, September 22, 1894; "The Jefferson Parish Lynching," *SWCA*, September 28, 1893; "The Growth of a Better Sentiment in Favor of the Negro," *SWCA*, April 27, 1893; "Southern View of the Lynch Code," *SWCA*, December 7, 1893. See also "In League with Evil," *SWCA*, October 31, 1895. For other calls for white Christians to reject lynching as incompatible with Christianity and to use their significant influence to end the practice, see "Report of Committee on State of the Church," *SWCA*, July 14, 1892; N. H. Speight, "Race Pride," *SWCA*, October 19, 1893; John Braden, "Thou Shalt Not Kill," *SWCA*, September 20, 1894.

46. [Untitled editorial], *Christian Index*, July 4, 1891; "'Is It Just?'" *SWCA*, August 23, 1894; "Looking Backward," *SWCA*, January 26, 1893.

47. "The Jefferson Parish Lynching," *SWCA*, September 28, 1893. These sentences in the article were quoted from the *Chicago Inter-Ocean* and included with additional editorial comments in the *Southwestern Christian Advocate*. Stowe, *Uncle Tom's Cabin*.

48. "Brutalizing a Race," *SWCA*, September 28, 1893. For efforts to oppose lynching by quoting Mrs. Jefferson Davis, see L. J. S. Bell, "The Negro and His Late Master," *SWCA*, June 22, 1893.

49. "Race Gleanings," *Christian Index*, August 25, 1894; "A Bishop Disgraces Himself," *SWCA*, June 9, 1892.

50. J. W. Hudson and W. S. Harris, "Resolutions Passed by the New Orleans Preachers' Meeting," *SWCA*, May 4, 1893; "The Proposed Day of Fasting," *SWCA*, May 11, 1893. See also "Thanksgiving and Invocation Day," *SWCA*, May 25, 1893; "The Lord Reigneth!" *SWCA*, June 1, 1893. There were similar days of prayer called in 1892 and 1893.

51. "Lesson from the Day of Prayer," *SWCA*, June 16, 1892; "Brutalizing a Race," *SWCA*, September 28, 1893; "Sowing to the Whirlwind," *SWCA*, January 5, 1893. The internal quotations were from Romans 2:5 and Song of Solomon 6:10, respectively (King James Version). See also J. C. Lewis, "The Crime of Lynching," *SWCA*, April 20, 1899.

52. "Sowing to the Whirlwind," *SWCA*, January 5, 1893; "Oh, Lord! How Long?" *SWCA*, August 2, 1894. For similar biblical cries of lamentation, see Psalm 6:3; Psalm 13:1, Psalm 35:17, and Psalm 80:4 (King James Version).

53. "Brutalizing a Race," *SWCA*, September 28, 1893.

54. "Our Thanksgiving," *SWCA*, November 28, 1895. "Blessed are they which are persecuted for righteousness' sake: for theirs is the kingdom of heaven." Matthew 5:10 (King James Version). The second-century Christian writer Tertullian is credited with the statement that "the blood of the martyrs is the seed of the church." The Protestant embrace of the idea dates back to the Reformation and could be seen in the legacy of Foxe's *Book of Martyrs*. On the translation of these ideas across the Atlantic in early America, see Weimer, *The Martyr's Mirror*.

55. David Chappell has argued that black Christians' prophetic lament against white racism protected them from the naïveté of liberal whites who underestimated southern

whites' opposition to black citizens' equal civil and political rights. Chappell, *A Stone of Hope*.

56. Harrison, *The Gospel Among the Slaves*, 26–28. Harrison noted that most of the primary sources he reprinted had been collected by Miss Annie Marie Barnes, further indicating white women's role in memorializing fictions of antebellum history, but Harrison supplied the commentary linking theses many antebellum and postemancipation sources. Harrison, *The Gospel Among the Slaves*, 3.

57. Harrison, *The Gospel Among the Slaves*, 300.

58. Harrison, *The Gospel Among the Slaves*, 318, 394, 387–88.

59. Holsey, *Autobiography, Sermons, Addresses and Essays*,10, 5–7. See Eskew, "Black Elitism."

60. Between 1895 and 1897, the minutes of the Louisiana Annual Conferences indicated between five and fifteen "Colored Members" alongside 28,000–29,000 white members. The 1898 minutes counted "White Members" and "Local Preachers" but omitted "Colored Members." In 1899, the minutes simply noted "Members." *Minutes of the Louisiana Annual Conference, Methodist Episcopal Church, South, Fiftieth Session*, 5; *Minutes of the Louisiana Annual Conference, Methodist Episcopal Church, South, Fifty-First Session*, 5; *Minutes of the Louisiana Annual Conference, Methodist Episcopal Church, South, Fifty-Second Session*, 5; *Minutes of the Louisiana Annual Conference, Methodist Episcopal Church, South, Fifty-Third Session*, 5; *Minutes of the Louisiana Annual Conference, Methodist Episcopal Church, South, Fifty-Fourth Session*, 5.

61. Leavell and Bailey, *A Complete History of Mississippi Baptists*, 61, 618; Jewell, *History of Methodism in Arkansas*, 382. Both works abound with the minutiae typical of local denominational histories. The authors recount persecutions that their denomination faced from other Christian groups, celebrated individual prominent ministers, and underlined the importance of seemingly minor theological disputes. Black Baptists appeared only in a brief appendix near the end of Volume 2 of Leavell and Bailey's work. Leavell and Bailey, *A Complete History of Mississippi Baptists*, 1449–58. Black Methodists similarly appeared in a concluding chapter of Jewell's work.

62. See chapter 1. For her United Daughters of the Confederacy work and financial ruin after the Civil War, see Broussard, *Stepping Lively in Place*, 185–87. On the UDC, see Janney, *Burying the Dead but Not the Past*; Cox, *Dixie's Daughters*.

63. "Speech at Park's Grove, August 28, 1897," Fontaine Richard Earle Papers, University of Arkansas–Fayetteville; McCurry, *Confederate Reckoning*.

64. Galloway, *The South and the Negro*, 6, 9.

65. Galloway, *The South and the Negro*, 7–8.

66. Quincy Ewing, "How Can Lynching be Checked in the South?" *The Outlook*, October 12, 1901. *The Outlook* was a New York–based Christian periodical of the American Sabbath Tract Society. Ewing prefaced these statements with arguments for why northern whites were implicated in lynching, arguing that northern whites should not feel morally superior to southern whites. His earlier sermon had been quoted in a previous editorial in *The Outlook* against lynching. In it, he called for the state legislature to levy a tax on any county where a lynching occurred and for any sheriff who surrendered a prisoner to a mob to be removed from office. "The Epidemic of Savagery," *The Outlook*, September 7, 1901. Jacqueline Dowd Hall wrote the definitive work on Jessie Daniel Ames's work. Hall, *Revolt Against Chivalry*.

Conclusion

1. First quoted in Gilmore, *Gender and Jim Crow*, 201; Brown, "Speaking Up for the Race at Memphis, Tennessee, October 8, 1920," in Lerner, ed., *Black Women in White America*, 467–72.

2. Rev. Samuel G. Wright to Rev. George Whipple, Natchez, Mississippi, March 9, 1864, AMA Archives, 71610; J. W. McNeil, "The Colored Methodist Episcopal Church of America," *NOCA*, December 6, 1877; *Constitution of the State of Mississippi*, Article XIV, Section 263. On the centrality of sex and gender in the creation of white supremacy, see Hodes, *White Women, Black Men*; Hale, *Making Whiteness*.

3. Examining antislavery Christians' arguments that slavery as an institution—rather than the action of individual slaveowners—was sinful, Molly Oshatz places that shift at the center of an intellectual history of liberal Protestantism, offering a corollary to my arguments about how southern proslavery readings transformed conservative Bible-reading practices. Oshatz, *Slavery and Sin*.

4. Wilson, *Baptized in Blood*; Blight, *Race and Reunion*; Blum, *Reforging the White Republic*.

5. Historians have shown that Freedmen's Bureau policies sought to bolster marriage in decisions such as broad declarations that all couples cohabiting on a given date were legally married. These moves clumsily tried to address enslaved people's lack of access to marriage, and they showed that local and state governments preferred households headed by a man who oversaw the labor of his wife and children. Cott, *Public Vows*, 77–104; Bercaw, *Gendered Freedoms*, 117–34; Frankel, *Freedom's Women*, 79–122; O'Donovan, *Becoming Free in the Cotton South*, 193–98.

6. See chapter 5. "Iola's Corner: Mrs. Morrell's Idea," *Christian Index*, March 2, 1889; "Iola's Corner," *Christian Index*, June 29, 1889; "Iola's Corner," *Christian Index*, May 16, 1891; Wells, *Southern Horrors*.

7. Dixon, *The Clansman*; Grimké, *Rachel*; Baker, *Gospel According to the Klan*.

8. Hall, *Revolt Against Chivalry*; Smith, *The Gender of History*; Mitchell, *Gone with the Wind*.

9. Among the voluminous literature on the rise of the religious right, Randall Balmer argues that its origin did not relate to abortion or feminism, but to white Christians' intent to evade civil rights laws against segregation. The argument that feminism and gender norms drove the religious right is more common and can be seen in Seth Dowland, among others. As exceptions to this general trend, Marie Griffith and Jane Dailey have shown that fears of sex across the color line were central to concerns about segregation and sex. Balmer, "Forum"; Dowland, *Family Values*; Griffith, *Moral Combat*; Dailey, "Sex, Segregation, and the Sacred after *Brown*."

10. Du Bois, *The Souls of Black Folk*, vii.

11. Longfield's chapter on Machen's role in Presbyterian fundamentalist conflicts argues that Southern Presbyterianism was Machen's primary influence. His mother, Minnie Gresham Machen, to whom the never-married Machen remained close as an adult, taught him to venerate the Scottish common sense philosophy that proslavery stalwart James Henley Thornwell taught. Her father was an elder in a Southern Presbyterian Church in Macon, Georgia, until his death in 1891. Longfield, *The Presbyterian Controversy*, 28–53.

Bibliography

Archival Sources

Amistad Research Center, Tulane University, New Orleans, LA
  American Missionary Association Archives
  Catalog of the American Missionary Association
Archives and Special Collections, Centenary College of Louisiana, Shreveport, LA
  Minutes of the Louisiana Annual Conference, Methodist Episcopal Church, South, Fiftieth Session, Jackson, La., December 11–16, 1895. New Orleans: Hopkins' Printing Office, n.d.
  Minutes of the Louisiana Annual Conference, Methodist Episcopal Church, South, Fifty-First Session, Ruston, La., December 9–14, 1896. New Orleans: Hopkins' Printing Office, n.d.
  Minutes of the Louisiana Annual Conference, Methodist Episcopal Church, South, Fifty-Second Session, Crowley, La., January 6–10, 1898. New Orleans: Hopkins' Printing Office, n.d.
  Minutes of the Louisiana Annual Conference, Methodist Episcopal Church, South, Fifty-Third Session, Mansfield, La., December 15–19, 1898. New Orleans: Hopkins' Printing Office, n.d.
  Minutes of the Louisiana Annual Conference, Methodist Episcopal Church, South, Fifty-Fourth Session, Monroe, La., December 7–11th, 1899. New Orleans: New Orleans Advocate Print, 1900.
  MS 77, Walter M. Lowrey Papers
Benjamin Arnett Papers, Rembert E. Stokes Library and Information Commons, Wilberforce University, Wilberforce, OH (BAP)
  Johnston, Moses R., Ed. *Louisiana Conference Annual Consisting of Sermons Preached Before the Louisiana Annual Conference of the African M.E. Church, at Its Eleventh Annual Session, Held in New Orleans, La., Commencing January 7th, 1876.* Nashville, TN: Caruthers & Kirk, 1876.
  Journal and Reports of the Ninth Session of the North Louisiana Annual Conference of the African M.E. Church Held in Mount Calvary Chapel, at Homer, La. from December 18th to December 21st, 1890. n.p., n.d.
  Journal of the Sixteenth Annual Session of the Mississippi Annual Conference, African Methodist Episcopal Church, Held in St. Peter's Chapel, A.M.E. Church, Port Gibson, Miss., from December 12 to 19, 1883. Natchez, MS: Democrat Book and Job Print, 1884.
  Minutes of the Eighth Session of the Tennessee Conference of the African Methodist Episcopal Church, Held in Avery Chapel, Memphis, from October 6 to October 14, 1875. Memphis, TN: Price, Jones & Co., 1875.
  Minutes of the Eleventh Annual Conference of the African Methodist Episcopal Church in Louisiana Annual Conference. n.p., January 1876.
  Minutes of the Fifteenth Quadrennial Session of the General Conference of the African Methodist Episcopal, Place of Session, Nashville, Tennessee, May 6, 1872. n.p., n.d.

Minutes of the Fifteenth Session of the South Arkansas Annual Conference of the African Methodist Episcopal Church Held in New Hope A.M.E. Church Holly Grove, Arkansas, Dec. 4th to Dec. 10th, '90. Nashville, TN: Publishing House of the AME Sunday-School Union, 1891.

Minutes of the First Session of the Tennessee Annual Conference of the African Methodist E. Church, Convened as per Appointment in St. John Chapel, Nashville, Tenn., September 10th, 1868, for the Purpose of Organization. Nashville, TN: Press and Times Company's Book and Job Rooms, 1868.

Minutes of the Fourth Session of the West Tennessee Conference of the African Methodist Episcopal Church, Held at Huntington, Tennessee from November 25th–December 1st, 1879. Clarksville, TN: Tobacco Leaf Office, 1880.

Minutes of the Seventh Annual Session of Louisiana Conference African Methodist Episcopal Church, Held in St. James' Chapel, Roman St., Bet. Customhouse and Bienville, New Orleans, January 25th, 1872. n.p., n.d.

Minutes of the Seventh Session of the North Mississippi Annual Conference Held in Bethel A.M.E. Church, in the City of Vicksburg, Mississippi, from January 9th to Jan. 17th A.D. 1884. Vicksburg, MS: Vicksburg Printing and Publishing Company, 1884.

Minutes of the Sixteenth Session of the Louisiana Annual Conference of the African Methodist Episcopal Church. n.p., n.d. [1881].

Minutes of the Tenth Annual Conference of the African Methodist Episcopal Church Held in Bethel Chapel, A.M.E. Church. Baton Rouge La. Commencing January 30th, 1875. n.p., n.d.

Minutes of the Third Session of the Arkansas Annual Conference of the African M.E. Church, Convened in Citizen's Chapel, Helena, Ark., September 28, 1870. Little Rock, AR: State Journal Print, 1870.

Minutes of the Third Session of the Tennessee Annual Conference of the African M.E. Church, Held in Murfreesboro, from Sep. 7th to 15th, 1870. Nashville, TN: Bailey's Cottage Printing House, 1870.

Minutes of the Twenty-Sixth Annual Session of the African Methodist Episcopal Church in Louisiana. n.p., n.d. [1891].

Christian Methodist Episcopal Church Archives, Memphis, TN
    Manuscript CME Church General Conference Minutes, 1870–1906
David M. Rubenstein Rare Book and Manuscript Library, Duke University, Durham, NC
    Kate D. Foster Diary, 1863–72
J. B. Cain Archives of Mississippi Methodism, Millsaps College, Jackson, MS
    MS 10, John Griffing Jones Autobiography and Sermons, 1830–88 (JGJ)
Stuart A. Rose Manuscript, Archives, and Rare Book Library (MARBL), Emory University, Atlanta, GA
    The Doctrines and Disciplines of the Colored Methodist Episcopal Church in America. Byhalia, MS: E. Cottrell, Agent, for the Colored ME Church in America, 1883.
    MS 807, Bailey and Thurman Families Papers Circa 1882–1995, Series 1, Box 1.
    "Paine Institute, Augusta, Georgia: Under the Auspice of the Methodist Episcopal Church, South, and the Colored Methodist Episcopal Church in America." 1885 pamphlet.

Mississippi Department of Archives and History (MDAH), Jackson, MS

Catherine (Kate) Olivia Foster Diary, 1863–72

Douglas, William K. *Christian Priest Taken from Among Men: Sermon Preached in the Church of the Holy Comforter, Dry Grove, Miss., at the Ordination of Mr. George H. Jackson (Colored) to the Diaconate of the Protestant Episcopal Church, May 14th, 1874.* Vicksburg, MS: Rogers & Groome, 1874.

Pitts Theological Library, Emory University, Atlanta, GA

Holsey, Lucius H., A. H. Spencer, and Emanuel Asberry. *Sketch of the Life of Richard H. Vanderhorst: The Second Bishop,* edited by Randall A. Carter and John B. Cade. Jackson, TN: CME Publishing House, 1929.

MS 091, Linus Parker Papers

Southern Historical Collection (SHC), Wilson Library, University of North Carolina at Chapel Hill, Chapel Hill, NC

MS 1608, Wyche-Otey Papers, Subseries 3.2, Octavia Otey Diary, 1864–88

MS 1918, William Kirtland Douglas Papers, 1775–1898

Special Collections, J. D. Williams Library, University of Mississippi, Oxford, MS (JDWL)

Journal of the Forty-Eighth Annual Council of the Protestant Episcopal Church of the Diocese of Mississippi, Held in Christ Church, Vicksburg, on the 5th, 6th, and 7th Days of May, A.D., 1875. Vicksburg, MS: Rogers & Groome, Steam Book and Job Printers, 1875.

Journal of the Forty-First Annual Convention of the Protestant Episcopal Church in the Diocese of Mississippi, Held in Grace Church, Canton, On the 29th and 30th Days of April, and 1st Day of May, 1868. New Orleans: L. R. Simmons & Co, 1868.

Journal of the Forty-Fourth Annual Council of the Protestant Episcopal Church of the Diocese of Mississippi, Held in Trinity Church, Natchez, on the 27th, 28th, and 29th Days of April, A.D., 1871. Jackson, MS: Clarion Steam Printing, 1871.

McDonald. A. C. *"Mississippi and Its Future": A Sermon for the Times, Delivered on the Day of General Thanksgiving in the Hall of Representatives, April 21, 1870.* Jackson, MS: Kimball, Raymond & Co., 1870.

Special Collections, University of Arkansas–Fayetteville, Fayetteville, AR

Lives Transformed: The People of Southland College, Digital Collection.

MS 68, Fontaine Richard Earle Papers

Newspapers and Periodicals

Christian Index (Jackson, TN)

Clarion Ledger (Jackson, MS)

Daily Arkansas Gazette (Little Rock, AR)

Daily Picayune (New Orleans, LA)

Donaldson Chief (Donaldson, LA)

Hinds County Gazette (Raymond, MS)

Little Rock Daily Gazette (Little Rock, AR)

Louisiana Sugar-Bowl (New Iberia, LA)

Memphis Daily Appeal (Memphis, TN)

Milan Exchange (Milan, TN)

New Mississippian (Jackson, MS)

New Orleans Christian Advocate (NOCA) (New Orleans, LA)

New Orleans Daily Democrat (New Orleans, LA)

Ouachita Telegraph (Monroe, LA)

The Outlook (New York, NY)

Public Ledger (Memphis, TN)

Southern Presbyterian Review (Columbia, SC)

South-Western Presbyterian (New Orleans, LA)   *The Times* (Shreveport, LA)
Southwestern (Christian) Advocate   *Times-Democrat* (New Orleans, LA)
  (*SWCA*) (New Orleans, LA)   *The Weekly Clarion* (Jackson, MS)

Published Primary Sources

African-American Baptist Annual Reports 1865–1990s. American Baptist Historical Society. Wilmington, DE: Scholarly Resources Inc., 1999.

Ames, Blanche Butler, Compiler. *Chronicles from the Nineteenth Century: Family Letters of Blanche Butler and Adelbert Ames Married July 21st, 1870*, vol. 1. Clinton, MA: Privately published, 1957.

Berlin, Ira, Barbara J. Fields, Steven F. Miller, Joseph P. Reidy, and Leslie S. Rowland, Eds. *Free at Last: A Documentary History of Slavery, Freedom, and the Civil War*. New York: New Press, 1992.

Cade, John Brother. *Holsey—The Incomparable*. New York: Pageant Press, 1965.

Constitution of the State of Mississippi, Adopted November 1, 1890. Jackson, MS: E. L. Martin, Convention Printer, 1891.

Constitution of the State of Tennessee, Adopted at Convention at Nashville, February 23rd A.D. 1870. Tennessee Virtual Archive. https://cdm15138.contentdm.oclc.org/digital /collection/tfd/id/584, accessed May 19, 2019.

Dabney, Robert L. *A Defence of Virginia, and Through Her, of the South, in Recent and Pending Contests Against the Sectional Party*. New York: E. J. Hale & Son, 1867.

Dixon, Thomas. *The Clansman: A Historical Romance of the Ku Klux Klan*. New York: Grosset & Dunlap, 1905.

Douglass, Frederick. *Narrative of the Life of Frederick Douglass, an American Slave*. Boston: Anti-Slavery Office, 1845. https://docsouth.unc.edu/neh/douglass/douglass.html.

Du Bois, W. E. B. *Black Reconstruction in America: Toward a History of the Part Which Black Folk Played in the Attempt to Reconstruct Democracy in America 1860–1880*. New York: Harcourt Brace, 1935.

———. *The Negro Church: Report of a Social Study Made Under the Direction of Atlanta University; Together with the Proceedings of the Eighth Conference for the Study of the Negro Problems, Held at Atlanta University, May 26th, 1903*. Walnut Creek, CA: AltaMira Press of Rowman & Littlefield, 2003 [1903].

———. *The Souls of Black Folk: Essays and Sketches*. Chicago: A. C. McClurg & Co., 1903.

Du Bose, Horace M. *A History of Methodism: Being a Volume Supplemental to "A History of Methodism" by Holland N. McTyeire, D.D. Late One of the Bishops of the Methodist Episcopal Church, South, Bringing the Story of Methodism, with Special Reference to the History of the Methodist Episcopal Church, South, down to the Year 1916*. Nashville, TN: Publishing House of the ME Church, South, 1916.

Earle, Fontaine Richard, Robert E. Waterman, and Thomas Rothrock. "The Earle-Buchanan Letters of 1861–1876." *Arkansas Historical Quarterly* 33(2) (Summer 1974): 99–174.

Foner, Philip S., and George E. Walker, Eds. *Proceedings of the Black National and State Conventions, 1865–1900*, vol. 1. Philadelphia: Temple University Press, 1986.

Furman, Richard. *Exposition of the Views of the Baptists Relative to the Colored Population the United States in a Communication to the Governor of South Carolina*. Charleston, SC: A. E. Miller, 1823.

Galloway, Charles Betts. *The South and the Negro: An Address Delivered at the Seventh Annual Conference for Education in the South, Birmingham, Ala., April 26th, 1904*. New York: Southern Education Board, 1904.

Grimké, Angelina Weld. *Rachel, A Play in Three Acts*. Boston: Cornhill Company, 1920.

Harrison, W. P. *The Gospel Among the Slaves: A Short Account of Missionary Operations Among the African Slaves of the Southern States*. Nashville, TN: Publishing House of the ME Church, South, 1893.

Hawkins, John Russell. *Centennial Encyclopedia of the African Methodist Episcopal Church*. Philadelphia: Book Concern of the AME Church, 1916.

Haygood, Atticus G. *Our Brother in Black: His Freedom and His Future*. Nashville, TN: Southern Methodist Publishing House, 1881.

Hicks, William. *History of Louisiana Negro Baptists, from 1804 to 1914*. Nashville, TN: National Baptist Publishing Co., [1915]. http://docsouth.unc.edu/church/hicks/hicks.html.

Hodge, Charles. "Bible Argument on Slavery." In *Cotton Is King, and Pro-Slavery Arguments: Comprising the Writings of Hammond, Harper, Christy, Stringfellow, Hodge, Bledsoe, and Cartwright, on This Important Subject*, edited by E. N. Elliott, 841–77. Augusta, GA: Pritchard, Abbott & Loomis, 1860.

Holsey, Lucius H. *Autobiography, Sermons, Addresses and Essays of Bishop L. H. Holsey*. Atlanta, GA: Franklin Printing and Publishing, 1898. http://docsouth.unc.edu/neh/holsey/holsey.html.

Index to Reports of Committees of the House of Representatives for the Second Session of the Forty-Third Congress, 1874–1875. Washington, DC: Government Printing Office, 1875.

Irving, Washington. *The Works of Washington Irving*, vol. 2: *The Sketch-Book*, new ed., rev. New York: G. P. Putnam, 1860.

Jacobs, Harriet A. *Incidents in the Life of a Slave Girl, Written by Herself*, edited by L. Maria Child and Jean Fagan Yellin. Cambridge, MA: Harvard University Press, 1987.

Jewell, Horace. *History of Methodism in Arkansas*. Little Rock, AR: Press Printing Company, 1892.

Jones, John G. *A Concise History of the Introduction of Protestantism into Mississippi and the Southwest*. St. Louis: P. M. Pinckard, 1866.

Journal of the Proceedings of the Constitutional Convention, of the State of Mississippi: Begun at the City of Jackson on August 12, 1890, and Concluded November 1, 1890. Jackson, MS: E. L. Martin, 1890.

Lane, Isaac. *Autobiography of Bishop Isaac Lane, LL.D. with a Short History of the C.M.E. Church in America and of Methodism*. Nashville, TN: Publishing House of the ME Church, South, 1916. http://docsouth.unc.edu/fpn/lane/lane.html.

Laws of the State of Mississippi: Passed at a Regular Session of the Mississippi Legislature: Held in the City of Jackson, October, November and December 1865. Jackson, MS: J. J. Shannon, State Printer, 1866.

Leavell, Z. T., and T. J. Bailey, *A Complete History of Mississippi Baptists, from the Earliest Times,* vols. 1 and 2. Jackson, MS: Mississippi Baptist Publishing, 1904.

Lerner, Gerda, Ed. *Black Women in White America: A Documentary History.* New York: Random House, 1972.

Marshall, C. K. *The Colored Race Weighed in the Balance.* Nashville, TN: Southern Methodists Publishing House, 1883.

McAfee, Sara J. *History of the Woman's Missionary Society in the Colored Methodist Episcopal Church, Comprising Its Founders, Organizations, Pathfinders, Subsequent Developments and Present Status.* Phenix City, AL: Phenix City Herald, 1945.

Minutes of the Annual Conferences of the Methodist Episcopal Church, Spring Conference 1879. Cincinnati, OH: Hitchcock & Walden, 1879.

Minutes of the Annual Conferences of the Methodist Episcopal Church, Spring Conference 1880. Cincinnati, OH: Walden & Stowe, 1880.

Minutes of the Annual Conferences of the Methodist Episcopal Church, Spring Conferences 1880. New York: Phillips & Hunt, 1880.

Minutes of the Annual Conferences of the Methodist Episcopal Church, Spring Conference 1888. Cincinnati, OH: Cranston & Stowe, 1888.

Minutes of the Annual Conferences of the Methodist Episcopal Church, Spring Conference 1889. Cincinnati, OH: Cranston & Stowe, 1889.

Minutes of the Annual Conferences of the Methodist Episcopal Church, Spring Conference 1891. Cincinnati, OH: Cranston & Stowe, 1891.

Minutes of the Annual Conferences of the Methodist Episcopal Church, Spring Conference 1899. Cincinnati, OH: Curts & Jennings, 1899.

Minutes of the Annual Conferences of the Methodist Episcopal Church, Spring Conference 1900. Cincinnati, OH: Jennings & Pye, 1900.

Minutes of the Memphis Conference of the Methodist Episcopal Church, South, for the Years 1862–1867, Published for the Bicentennial of American Methodism. Memphis, TN: Commission on Archives and History Memphis Conference, United Methodist Church, 1984. https://www.memphis-umc.net /journals1862topresent.

Minutes of the State and Sunday-School Convention Held with the Paradise Baptist Church, Marianna. Lee County, August 23, 24, 25, 26, and 27, 1882. Pine Bluff, AR: Pine Bluff Commercial Job Office, 1882.

Mississippi in 1875. Report of the Select Committee to Inquire into the Mississippi Election of 1875, with the Testimony and Documentary Evidence. Washington, DC: Government Printing Office, 1876.

Mitchell, Margaret. *Gone with the Wind.* New York: Avon Books, 1936.

Palmer, B. M. *The Family, in Its Civil and Churchly Aspects, an Essay in Two Parts.* Richmond, VA: Presbyterian Committee of Publication, 1876.

———. *Thanksgiving Sermon, Delivered at the First Presbyterian Church, New Orleans, on Thursday, November 29, 1860.* New York: George F. Nesbitt & Co, 1861.

Phillips, Charles Henry. *The History of the Colored Methodist Episcopal Church in America: Comprising Its Organization, Subsequent Development and Present Status.* Jackson, TN: Publishing House of the CME Church, 1898.

———. *The History of the Colored Methodist Church in America: Comprising Its Organization, Subsequent Development and Present Status.* Jackson, TN: Publishing House of the CME Church, 1925. http://docsouth.unc.edu/church/phillips/phillips.html.

Report of the Board of Education of the Methodist Episcopal Church to the General Conference of 1880. Syracuse, NY: Masters & Stone, 1880.

Rivers, R. H. *The Life of Robert Paine D.D., Bishop of the Methodist Episcopal Church, South.* Nashville, TN: Southern Methodist Publishing House, 1884.

Ross, Frederick Augustus. *Slavery Ordained of God.* Philadelphia: J. B. Lippincott, 1857.

Smith, Charles Spencer. *A History of the African Methodist Episcopal Church, Being a Volume Supplemental to a History of the African Methodist Episcopal Church, by Daniel Alexander Payne, D.D., LL.D., Late One of Its Bishops, Chronicling the Principal Events in the Advance of the African Methodist Episcopal Church from 1856 to 1922.* Philadelphia: Book Concern of the AME Church, 1922. https://docsouth.unc.edu/church/cssmith/smith.html.

Smith, William A. *Lectures on the Philosophy and Practice of Slavery, as Exhibited in the Institution of Domestic Slavery in the United States,* edited by Thomas O. Summers. Nashville, TN: Stevenson & Evans, 1856. http://docsouth.unc.edu/church/smith/menu.html.

State Convention of the Colored Citizens of Tennessee. *Proceedings of the Colored State Convention, Held in Nashville, Feb. 22d, 23d, 24th & 25th.* Nashville, TN: C. LeRoi, 1871. http://coloredconventions.org/items/show/309, accessed June 3, 2019.

Stewart, Maria W. *Meditations from the Pen of Mrs. Maria W. Stewart . . . Presented in 1832 to the First African Baptist Church and Society of Boston, Mass.* Washington, DC: n.p., 1879.

Stowe, Harriet B. *Uncle Tom's Cabin: Or Life Among the Lowly.* Boston: J. P. Jewett, 1852.

Summers, Thomas O., Ed. *Journal of the General Conference of the Methodist Episcopal Church, South, Held in Louisville, Kentucky, May 1874.* Nashville, TN: Publishing House of the Methodist Episcopal Church South, 1874.

———, Ed. *Journal of the General Conference of the Methodist Episcopal Church, South, Held in Memphis, 1870.* Nashville, TN: Publishing House of the Methodist Episcopal Church South, 1870.

———, Ed. *Journal of the General Conference of the Methodist Episcopal Church, South, Held in New Orleans, May 1866.* Nashville, TN: Publishing House of the Methodist Episcopal Church South, 1866.

Tucker, J. L. *The Relations of the Church to the Colored Race: Speech of the Rev. J. L. Tucker, D.D., of Jackson, Mississippi, Before the Church Congress Held in Richmond, Va., on 24–28 Oct, 1882.* Jackson, MS: Charles Winkley, 1882.

Veblen, Thorstein. *The Theory of the Leisure Class: An Economic Study of Institutions.* New York: MacMillan, 1899.

Walker, David, *Walker's Appeal . . . to the Colored Citizens of the World, but in Particular, and Very Expressly to Those of the United States of America,* 2nd ed. Boston: n.p., 1830.

Washington, Booker T., et al. *The Negro Problem: A Series of Articles by Representative American Negroes of Today.* New York: James Pott & Company, 1903.

Webster, Noah. *An American Dictionary of the English Language.* Springfield, MA: George and Charles Merriam, 1850 and 1853.

———. *An American Dictionary of the English Language,* edited by Chauncey A. Goodrich and Noah Porter. Cambridge, MA: G. & C. Merriam Publishers, 1864 and 1866.

Wells, Ida B. *A Red Record*. Chicago: Donohue & Henneberry, 1895. Reprinted in *The Selected Works of Ida B. Wells-Barnett*. New York: Oxford University Press, 1991.
———. *Southern Horrors: Lynch Law in All Its Phases*. New York: New York Age Press, 1892.
Wells-Barnett, Ida B. *Crusade for Justice: The Autobiography of Ida B. Wells*, edited by Alfreda M. Duster. Chicago: University of Chicago Press, 1970.
Woodson, Carter G. *The History of the Negro Church*. Washington, DC: Associated Publishers, 1921.

Secondary Sources

Angell, Stephen Ward. *Bishop Henry McNeal Turner and African-American Religion in the South*. Knoxville: University of Tennessee Press, 1992.
Ash, Stephen V. *A Massacre in Memphis: The Race Riot That Shook the Nation One Year After the Civil War*. New York: Hill & Wang, 2013.
Bailey, Julius. *Around the Family Altar: Domesticity in the African Methodist Episcopal Church, 1865–1900*. Gainesville: University Press of Florida, 2005.
Baker, Kelly J. *Gospel According to the Klan: The KKK's Appeal to Protestant America, 1915–1930*. Lawrence: University Press of Kansas, 2011.
Balmer, Randall. "Forum: Studying Religion in the Age of Trump." *Religion and American Culture* 17 (2017): 3–7.
Baptist, Edward. *The Half Has Never Been Told: Slavery and the Making of American Capitalism*. New York: Basic Books, 2014.
Bardaglio, Peter W. *Reconstructing the Household: Families, Sex, and the Law in the Nineteenth-Century South*. Chapel Hill: University of North Carolina Press, 1995.
Bebbington, D. W. *Evangelicalism in Modern Britain: A History from the 1730s to the 1980s*. Boston: Unwin Hyman, 1989.
Beckert, Sven. *Empire of Cotton: A Global History*. New York: Knopf, 2014.
Bederman, Gail. *Manliness and Civilization: A Cultural History of Gender and Race in the United States, 1880–1917*. Chicago: University of Chicago Press, 1995.
Bendroth, Margaret Lamberts. *Fundamentalism and Gender, 1875 to the Present*. New Haven, CT: Yale University Press, 1996.
Bennett, James. *Religion and the Rise of Jim Crow in New Orleans*. Princeton, NJ: Princeton University Press, 2005.
Bercaw, Nancy. *Gendered Freedoms: Race, Rights, and the Politics of Household in the Delta, 1861–1875*. Gainesville: University Press of Florida, 2003.
Blight, David. *Race and Reunion: The Civil War in American Memory*. Cambridge, MA: Belknap Press of Harvard University Press, 2001.
Blum, Edward J. "The Crucible of Disease: Trauma, Memory, and National Reconciliation." *Journal of Southern History* 69 (2003): 791–820.
———. *Reforging the White Republic: Race, Religion, and American Nationalism, 1865–1898*. Baton Rouge: Louisiana University Press, 2005.
———. *W. E. B. Du Bois, American Prophet*. Philadelphia: University of Pennsylvania Press, 2009.

Blum, Edward J., and Paul Harvey. *The Color of Christ: The Son of God and the Saga of Race in America*. Chapel Hill: University of North Carolina Press, 2012.

Blum, Edward J., and W. Scott Poole. *Vale of Tears: New Essays on Religion and Reconstruction*. Macon, GA: Mercer University Press, 2005.

Bordin, Ruth. *Woman and Temperance: The Quest for Power and Liberty, 1873–1900*. Philadelphia: Temple University Press, 1981.

Brekus, Catherine A. *Sarah Osborn's World: The Rise of Evangelical Christianity in Early America*. New Haven, CT: Yale University Press, 2013.

————. "Writing as a Protestant Practice: Devotional Diaries in Early New England." In *Practicing Protestants: Histories of Christian Life in America, 1630–1965*, edited by Laurie F. Maffly-Kipp, Leigh E. Schmidt, and Mark Valeri, 19–34. Baltimore: Johns Hopkins University Press, 2006.

Broussard, Joyce Linda. *Stepping Lively in Place: The Not-Married, Free Women of Civil-War-Era Natchez, Mississippi*. Athens: University of Georgia Press, 2016.

Brown, Canter, Jr., and Larry E. Rivers. *For a Great and Grand Purpose: The Beginnings of the AMEZ Church in Florida, 1865–1905*. Gainesville: University Press of Florida, 2004.

Brown, Kathleen M. *Good Wives, Nasty Wenches, and Anxious Patriarchs: Gender, Race, and Power in Colonial Virginia*. Chapel Hill: University of North Carolina Press, 1996.

Brundage, Fitzhugh. *The Southern Past: A Clash of Race and Memory*. Cambridge, MA: Harvard University Press, 2005.

Butchard, Ronald E. *Schooling the Freed People: Teaching, Learning, and the Struggle for Black Freedom, 1861–1876*. Chapel Hill: University of North Carolina Press, 2010.

Butler, Anthea D. "'Only a Woman Would Do': Bible Reading and African American Women's Organizing Work." In *Women and Religion in the African Diaspora: Knowledge, Power, and Performance*, edited by R. Marie Griffith and Barbara Dianne Savage, 155–78. Baltimore: Johns Hopkins University Press, 2006.

————. *Women in the Church of God in Christ: Making a Sanctified World*. Chapel Hill: University of North Carolina Press, 2007.

Carrigan, William D., Ed. *Lynching Reconsidered: New Perspectives in the Study of Mob Violence*. New York: Routledge, 2008.

Carwardine, Richard. *Evangelicals and Politics in Antebellum America*. New Haven, CT: Yale University Press, 1993.

Chang, Derek. *Citizens of a Christian Nation: Evangelical Mission and the Problem of Race in the Nineteenth Century*. Philadelphia: University of Pennsylvania Press, 2012.

Chappell, David L. *A Stone of Hope: Prophetic Religion and the Death of Jim Crow*. Chapel Hill: University of North Carolina Press, 2004.

Clark, Emily Suzanne. *A Luminous Brotherhood: Afro-Creole Spiritualism in Nineteenth-Century New Orleans*. Chapel Hill: University of North Carolina Press, 2016.

Clinton, Catherine. *The Plantation Mistress: Woman's World in the Old South*. New York: Pantheon Books, 1982.

Coker, Joe L. *Liquor in the Land of the Lost Cause: Southern White Evangelicals and the Prohibition Movement*. Lexington: University Press of Kentucky, 2007.

Collier-Thomas, Bettye. *Jesus, Jobs, and Justice: African American Women and Religion*. New York: Knopf, 2010.

Cott, Nancy F. "Marriage and Women's Citizenship in the United States, 1830–1934."
    American Historical Review 103 (1998): 1440–74.
———. *Public Vows: A History of Marriage and the Nation.* Cambridge, MA: Harvard
    University Press, 2000.
Cox, Karen L. *Dixie's Daughters: The United Daughters of the Confederacy and the
    Preservation of Confederate Culture.* Gainesville: University Press of Florida, 2003.
Dailey, Jane. *Before Jim Crow: The Politics of Race in Postemancipation Virginia.* Chapel Hill:
    University of North Carolina Press, 2000.
———. "Sex, Segregation, and the Sacred after *Brown*." *Journal of American History* 91
    (2004): 119–44.
Dowland, Seth. *Family Values and the Rise of the Christian Right.* Philadelphia: University
    of Pennsylvania Press, 2015.
Downs, Gregory P., and Kate Masur, Eds. *The World the Civil War Made.* Chapel Hill:
    University of North Carolina Press, 2015.
Downs, Jim. *Sick from Freedom: African-American Illness and Suffering During the Civil War
    and Reconstruction.* New York: Oxford University Press, 2012.
Dvorak, Katharine L. *An African-American Exodus: The Segregation of the Southern
    Churches.* Brooklyn, NY: Carlson Publishing, 1991.
Edwards, Laura. *Gendered Strife and Confusion: The Political Culture of Reconstruction.*
    Bloomington: Indiana University Press, 1997.
Eskew, Glenn. "Black Elitism and the Failure of Paternalism in Postbellum Georgia: The
    Case of Bishop Lucius Henry Holsey." *Journal of Southern History* 58(4) (1992): 637–66.
Evans, Curtis J. *The Burden of Black Religion.* New York: Oxford University Press, 2008.
Faust, Drew Gilpin. *The Creation of Confederate Nationalism: Ideology and Identity in the
    Civil War South.* Baton Rouge: Louisiana State University Press, 1988.
———, Ed. *The Ideology of Slavery: Proslavery Thought in the Antebellum South, 1830–1860.*
    Baton Rouge: University of Louisiana Press, 1981.
———. *Mothers of Invention: Women of the Slaveholding South in the American Civil War.*
    Chapel Hill: University of North Carolina Press, 1996.
———. *This Republic of Suffering: Death and the American Civil War.* New York: Knopf, 2008.
Feimster, Crystal. *Southern Horrors: Women and the Politics of Rape and Lynching.*
    Cambridge, MA: Harvard University Press, 2009.
Ferris, Marcie Cohen, and Mark I. Greenberg, Eds. *Jewish Roots in Southern Soil: A New
    History.* Waltham, MA: Brandeis University Press, 2006.
Foner, Eric. *Reconstruction: America's Unfinished Revolution, 1863–1877.* New York: Harper &
    Row, 1988.
Ford, Bridget. *Bonds of Union: Religion, Race, and Politics in a Civil War Borderland.* Chapel
    Hill: University of North Carolina Press, 2016.
Fountain, Daniel L. *Slavery, Civil War, and Salvation: African American Slaves and
    Christianity, 1830–1870.* Baton Rouge: University of Louisiana Press, 2010.
Fox-Genovese, Elizabeth. *Within the Plantation Household: Black and White Women of the
    Old South.* Chapel Hill: University of North Carolina Press, 1988.
Fox-Genovese, Elizabeth, and Eugene D. Genovese. "Divine Sanction of Social Order:
    Religious Foundations of the Southern Slaveholders' World View." *Journal of the
    American Academy of Religion* 55(2) (1987): 211–33.

Frankel, Noralee. *Freedom's Women: Black Women and Families in Civil War Era Mississippi.* Bloomington: Indiana University Press, 1999.

Fredrickson, George. *The Black Image in the White Mind: The Debate on Afro-American Character and Destiny, 1817–1914.* New York: Harper and Row, 1971.

Friedman, Jean E. *The Enclosed Garden: Women and Community in the Evangelical South, 1830–1900.* Chapel Hill: University of North Carolina Press, 1985.

Gardner, Martha. *The Qualities of a Citizen: Women, Immigration, and Citizenship, 1870–1965.* Princeton, NJ: Princeton University Press, 2005.

Genovese, Eugene. *Roll Jordan Roll: The World the Slaves Made.* New York: Vintage, 1974.

Gerbner, Katharine. *Christian Slavery: Conversion and Race in the Protestant Atlantic World.* Philadelphia: University of Pennsylvania Press, 2018.

Giddings, Paula J. *Ida: A Sword Among Lions: Ida B. Wells and the Campaign Against Lynching.* New York: Harper Collins, 2008.

Giggie, John. *After Redemption: Jim Crow and the Transformation of African American Religion in the Delta, 1875–1915.* New York: Oxford University Press, 2008.

Gilmore, Glenda. *Gender and Jim Crow: Women and the Politics of White Supremacy in North Carolina, 1896–1920.* Chapel Hill: University of North Carolina Press, 1996.

Glymph, Thavolia. *Out of the House of Bondage: The Transformation of the Plantation Household.* New York: Cambridge University Press, 2008.

Goen, C. C. *Broken Churches, Broken Nation: Denominational Schisms and the Coming of the Civil War.* Macon, GA: Mercer University Press, 1985.

Goetz, Rebecca. *The Baptism of Early Virginia: How Christianity Created Race.* Baltimore: Johns Hopkins University Press, 2012.

Goldstein, Eric. *The Price of Whiteness: Jews, Race, and American Identity.* Princeton, NJ: Princeton University Press, 2006.

Graham, John H. *Mississippi Circuit Riders, 1865–1965.* Nashville, TN: Parthenon Press, 1967.

Gravely, William B. "The Social, Political and Religious Significance of the Formation of the Colored Methodist Episcopal Church (1870)." *Methodist History* 18 (October 1979): 3–25.

Greeson, Jennifer R. *Our South: Geographic Fantasy and the Rise of National Literature.* Cambridge, MA: Harvard University Press, 2010.

Griffith, R. Marie. *Moral Combat: How Sex Divided American Christians and Fractured American Politics.* New York: Basic Books, 2017.

Hahn, Steven. *A Nation Under Our Feet: Black Political Struggles in the Rural South from Slavery to the Great Migration.* Cambridge, MA: Belknap Press of Harvard University Press, 2003.

Hale, Grace Elizabeth. *Making Whiteness: The Culture of Segregation in the South, 1890–1940.* New York: Pantheon Books, 1998.

Hall, Jacquelyn Dowd. *Revolt Against Chivalry: Jessie Daniel Ames and the Women's Campaign Against Lynching.* New York: Columbia University Press, 1979.

Harlow, Luke E. "The Civil War and the Making of Conservative American Evangelicalism." In *Turning Points in the History of American Evangelicalism,* edited by Heath Carter and Laura Porter. Grand Rapids, MI: Eerdmans, 2017.

———. *Religion, Race, and the Making of Confederate Kentucky, 1830–1880.* New York: Cambridge University Press, 2014.

———. "Slavery, Race, and Political Ideology in the White Christian South Before and After the Civil War." In *Religion and American Politics: From the Colonial Period to the Present*, 2nd ed., edited by Mark A. Noll and Luke E. Harlow. New York: Oxford University Press, 2007.

Harper, Matthew. *The End of Days: African American Religion and Politics in the Age of Emancipation*. Chapel Hill: University of North Carolina Press, 2016.

Harrill, J. Albert. "The Use of the New Testament in the American Slave Controversy: A Case History in the Hermeneutical Tension Between Biblical Criticism and Christian Moral Debate." *Religion & American Culture: A Journal of Interpretation* 10(2) (2000): 149–86.

Harvey, Paul. *Christianity and Race in the American South: A History*. Chicago: University of Chicago Press, 2016.

———. *Freedom's Coming: Religious Culture and the Shaping of the South from the Civil War Through the Civil Rights Era*. Chapel Hill: University of North Carolina Press, 2005.

———. *Redeeming the South: Religious Cultures and Racial Identities Among Southern Baptists, 1865–1920*. Chapel Hill: University of North Carolina Press, 1997.

Haynes, Stephen. *Noah's Curse: The Biblical Justification of American Slavery*. New York: Oxford University Press, 2002.

Hempton, David N. *Methodism: Empire of the Spirit*. New Haven, CT: Yale University Press, 2005.

Hewitt, Nancy A., and Suzanne Lebsock, Eds. *Visible Women: New Essays on American Activism*. Urbana: University of Illinois Press, 1993.

Higginbotham, Evelyn Brooks. "African-American Women's History and the Metalanguage of Race." *Signs* 17(2) (1992): 251–74.

———. *Righteous Discontent: The Women's Movement in the Black Baptist Church, 1880–1920*. Cambridge, MA: Harvard University Press, 1993.

Hildebrand, Reginald F. *The Times Were Strange and Stirring: Methodist Preachers and the Crisis of Emancipation*. Durham, NC: Duke University Press, 1995.

Hill, Samuel S., Ed. *Religion in the Southern States: A Historical Study*. Macon, GA: Mercer University Press, 1984.

Hill, Samuel S., Charles H. Lippy, and Charles Reagan Wilson, Eds. *Encyclopedia of Religion in the South*. Macon, GA: Mercer University Press, 2005.

Hobson, Christopher Z. *The Mount of Vision: African American Prophetic Tradition, 1800–1915*. New York: Oxford University Press, 2010.

Hodes, Martha. *White Women, Black Men: Illicit Sex in the 19th-Century South*. New Haven, CT: Yale University Press, 1997.

Hogue, James. *Uncivil War: Five New Orleans Street Battles and the Rise and Fall of Radical Reconstruction*. Baton Rouge: Louisiana State University Press, 2006.

Holifield, E. Brooks. *The Gentlemen Theologians: American Theology in Southern Culture, 1795–1860*. Durham, NC: Duke University Press, 1978.

Hollandsworth, James G. *An Absolute Massacre: The New Orleans Race Riot of July 30, 1866*. Baton Rouge: Louisiana State University Press, 2004.

Holm, April. *A Kingdom Divided: Evangelicals, Loyalty, and Sectionalism in the Civil War Era*. Baton Rouge: Louisiana State University Press, 2017.

Holt, Sharon Ann. *Making Freedom Pay: North Carolina Freedpeople Working for Themselves, 1865–1900*. Athens: University of Georgia, 2000.

Hsia, R. Po-chia. *The World of Catholic Renewal, 1540–1770*, rev. ed. New York: Cambridge University Press, 2005.

Hunter, Tera W. *Bound in Wedlock: Slave and Free Black Marriage in the Nineteenth Century*. Cambridge, MA: Belknap Press of Harvard University Press, 2016.

Irons, Charles. *The Origins of Proslavery Christianity: White and Black Evangelicals in Colonial and Antebellum Virginia*. Chapel Hill: University of North Carolina Press, 2009.

Jackson, Alicia K. "The Colored Methodist Episcopal Church and Their Struggle for Autonomy and Reform in the New South." PhD dissertation, University of Mississippi, 2004.

Janney, Caroline E. *Burying the Dead but Not the Past: Ladies' Memorial Associations and the Lost Cause*. Chapel Hill: University of North Carolina Press, 2008.

Johnson, Walter. "On Agency." *Journal of Social History* 37(1) (2003): 113–24.

———. *River of Dark Dreams: Slavery and Empire in the Cotton Kingdom*. Cambridge, MA: Belknap Press of Harvard University Press, 2013.

———. *Soul by Soul: Life Inside the Antebellum Slave Market*. Cambridge, MA: Harvard University Press, 2000.

Jones, Martha. *Birthright Citizens: A History of Race and Rights in Antebellum America*. New York: Cambridge University Press, 2018.

Jones-Rogers, Stephanie E. *They Were Her Property: White Women as Slave Owners in the American South*. New Haven, CT: Yale University Press, 2019.

Jordan, Winthrop. *White over Black: American Attitudes Toward the Negro, 1550–1812*. Chapel Hill: University of North Carolina Press, 1968.

Kantrowitz, Stephen David. *Ben Tillman and the Reconstruction of White Supremacy*. Chapel Hill: University of North Carolina Press, 2000.

Kennedy, Thomas C. *The History of Southland College: The Society of Friends and Black Education in Arkansas*. Fayetteville: University of Arkansas Press, 2009.

Kerber, Linda K. "The Meaning of Citizenship." *Journal of American History* 84(3) (1997): 833–54.

———. "The Paradox of Women's Citizenship in the Early Republic: The Case of *Martin v. Commonwealth*, 1805." *American Historical Review* 97 (1992): 349–78.

Kerrison, Catherine. *Claiming the Pen: Women and Intellectual Life in the Early American South*. Ithaca, NY: Cornell University Press, 2006.

Kidd, Colin. *The Forging of Races: Race and Scripture in the Protestant Atlantic World, 1600–2000*. New York: Cambridge University Press, 2006.

Lakey, Othal. *The History of the CME Church (Revised)*. Memphis, TN: Christian Methodist Episcopal Church Publishing House, 1995.

———. *The Rise of "Colored Methodism": A Study of the Background and the Beginnings of the Christian Methodist Episcopal Church*. Dallas: Crescendo Book Publications, 1972.

Lakey, Othal Hawthorne, and Betty Beene Stephens. *God in My Mama's House: The Women's Movement in the CME Church*. Memphis, TN: CME Publishing House, 1994.

Lee, Susanna Michelle. *Claiming the Union: Citizenship in the Post-Civil War South*. New York: Cambridge University Press, 2014.

Lippy, Charles H., Ed. *Religion in South Carolina*. Columbia: University of South Carolina Press, 1993.

Longfield, Bradley J. *The Presbyterian Controversy: Fundamentalists, Modernists, and Moderates*. New York: Oxford University Press, 1991.

Maffly-Kipp, Laurie F. *Setting Down the Sacred Past: African-American Race Histories*. Cambridge, MA: Belknap Press of Harvard University Press, 2010.

Martin, Sandy Dwayne. *For God and Race: The Religious and Political Leadership of AMEZ Bishop James Walker Hood*. Columbia: University of South Carolina Press, 1999.

Mason, Patrick Q. *The Mormon Menace: Violence and Anti-Mormonism in the Postbellum South*. New York: Oxford University Press, 2011.

Masur, Kate. *An Example for All the Land: Emancipation and the Struggle over Equality in Washington, D.C.* Chapel Hill: University of North Carolina Press, 2010.

Mathews, Donald G. *Religion in the Old South*. Chicago: University of Chicago Press, 1976.

McCurry, Stephanie. *Confederate Reckoning: Power and Politics in the Civil War South*. Cambridge, MA: Harvard University Press, 2010.

———. *Masters of Small Worlds: Yeomen Households, Gender Relations, & the Political Culture of the Antebellum South Carolina Low Country*. New York: Oxford University Press, 1995.

———. *Women's War: Fighting and Surviving the American Civil War*. Cambridge, MA: Belknap Press of Harvard University Press, 2019.

McGreevy, John T. *Catholicism and American Freedom: A History*. New York: W. W. Norton, 2003.

McPherson, Tara. *Reconstructing Dixie: Race, Gender, and Nostalgia in the Imagined South*. Durham, NC: Duke University Press, 2003.

Miller, Albert G. *Elevating the Race: Theophilus G. Steward, Black Theology, and the Making of an African American Civil Society, 1865–1924*. Knoxville: University of Tennessee Press, 2003.

Miller, Gene Ramsey. *A History of North Mississippi Methodism*. Nashville, TN: Parthenon Press, 1966.

Montgomery, William E. *Under Their Own Vine and Fig Tree: The African-American Church in the South, 1865–1900*. Baton Rouge: Louisiana State University Press, 1993.

Morrow, Ralph E. *Northern Methodism and Reconstruction*. East Lansing: Michigan State University Press, 1956.

Nieman, Donald G., Ed. *Church and Community Among Black Southerners, 1865–1900*. New York: Garland Publishing, 1994.

Noll, Mark A. *America's God: From Jonathan Edwards to Abraham Lincoln*. New York: Oxford University Press, 2002.

———. *The Civil War as a Theological Crisis*. Chapel Hill: University of North Carolina Press, 2006.

———. *God and Race in American Politics: A Short History*. Princeton, NJ: Princeton University Press, 2008.

O'Donovan, Susan. *Becoming Free in the Cotton South*. Cambridge, MA: Harvard University Press, 2007.

Oshatz, Molly. *Slavery and Sin: The Fight Against Slavery and the Rise of Liberal Protestantism*. New York: Oxford University Press, 2012.

Paddison, Joshua. *American Heathens: Religion, Race, and Reconstruction in California.* Berkeley: University of California Press, 2012.

Painter, Nell Irvin. "Of *Lily*, Linda Brent, and Freud: A Non-Exceptionalist Approach to Race, Class, and Gender in the Slave South." *Georgia Historical Quarterly* 76(2) (Summer 1992): 241–59.

Pascoe, Peggy. *What Comes Naturally: Miscegenation Law and the Making of Race in America.* New York: Oxford University Press, 2009.

Prince, K. Stephen. *Stories of the South: Race and the Reconstruction of Southern Identity, 1865–1915.* Chapel Hill: University of North Carolina, 2014.

Rable, George C. *But There Was No Peace: The Role of Violence in the Politics of Reconstruction.* Athens: University of Georgia Press, 2007.

———. *God's Almost Chosen People: A Religious History of the American Civil War.* Chapel Hill: University of North Carolina, 2010.

Raboteau, Albert J. *Slave Religion: The "Invisible Institution" in the Antebellum South,* rev. ed. New York: Oxford University Press, 2004.

Remillard, Arthur. *Southern Civil Religions: Imagining the Good Society in the Post-Reconstruction Era.* Athens: University of Georgia Press, 2011.

Richardson, Joe M. *Christian Reconstruction: The American Missionary Association and Southern Blacks, 1861–1890.* Tuscaloosa: University of Alabama Press, 2008.

Rivers, Larry Eugene, and Canter Brown, Jr. *Laborers in the Vineyard of the Lord: The Beginnings of the AME Church in Florida, 1865–1895.* Gainesville: University Press of Florida, 2001.

Rosen, Hannah. *Terror in the Heart of Freedom: Citizenship, Sexual Violence, and the Meaning of Race in the Postemancipation South.* Chapel Hill: University of North Carolina Press, 2009.

Rubin, Anne Sarah. *A Shattered Nation: The Rise and Fall of the Confederacy, 1861–1868.* Chapel Hill: University of North Carolina Press, 2005.

Rushdy, Ashraf H. A. *American Lynching.* New Haven, CT: Yale University Press, 2012.

Sarna, Jonathan. *When General Grant Expelled the Jews.* New York: Shocken Books, 2012.

Savage, Barbara Dianne. *Your Spirits Walk Beside Us: The Politics of Black Religion.* Cambridge, MA: Belknap Press of Harvard University Press, 2008.

Schechter, Patricia A. *Ida B. Wells-Barnett and American Reform, 1880–1930.* Chapel Hill: University of North Carolina Press, 2001.

Schweiger, Beth Barton, and Donald G. Mathews, Eds. *Religion in the American South: Protestants and Others in History and Culture.* Chapel Hill: University of North Carolina Press, 2006.

Scott, Ann Firor. *The Southern Lady: From Pedestal to Politics, 1830–1930.* Chicago: University of Chicago Press, 1970.

Scully, Randolph Ferguson. *Religion and the Making of Nat Turner's Virginia: Baptist Community and Conflict, 1740–1840.* Charlottesville: University of Virginia Press, 2008.

Shattuck, Gardiner H. *A Shield and Hiding Place: The Religious Life of Civil War Armies.* Macon, GA: Mercer University Press, 1987.

Smith, Bonnie G. *The Gender of History: Men, Women, and Historical Practice.* Cambridge, MA: Harvard University Press, 1998.

Smith, John David. *An Old Creed for the New South: Proslavery Ideology and Historiography, 1865–1918.* Westport, CT: Greenwood Press, 1985.

Sommerville, Raymond R. *An Ex-Colored Church: Social Activism in the CME Church, 1870–1970.* Macon, GA: Mercer University Press, 2004.

Span, Christopher. *From Cotton Field to Schoolhouse: African American Education in Mississippi, 1862–1875.* Chapel Hill: University of North Carolina Press, 2009.

Sparks, Randy J. *On Jordan's Stormy Banks: Evangelical Religion in Mississippi, 1773–1876.* Athens: University of Georgia, 1994.

———. "'The White People's Arms Are Longer Than Ours': Blacks, Education, and the American Missionary Association in Reconstruction Mississippi." *Journal of Mississippi History* 54(1) (1992): 1–28.

Spragin, Ore L. *The History of the Christian Methodist Episcopal Church (1870–2009): Faithful to the Vision.* Lima, OH: Wyndham Hall Press, 2011.

Stern, Andrew. *Southern Cross, Southern Crucifix: Catholic-Protestant Relations in the Old South.* Tuscaloosa: University of Alabama Press, 2012.

Stout, Harry. *Upon the Altar of the Nation: A Moral History of the Civil War.* New York: Viking, 2006.

Stowell, Daniel. *Rebuilding Zion: The Religious Reconstruction of the South, 1863–1877.* New York: Oxford University Press, 1998.

Thompson, H. Paul. *A Most Stirring and Significant Episode: Religion and the Rise and Fall of Prohibition in Black Atlanta, 1865–1887.* DeKalb: Northern Illinois University Press, 2013.

Thompson, Julius E. *Black Life in Mississippi: Essays on Political, Social, and Cultural Studies in a Deep South State.* Lanham, MD: University Press of America, 2001.

———. *Lynchings in Mississippi: A History, 1865–1965.* Jefferson, NC: McFarland & Company, 2001.

Tigert, Jonathan J. *Bishop Holland Nimmons McTyeire: Ecclesiastical and Educational Architect.* Nashville, TN: Vanderbilt University Press, 1955.

Varon, Elizabeth R. *We Mean to Be Counted: White Women & Politics in Antebellum Virginia.* Chapel Hill: University of North Carolina Press, 1998.

Walker, Clarence E. *A Rock in a Weary Land: The African Methodist Episcopal Church During the Civil War and Reconstruction.* Baton Rouge: Louisiana State University Press, 1982.

Weimer, Adrian Chastain. *The Martyr's Mirror: Persecution and Holiness in Early New England.* New York: Oxford University Press, 2011.

Weisenfeld, Judith F. *African American Women and Christian Activism: New York's YWCA, 1905–1945.* Cambridge, MA: Harvard University Press, 1997.

———. *New World A-Coming: Black Religion and Racial Identity During the Great Migration.* New York: New York University Press, 2016.

White, Deborah Gray. *Ar'n't I a Woman? Female Slaves in the Plantation South.* New York: W. W. Norton, 1985.

Whites, LeeAnn. *The Civil War as a Crisis in Gender: Augusta, Georgia, 1860–1890.* Athens: University of Georgia Press, 1995.

Williams, Heather Andrea. *Self-Taught: African American Education in Slavery and Freedom.* Chapel Hill: University of North Carolina Press, 2005.

Willis, John C. *Forgotten Time: The Yazoo-Mississippi Delta After the Civil War.* Charlottesville: University Press of Virginia, 2000.

Wilson, Charles Reagan. *Baptized in Blood: The Religion of the Lost Cause, 1865–1920,* rev. ed. Athens: University of Georgia Press, 2009.

Winter, R. Milton. "James A. Lyon: Southern Presbyterian Apostle of Progress." *Journal of Presbyterian History (1962–1985)* 60(4) (1982): 314–35.

Wolcott, Victoria. *Remaking Respectability: African American Women in Interwar Detroit.* Chapel Hill: University of North Carolina Press, 2001.

Wood, Amy Louise. *Lynching and Spectacle: Witnessing Racial Violence in America, 1890–1940.* Chapel Hill: University of North Carolina Press, 2009.

Wood, Kirsten. *Masterful Women: Slaveholding Widows from the American Revolution to the Civil War.* Chapel Hill: University of North Carolina Press, 2004.

Woods, James M. *A History of the Catholic Church in the American South, 1513–1900.* Gainesville: University Press of Florida, 2011.

Woodward, C. Vann. *The Burden of Southern History.* Baton Rouge: Louisiana State University Press, 1960.

———. *The Strange Career of Jim Crow.* New York: Oxford University Press, 2002.

Woodworth, Steven E. *While God Is Marching On: The Religious World of Civil War Soldiers.* Lawrence: University Press of Kansas, 2001.

Index

9 781469 659695